Ellipsis

SUNY series in Contemporary Continental Philosophy
Dennis J. Schmidt, editor

Ellipsis

Of Poetry and the Experience of Language after Heidegger, Hölderlin, and Blanchot

William S. Allen

STATE UNIVERSITY OF NEW YORK PRESS

Published by
State University of New York Press, Albany

Printed in the United States of America

For information, contact State University of New York Press, Albany, NY
www.sunypress.edu

Production by Michael Haggett & Marilyn Semerad
Marketing by Anne M. Valentine

Library of Congress Cataloging in Publication Data

Allen, William S., 1971–
Ellipsis : of poetry and the experience of language after Heidegger, Hölderlin, and Blanchot / William S. Allen.
p. cm. — (SUNY series in contemporary continental philosopy)
Includes bibliographical references and index.
ISBN-13: 978-0-7914-7151-7 (hardcover : alk. paper)
ISBN-13: 978-0-7914-7152-4 (pbk. : alk. paper) 1. Philosophy, Modern—20th century. 2. Poetry. 3. Language and languages—Philosophy. 4. Heidegger, Martin, 1889–1976. 5. Hölderlin, Friedrich, 1770–1843. 6. Blanchot, Maurice. I. Title.

B804.A435 2007
121'.68—dc22

2006032535

10 9 8 7 6 5 4 3 2 1

Nur das Einmalige ist wieder-holbar
(Only the singular is re-peatable)

Martin Heidegger, 1936–37

Tu appelleras désormais poème une certaine passion de la marque singulière
(You will call poem from now on a certain passion of the singular mark)

Jacques Derrida, November 1988

Contents

PART TWO: THE REPETITION OF LANGUAGE

Acknowledgments

I must express my gratitude firstly to Paul Davies, Chris Fynsk, and to an anonymous reader at the State University of New York Press who carefully read earlier drafts of this work and who gave some much needed support and critical commentary. Above all, the development of this work has been made possible by two very significant figures in my life: Miguel de Beistegui and Anna Johnson. Miguel has provided the essence of careful and discreet guidance, constantly surprising me with the precision of his comments and the generosity of his support. Anna's presence breathes through every word and phrase of this work as a persistent reminder of why I should be doing it, why the perseverance and the exactitude required by such a project have an importance far beyond the project itself; it is thus to her that this work is dedicated.

Abbreviations

Citations give page references to the original and then the English translation, where appropriate. Translations have occasionally been modified in the interests of accuracy, consistency, or subtlety.

BPE Martin Heidegger, *Beiträge zur Philosophie (Vom Ereignis)*, ed. Friedrich-Wilhelm von Herrmann (Frankfurt am Main: Vittorio Klostermann, 1989); tr. Parvis Emad and Kenneth Maly as *Contributions to Philosophy (From Enowning)* (Bloomington: Indiana University Press, 1999).

ED Maurice Blanchot, *L'écriture du désastre* (Paris: Gallimard, 1980); tr. Ann Smock as *The Writing of the Disaster* (Lincoln: University of Nebraska Press, 1986).

EHD Heidegger, *Erläuterungen zu Hölderlins Dichtung*, ed. Friedrich-Wilhelm von Herrmann (Frankfurt am Main: Vittorio Klostermann, 1996); tr. Keith Hoeller as *Elucidations of Hölderlin's Poetry* (Amherst, NY: Humanity Books, 2000).

EI Blanchot, *L'entretien infini* (Paris: Gallimard, 1969); tr. Susan Hanson as *The Infinite Conversation* (Minneapolis: University of Minnesota Press, 1992).

EM Heidegger, *Einführung in die Metaphysik*, ed. Petra Jaeger (Frankfurt am Main: Klostermann, 1983); tr. Gregory Fried and Richard Polt as *Introduction to Metaphysics* (New Haven: Yale University Press, 2000).

H Heidegger, *Holzwege*, ed. Friedrich-Wilhelm von Herrmann (Frankfurt am Main: Vittorio Klostermann, 1994); tr. and ed. Julian Young and Kenneth Haynes as *Off the Beaten Track* (Cambridge: Cambridge University Press, 2002).

Kahn Charles Kahn, *The Art and Thought of Heraclitus* (Cambridge: Cambridge University Press, 1979).

PAD Blanchot, *Le pas au-delà* (Paris: Gallimard, 1973); tr. Lycette Nelson as *The Step Not Beyond* (Albany: State University of New York Press, 1992).

PF Blanchot, *La part du feu* (Paris: Gallimard, 1949); tr. Charlotte Mandell as *The Work of Fire* (Stanford: Stanford University Press, 1995).

PI Jacques Derrida, *Points . . . : Interviews, 1974–1994*, ed. Elisabeth Weber, tr. Peggy Kamuf et al. (Stanford: Stanford University Press, 1995).

S Heidegger, *Seminare*, ed. Curd Ochwadt (Frankfurt am Main: Vittorio Klostermann, 1986); partly tr. Andrew Mitchell and François Raffoul, in *Four Seminars: Le Thor 1966, 1968, 1969, Zähringen 1973* (Bloomington: Indiana University Press, 2003).

SI Heidegger, "Der Satz der Identität," in *Identity and Difference* (New York: Harper, 1969), 85–106; tr. Joan Stambaugh as "The Principle of Identity," in *Identity and Difference*, 23–41.

SW Friedrich Hölderlin, *Sämtliche Werke*, ed. Friedrich Beißner (Stuttgart: Kohlhammer, 1943–85), 8 volumes listed by volume number; partly tr. and ed. Thomas Pfau, in *Essays and Letters on Theory* (Albany: State University of New York Press, 1988).

SZ Heidegger, *Sein und Zeit* (Tübingen: Max Niemeyer, 1953); tr. John Macquarrie and Edward Robinson as *Being and Time* (Oxford: Blackwell, 1962).

US Heidegger, *Unterwegs zur Sprache*, ed. Friedrich-Wilhelm von Herrmann (Frankfurt am Main: Vittorio Klostermann, 1985); tr. Peter D. Hertz and Joan Stambaugh, in *On the Way to Language* (New York: Harper, 1971); Albert Hofstadter, in *Poetry, Language, Thought* (New York: Harper, 1971).

VA Heidegger, *Vorträge und Aufsätze* (Pfullingen: Günther Neske, 1954), 3 volumes listed by volume number; partly tr. Albert Hofstadter, in *Poetry, Language, Thought* (New York: Harper, 1971); David Farrell Krell and Frank A. Capuzzi, in *Early Greek Thinking* (New York: Harper, 1975); William Lovitt, in *The Question*

Concerning Technology and Other Essays (New York: Harper, 1977); David Farrell Krell, in *Nietzsche: The Eternal Recurrence of the Same* (New York: Harper, 1984).

W Heidegger, *Wegmarken*, ed. Friedrich-Wilhelm von Herrmann (Frankfurt am Main: Vittorio Klostermann, 1967); tr. as *Pathmarks*, ed. William McNeill (Cambridge: Cambridge University Press, 1998).

WHD Heidegger, *Was heißt Denken?* (Tübingen: Max Niemeyer, 1954); tr. J. Glenn Gray and Fred D. Wieck as *What Is Called Thinking?* (New York: Harper, 1968).

ZBP Heidegger, *Zur Bestimmung der Philosophie*, ed. Bernd Heimbüchel (Frankfurt am Main: Vittorio Klostermann, 1999); tr. Ted Sadler as *Towards the Definition of Philosophy* (London: Athlone, 2000).

ZSD Heidegger, *Zur Sache des Denkens* (Tübingen: Max Niemeyer, 1988); tr. Joan Stambaugh as *On Time and Being* (New York: Harper, 1972).

Introduction

> I only know one thing: because meditation on language and being has determined my path of thinking from early on, therefore their discussion has stayed as far as possible in the background.
>
> —Heidegger, "From a Dialogue on Language," 1954

What is the experience of a poem? In both its reading and its writing, although in ways that need to be explicated, a poem appears as an instance of language that seems to evade or resist theoretical discourse. There is no general experience of a poem, and yet its language seems to present itself in such a way that even if, and perhaps because, we cannot bring it to any complete understanding, we still find it hard to turn aside. In a sense this ambiguity itself seems to mark the nature of the experience, and thus its resistance to generalization, because even if it seems to evade ordinary discourse a poem does not lack significance, and although it may not seem to refer to anything in particular beyond itself and in fact seems to refer to nothing, but itself, it is nevertheless a poem in the act of being a poem; the question of its own existence turned back on itself *as* its existence. But to understand the experience of such a poem we must first be clear about the meaning of "experience" here, for I would insist that we see it simply in terms of its etymology as a traversing of a certain limit, in this case, the limit of language as it presents itself.

However, it is at this point that we must start to differentiate the experience of reading from that of writing and in doing so provide a more concrete description of the nature of the language that is to be found in a poem. To help establish this inquiry on a more neutral, and thereby open, ground, I will turn to Maurice Blanchot's use of "fiction" or "literature," which in its generalized anonymity moves us away from the particularities of genre analysis—poetry as opposed to prose, for example—and toward the broader question of a language that does not act as an instrument of expression or communication. While I would not deny that there is in the experience of a poem a certain sense of communication, I would distinguish poetic language from those forms that seem to be fully used up in the act of communication and thus appear to be transparent. What is to be found in fiction or literature is an experience of another kind of language that appears *as itself*, something that seems to be concentrated to a particular degree in a poem. In German the word for poetry and fictional works is *Dichtung*, which, although it is not etymologically linked to it, carries a resonance with *dicht*, meaning "thick" or "dense." This density, for me, seems to characterize the experience of a poem, but as a result this is an extremely strange and elusive experience, for as Blanchot's works persistently recall, this thickening of language *as* language carries unknown consequences: "What is the result of the fact that we have literature? What is implied about being (*Qu'en est-il de l'être*), if one says that 'something like Literature exists'"?[1]

This question will be at the heart of the following inquiry, but I will retain my focus on the experience of a poem as there is something particularly dense about its language, something that seems to draw us as both reader and writer before the very fact of language, before our own language as humans. In attempting to address ourselves to this question of literature we cannot avoid the fact that the very manner of our address may be a problem, for it is not given that the experience of a poem is something that can be addressed as a "what." Consequently, we cannot avoid the fact that in order to come to terms with the question of literature we have to consider the manner in which we are making this attempt, that is, we have to consider our own language, and thus what it implies to address that which perhaps cannot be addressed in any substantive terms. Already, even before we have begun to address it, the experience of a poem has begun to address ourselves, insofar as it has brought into question our very relation to language. If we cannot simply proceed by assuming that the experience of a poem is such that we can address it as a "what" to be uncovered, in the manner in which we would perhaps ordinarily uncover a referent to a phrase or sentence, then we must rethink our own relation to language as reference, and this is part of what Blanchot calls the question *of* literature, the question that literature itself raises by its very existence.

While this question has long been part of the discourse of continental philosophy, largely due to the writings of Blanchot and following him, Jacques Derrida, what is not so readily familiar is the fact that the terms of this debate were articulated in their current form by Martin Heidegger. In doing so Heidegger brought this debate onto a more rigorous philosophical footing by inquiring into the relation of poetry and ontology, which in turn reflects back onto the ancient debate on the difference between the language of poetry and the language of philosophy. The reason why this debate has persisted and still persists is because there is something peculiar about the language of poetry or literature that seems to exceed or undermine the attempts of philosophy to pursue an ontological inquiry, that is, to try and bring to language an understanding of the meaning or nature of being. Hence Blanchot's question about the implications for being of the fact that literature exists; for what can it mean that there is something that apparently exceeds or undermines the possibility of uncovering a language of being? It is this question that literature itself persistently raises, for it is the very question that literature itself is, in which case any attempt to pursue an ontological inquiry by way of poetic language, which is the course that Heidegger's later work follows, must contend with the possibility that poetry itself may exceed or undermine that inquiry.

Heidegger's role in this debate has largely been obscured by the critical reception given to it by Blanchot and Derrida, but this not only misreads Heidegger, but also Blanchot and Derrida as well, as the very fact that they were prompted to take up this question in part comes from the seriousness and sophistication with which Heidegger treated this issue. Consequently, the aim of the present work is to demonstrate the necessity of grounding the contemporary debate on the question of literature within the ontological terms laid out by Heidegger. This is not to simply replace the language of literary theory with that of ontology, but more pointedly, to show that the question of literature implicates our own existence: the nature of human being. In this way the nature of poetic or literary language is such that it exposes, by way of its peculiar relation to ontology, something excessive about the nature of language itself, and thus also our relation to ourselves, our history, and others.

However, Heidegger's thinking presents us with a taxing problem, for it is at once the most developed examination of this linguistic (un)grounding of the human, but by virtue of this it is also the most overwhelming. It is necessary then to take a piecemeal approach, by which we can seek to find points of entry to his work that are also points of egress—points where it is possible to begin to defamiliarize his thinking, to stretch it beyond its own limits. These limits are accessible at precisely those points where the relation of philosophy to literature is engaged, which is where the philosophical nature of Heidegger's thinking is most at issue. For it is by way of literature that philosophy is forced to negotiate its own unstable grounding, its own porous limits. In teasing out these points Heidegger's work is not thereby surpassed or rendered irrelevant, nor does it simply transform Heidegger into Derrida; rather it is a way of reposing Heidegger's questions *after* Heidegger. Hence, although this approach may begin to stretch Heidegger's thinking beyond recognition, this is anything but unwarranted, for it is precisely in its estrangement that his legacy is most profound, and equally, this grants the best possible position from which to assess the most foreshortening limits of his thinking—its relation to history and textuality.

Of course, by turning back to Heidegger in this way, I am doing so by way of the impetus that Blanchot's question has raised, but the more the two writers are placed in dialogue, the more divergent their perspectives become. So while this might seem to reveal a Blanchotian Heidegger, it only does so insofar as it radicalizes and estranges Blanchot's work as well. This leaves each utterly distinct from the other, something that can only be appreciated if we do not assume a priori that one refutes or negates the other. This point is made all the more forcefully when the third partner in this dialogue is introduced: Friedrich Hölderlin. Again, the conventional discourse on Heidegger's relation to Hölderlin is such that it erases the singularity of each in favor of a partisan analysis. But the issue of singularity is central to both the matter and the terms of any discussion of the nature of literature and poetic experience, and it can only be understood once we realize how singularity dissembles itself and thereby suspends any relation we may attempt to establish with it. This returns us directly to the problem facing any ontological inquiry that seeks to address that which exceeds it, and as Heidegger, Hölderlin, and Blanchot would each insist, in their own ways, this problem is inherent to any ontological inquiry. Excession *is* the question raised by the issue of poetic ontology, and that to which the experience of a poem inevitably leads, something that Heidegger, Hölderlin, and Blanchot have, by their divergent responses, each given singular expression to, something that we can in our own way only attempt to repeat.

There is a pressing need for this research insofar as there is a general disinterest in the ontology of language and the issues it raises, which seems to derive from a disbelief in the value of this kind of philosophical and literary approach. Because this approach to language does not conform to the instrumental standards of accountability and transparency, where one is supposedly able to see any results immediately, it is deemed obscure and worthless. However, the ontological depth of this approach, which seeks to address itself to the human relation of language, is such that it can thereby expose what is most obscure and difficult about language, its finitude, which becomes apparent in our encounters with death, loss, or trauma. These encounters are what the writings of Heidegger, Hölderlin, and Blanchot have attempted to explore and as a result their works indicate something of the nature of what it is to be by way of this finitude, that is, how the claim of language exposes our humanity. It is thus the case that these exercises in and of language are also exercises of being.

. . .

The "quarrel between philosophy and poetry" that is discussed in Plato's *Politeia,* which as Socrates pointed out was already ancient by their time, has as its central focus the differing relation to truth that inheres in poetry and philosophy. As this quarrel is debated it becomes apparent that the difference lies in the fact that philosophy, for Plato, has a direct relation to truth, while in poetry truth becomes distorted. Heidegger refers to this debate in his lectures on Nietzsche's understanding of the will to power as art in the winter semester of 1936–37, in which Nietzsche's self-proclaimed "inverted Platonism" is grounded precisely in this problematic relation of art and truth. As Heidegger points out, it is necessary to understand what Plato understood by truth before we can ascertain how or whether Nietzsche inverted it, and for Heidegger, Plato's understanding of truth is grounded in the nature of appearance, such that truth lies not in the appearance of beings but in their essence, which Plato termed *eidos* and that subtends their sensible appearance. Philosophy is thus itself true in that thought is able to apprehend this essence directly, by *theoria,* in the supersensible appearance of the Idea, whereas poetry, by recapitulating this appearance in another mode, by way of sensible images, is only able to apprehend it indirectly and thus its truth is obscured and distorted. The word that Plato uses for this action of art in general is *mimēsis*, or "imitation," for by rendering appearance in another mode poetry or art repeats it and thereby dissembles its appearance. As a result art, for Plato, is distant from truth and thus subordinate to philosophy.

For Heidegger, Nietzsche's inversion of this model culminates in "How the 'True World' Finally Became a Fable" in *Twilight of the Idols*, where he relates how the true world of the *eidos* becomes progressively reified as it is transformed by Platonism and Kantianism, until with his own early work he recaptures a truth of the sensible world in the will to power as art. In this understanding, art is that mode of the will to power which, because of its inherence in the sensible rather than the supersensible, is our closest relation to the manner in which life extends and exceeds itself. Rather than seeing the truth of appearance in its Idea, which provides the constant background for what is, Nietzsche inverts this model by treating the variation and excession that occurs in the recapitulation of appearance in art, as the manner in which being most fully becomes what it is. But in this way *both* the true world and the sensible one are extinguished as their division is dissolved, and so Nietzsche doesn't simply invert but utterly removes himself from Platonism by finding truth *in* its appearances.

As Heidegger makes clear, this understanding of truth is to some extent already found in Plato's other works on the beautiful, as that which shines from out of itself, but in returning to this point Heidegger fails to also revisit the issue of *mimēsis* from the point of Nietzsche's revision of Platonism. This is an important omission, for if both the true world and the world of sensible appearances are extinguished, then there is no ground upon which to subordinate poetry to philosophy by saying that the former is *only* a *mimēsis* of truth. This is not simply a side issue in Heidegger's work for the issue of *mimēsis*, as the repetition of appearance, is at the heart of his transformation of phenomenology by way of poetry.

Twelve years before these Nietzsche lectures Heidegger had touched on the issue of *mimēsis* in his course on Plato's *Sophist*, where he describes how, in bringing forth an appearance by way of something other, *mimēsis* not only indicates its proximity to truth as that which subtends appearance, but also exposes its own existence as that which is but does not appear, and is thus to be understood, in a crucial ontological development, as *mē on*, "non-being." Thus, although *mimēsis* is dismissed on the one hand because of its distance from truth, it also brings about disruption on the other hand because it is too near to truth while not being it; *mimēsis* is both too close and too distant, for it allows the appearance of that which it is not, while itself disappearing in favor of an *other*. Hence, while *mimēsis* seems to remain in the secondary position of mere copying and thus subordinate production for Heidegger, it is nevertheless essential for the coming forth of language, for only out of its disappearance can there be appearance, only out of concealment can there by unconcealment; *mimēsis* is as the hidden (non)ground of truth.[2] It is to this issue of "supplementary" repetition that this work addresses itself, for it is central to the change that occurs in Heidegger's understanding of phenomenology in the period after *Being and Time*, in which he tries to respond to the question of poetry and thus to the ancient quarrel between philosophy and poetry.

Thus it is that the question of poetry leads directly into the issue of repetition, which then demands a rereading of *mimēsis*, as John Sallis has begun to sketch out over a number of works. This rereading not only exposes the relation of philosophy and poetry, but also and necessarily, exposes the limits of philosophy, which become apparent in its attempts to reach the ground of truth. Although no longer separated by a Platonic Idea, philosophy and poetry still diverge over their relation to repetition, in terms of the manner in which it occurs in the practice of thinking and poeticizing as writing. It is not the case that writing simply involves the obscurity and distortion previously ascribed to *mimēsis*, but that it brings out what Heidegger calls the abyssal untruth at the heart of truth: its endless finitude, which thereby renders elliptical our attempts to apprehend the truth of appearance, whether in thinking or poeticizing, although as we will see in substantially differing ways. That is, the repetition inherent in the appearance of appearance does not return to itself, but fragments, exposing an other relation to truth and language.

. . .

On 23 April 1934, following various disputes with his colleagues over the political direction of the institute, Heidegger resigned the rectorship of Freiburg University. That summer he had been scheduled to teach a course entitled "The State and Science," but on the first day of the course, at the beginning of May, Heidegger arrived and announced that he would be teaching a course on logic.[3] This turnaround led to a further and more radical development, for on the last day of the course, after examining the nature of logic and its relation to the essence of language, history, and people, he ended his course by declaring, by way of a conclusion on these interconnected themes, that "the original language is the language of poetry."[4] In doing so, Heidegger was not only setting out his position by re-establishing the terms of his philosophical work after the failure of his political engagements during his rectorship, but also was announcing the concerns of his next course in which he would examine Hölderlin's hymns "Germania" and "The Rhine." This turning to the language of poetry was no arbitrary choice arising from his disillusionment with the language of politics, but a deliberate move that would guide his thinking for the rest of his career. For as the following examination will show, Heidegger's concerns with poetry not only come from his lifelong love of literature initiated in his school days by readings of Hölderlin, Goethe, Rilke, and Trakl, but also, and more substantively, by his abiding concern with the language of philosophy.

Heidegger's interest in the nature of poetic language has often seemed to be obscure or eccentric, but as I will show, it is a concern that arises out of the heart of his thinking, for it is a concern with the nature of language, and specifically, with the question of what kind of language is capable of articulating the meaning of being. This question is central to any ontological inquiry, and for the young Heidegger this meant that he needed to start with an examination of the nature of logic, an examination that would guide his research for many years. Understanding the development of Heidegger's thinking in these early years is essential if we are to understand why and how he is drawn to the study of poetic language, and as a result I will briefly sketch out the main points of this development as they pertain to his analysis of the nature of logic and language before turning to the key rupture that occurs in this development: the issue of nothing.

For the young Heidegger, the traditional understanding of logic as the study of judgments could not explain how the correspondences that such judgments pertained to themselves arose. Thus the question of validity that logic concerned itself with had to be preceded by an analysis of the nature of meaning, that is, before we can assess the truth of meaning we have to understand the basis of that truth by looking for the origin of meaning. Resisting the idea that such meaning was imposed on matter from without or that its realm was limited to the analysis of propositional structures, Heidegger followed the work of Edmund Husserl and Emil Lask by suggesting that logic was not theoretical but arose out of the facticity, the sheer material presence, of existence as the very form of its materiality. For Husserl, this meant that existence was not mute but gave rise to its own categories as an excess, which it was then the task of phenomenology to reveal as the logic of phenomena. This uncovering of logic was achieved by what Lask described as a pure immersion or "dedication" to factical existence, by which these categories would reveal themselves through their own reflexivity. While Heidegger was greatly impressed by this approach, its findings were also disturbing, as the logic it revealed simply stated of existence that "it is." Phenomenology thus exposed the presence of being as that which is "there," its appearance simply appears, such that the meaning of being, its logic, would be the appearing of this appearance, the presencing of its presence. Meaning or logic would seem to arise as the *repetition* of existence, its excessive *tautology*.

The significance of this discovery in Heidegger's earliest lectures is pursued over the following years in a double strategy that inquires both into what form such a logic would take, and what it would reveal. Within the latter path Heidegger finds that the dedication that Lask advocated is an insufficient approach compared to the "limit-situations" studied by Karl Jaspers, who insisted that our awareness of existence is not revealed in everyday life but only when we encounter our limits: in death, struggle, guilt, or chance. This emphasis on finitude is at the heart of Heidegger's understanding of being, for it not only indicates the factical limits of our existence but also that the meaning of being can only be experienced when it is exposed to its limits, which implies that it is unsettling and difficult, if not impossible, to accept. But equally, as his reading of Wilhelm Dilthey shows, this also implies that this meaning occurs *as* the historicity of our being by way of its temporal horizons, thus revealing the phenomenological analysis of temporality as the meaning of being. The inquiry into the nature and form of such a logic develops by way of Heidegger's lengthy interrogation of Aristotle, which reveals the basis of logic as being grounded in the movement of *alētheia* (truth) as unconcealment. This movement is manifold and requires interpretation; hence the importance with which the logic of appearance, *logos apophantikos*, should be repeated by a hermeneutic logic. This repetition of logic does not move us further away from uncovering the meaning of being, but instead reverses the movement of the tautology of appearance from which it arises and thus implicates our own inquiry back into the explication of being.

On both counts then, in terms of our finitude and our interpretation, our own existence is made the heart of the possibility of understanding, and this gives to the development of a logic of being an irreducibly practical and historical project. Thus the question of the meaning of being becomes a question involving the nature of our own existence; it calls to us, as Heidegger repeatedly remarks, and thus both deeply affects us, unsettling our existence, and prompts us to respond, to open up its meaning through "care" to the manifold ways of "truthing" (*alētheuein*). Its question thus reveals a logic of finitude but also a creative logic, and the two are related, for in pursuing meaning we are pursuing our limits. But it is also a logic of deep duplicity or ambiguity, for in its facticity it is simply the appearance of appearance, the dia-phanous essence of phenomenology, which lets us see what is but also distorts. This is a significant issue for Heidegger's early work, as he is led, by way of a polarization of the movement of *alētheia* into the authentic and the everyday, to reduce the ambiguity of finitude and to emphasize the assumption of one's own limits in a moment of resolve. Although this horizonal schematization will soon disappear from Heidegger's language, the need for a violent logic of historical appropriation will persist into the 1930s.

Thus the turn to an inquiry into the nature of poetic language that then occurs is by no means unexpected, for poetry had long been a privileged mode of *alētheuein* for Heidegger, the only mode that could compare to thinking, as is evidenced by his brief but pointed comments from 1925 to 1927, when he was in the midst of an attempt to secure the "scientific" status of phenomenology. But this move from logic to *Dichtung* also conceals a move into the heart of Heidegger's own language and thus into the possibility for a greater awareness of its finitude and duplicity. It is within this later period that Heidegger's examination of language as the truth of being begins and that this work will follow by sketching out the major developments of his analysis of poetic language. As we have seen from this brief background survey, the appearance of *logos* is grounded in its relation to finitude and repetition, by which its appearance is rendered historical but also truthful, as it is a *logos* that is always *of* limits. Following his reading of Aristotle, Heidegger is made aware that the factical appearance of *logos* means that it is essentially related to *praxis* and is thus characterized by a deeply unsettling *pathos* that calls us to respond through "careful circumspection" (*fürsorgende Umsicht*, Heidegger's translation of *phronēsis*). Thus the language within which this *logos* appears must be capable of recovering this, for otherwise neither its finitude nor its historicity will be felt. It is because poetry, thus understood as neither *poiēsis* nor *theoria* but as *praxis*, answers to this demand that he finds its language more susceptible to truth than the language of science is, and it does so by repeating the turning of language that initially brought it about. For the turning *to* language that is *logos*, occurs *in* language by way of poetry; poetry is this turning of language onto itself; it is thus the *logos of logos*.

However, any attempt to follow this turning is faced with an extremely delicate hermeneutical challenge, for the attempt to interpret also occurs as an unfolding within language. While Heidegger explores the historical possibilities of this unfolding throughout the 1930s in an examination of the *alētheuein* of Hölderlin's poetry, it is not until the later works that he begins to approach the *pathos* of language's finitude. Here the "pain" of language that exposes us to our relation to death, reveals that it is through language that we uncover the meaning of our being, for it is through language that we are mortal. The response that we then need to make to the call of language, to the mark of finitude and historicity that it places on us, is left open by Heidegger, perhaps sensing the seriousness with which this hermeneutic challenge affects our existence. I will suggest though that the possibility of response already lies within the terms that Heidegger has drawn out, and that at least part of the work toward uncovering it has been started in the writings of Blanchot, who recognized that any experience of the finitude of language would also be an experience of alterity, for finitude is that which is endlessly other, thereby exposing the ethical dimension of our response: the demand and necessity of responding to finitude in its endless alterity. But the terms within which Blanchot finds this possibility carry their own limits, for our response to the alterity of language cannot be contained within the bounds of any hermeneutic "circle" since, as Hölderlin's writings show, it can never return to that which calls it, leaving it forever *elliptical*.

. . .

The centrality of the question of language to the writing of Heidegger's later works is indicated by his remark in the "Letter on 'Humanism'" that the project attempted in *Being and Time* failed because he could not find a language that was adequate to it (W: 159/249–250). From this failure Heidegger was forced to reconsider his approach and this change was first signaled in the essay that for many exemplifies the obscurity and absurdity of his later thinking: "What Is Metaphysics?" Here the rigorous analyses of fundamental ontology that had proved to be so impressive in *Being and Time* had seemingly given way to the mystical nonsense of nothing and its nihilation. My purpose here is not to rehearse the familiar debate between Heidegger and Rudolf Carnap, but to sketch out what is at stake in this new way of thinking and speaking.[5] For it is clear that if Heidegger turns to this way of using language because of the failure of the language he used in *Being and Time*, then this turning is what constitutes the work of his later writings, since to pursue the question of being through its manifold meanings is first and foremost to attempt to understand the relation of language and being.

"What Is Metaphysics?" is a pivotal paper in the development of Heidegger's early thinking, for in it he confronts the issue that has concerned him for the previous decade and in doing so signals the approach that will emerge in the following years. Throughout the 1920s, while he is developing his own understanding of phenomenology, Heidegger is also concerned with the status of phenomenology as a philosophical approach. As such, his work seeks to put phenomenology on a firm theoretical basis as fundamental ontology and thereby demonstrate its pre-eminence over the historical and scientific inquiries that dominated German thought at the time. After *Being and Time* had indicated the philosophical significance of fundamental ontology and its superiority over the historical sciences, it was necessary for Heidegger to then address himself to the language of the natural sciences. This was attempted by turning in the late 1920s to a "metontology" that would redirect fundamental ontology back into an analysis of the ontic or "worldly" sphere in which it arose, and in doing so address the natural world of "beings-as-a-whole" (*Seiende-im-Ganzen*). This approach was announced briefly at the end of *The Metaphysical Foundations of Logic* course in the summer of 1928 and again in *Kant and the Problem of Metaphysics*, which was published the following year after his lectures at Davos in March 1929.[6] It was at these lectures that Heidegger engaged in his critical debate with Ernst Cassirer over the cultural role of philosophy. While Cassirer believed in the idealistic possibilities of philosophy to raise humanity up into the transcendent values of symbolic cultural forms, Heidegger turned back to the earth, to the need for philosophy to thrust humanity into anxiety so that it could thereby encounter its own essence.

It is against the background of these diverging trends in his thinking that "What Is Metaphysics?" proclaimed Heidegger's position in his inaugural lecture at Freiburg University on 24 July 1929. It is not an exaggeration to suggest that there is a crisis in Heidegger's thinking in the late 1920s, in which he attempts to resolve the dilemma of legitimizing his thinking either by situating it in the traditional grounds of the natural and human sciences, or by grounding it on its own terms. This dilemma is firmly decided in favor of the latter in his inaugural lecture, but to do so Heidegger must first dispose of the necessity of grounding his thought in the language of scientific thinking, and thus confront the question that had concerned him since *Being and Time*; that of the status of ontological inquiry in the face of the natural sphere of beings as a whole. It is telling that in doing so Heidegger also phrases his new approach in terms that distance it from the traditional use of "logic," for he has been concerned over the previous decade with trying to understand the nature of logic and this has brought him to the point of questioning the very nature of what we mean by the term and what its relation to thinking might be. It is this radical shifting away from the traditional use of logic that has caused "What Is Metaphysics?" to be so misread, as Carnap has shown, but that has also shown for the first time the new ground of Heidegger's thinking, the earth that he had referred Cassirer to, which would set the course for all of his later thinking: *nothing*.

As he states at the very beginning of the lecture it will be necessary to pursue the question of metaphysics by way of a particular problem, rather than through a general inquiry, for it is only in the particular that metaphysics can find "the proper occasion to introduce itself" (W: 1/82). While this repeats the emphasis on the concrete begun in Heidegger's earlier phenomenological analyses, it is immediately revised by its comparison with the scientific methodological necessity of needing to refer to beings as a whole. At this point Heidegger addresses himself directly to what such an approach implies and in doing so he comes across the issue that will undermine its metaphysical legitimacy. For if science, in treating beings as a whole, directs itself to beings themselves, if these become the object and matter of its inquiry to the extent that nothing else is included, then there is an undisclosed linguistic conundrum at work here:

> precisely in the way scientific man secures to himself what is most properly his, he speaks, whether explicitly or not, of something different. What should be examined are beings only and otherwise—nothing; beings alone and further—nothing; solely beings and beyond that—nothing (*Erforscht werden soll nur das Seiende und sonst—nichts; das Seiende allein und weiter—nichts; das Seiende einzig und daraüber hinaus—nichts*). (W: 3/84)

This way of talking and writing seems fanciful; what is to be gained by taking up such an arbitrary turn of phrase into a philosophical inquiry? Heidegger's point, however, is that such a turn of phrase is anything but arbitrary, for its construction and usage indicate a concealed presumption about the scientific approach in which nothing is treated as nothing, that is, it is dismissed as meaningless and irrelevant although it is nevertheless still used as an essential tool for delimiting and thereby constituting the field of inquiry. Moreover, it is dismissed in this fashion without being seriously addressed; what is actually taking place when we talk in this way is passed over despite its clear rhetorical power.

It is thus that Heidegger moves us from the scientific methodology to its rhetorical basis, thereby shifting the grounds of the inquiry into the *language* in which such a method is developed. Ordinarily this would suggest a turning to the logical presuppositions of the scientific approach, but as Heidegger quickly demonstrates, this cannot help us here for it is precisely by means of these logical presuppositions that nothing is dismissed. A discrepancy has thus been exposed, for while logic assumes that "nothing" in these phrases has no meaning, its rhetorical power clearly persists. We know from Heidegger's earlier lectures on Aristotle that the nature of logic and its relation to rhetoric were key points in his ontological explorations, insofar as the nature of language is to be approached not only by the traditional logic of propositions, but also by its appearance in rhetoric, suggesting that the "logic" of language is much broader than our traditional assumptions may claim. Equally, as this "logic" is itself the *logos* of being, we can by way of the logic of language come to an understanding of the language of the *logos* itself: the logic of logic. In this way rhetoric does not simply constitute the style of a language, thereby indicating its points of emphasis, but actually directs us to the differential logic of language, which can reveal itself by way of propositions and statements but also by way of style and emphasis. For in both cases, the logic of language, the way that language itself works, reveals itself.

Thus, if we find that a scientific methodology proceeds from a point of delimiting its inquiry by treating it as "beings only and otherwise—nothing," then there is a very precise point of negotiation occurring here that would not have taken place if it had simply stated its field of inquiry as "beings only." Heidegger's point here is that in raising and then excluding "nothing," science has thereby exposed its own lack of concern with the question of the relation between being and nothing, and thus the nature of nothing, and as a result failed in its inquiry into beings. For what has been assumed is that the logical notion of nothing as the "not" of empty negation adequately covers the presence of nothing and its relation to being, while it is instead possible, as Heidegger will go on to indicate, that nothing has a very real status that cannot be so easily dismissed. It is this concrete particularity that Heidegger believes will open up the question of metaphysics for us, and that is addressed in the question—not of "what is nothing?" that would simply return us to the propositional problems of negation, for nothing "is" *not*—but of "how is it with nothing?" that refers us directly to the manner in which nothing "is" (W: 4–6/84–86).

As is evident, it is by adopting this approach to language and logic that Heidegger is announcing his response to the scientific methodology that provides the paradigm of legitimacy, not only for our inquiries into beings as whole, but also for our own status and position as inquirers. That is, it is by the manner of his treatment of these questions that Heidegger directs us to the possibility of understanding them anew, by way of their language, which is the manner in which his thinking will henceforth proceed. However, this only partly introduces us to the significance of Heidegger's new thinking here, for it is first necessary to understand *how* nothing is to be experienced. To begin, Heidegger points out how in a certain fundamental mood (*Stimmung*) like boredom or love we find ourselves by way of its disposition (*Befindlichkeit*) in the midst of beings as a whole, and that correlatively there are also moods in which this experience is removed, that is, in which the feeling of beings as whole is wholly removed (W: 8/87). This experience is encountered in the fundamental mood of anxiety (*Angst*): for when beings as a whole recede from us this receding itself oppresses us, exposing all things and ourselves to indifference, and in doing so nothing is thereby manifest and we are left suspended (W: 8–9/88). This uncanny experience "robs us of speech" but also exposes us to the very essence of our own existence, our being (Dasein), which is to say that being is *by way of* nothing, and that this is how nothing "is" (W: 9/89).

Thus, anxiety not only exposes us to being in the manner in which beings as a whole slip away, but also exposes us to nothing, and in the oppression of this slipping away, its repelling, is to be found the "nihilation" (*Nichtung*) of nothing, its essence: *how* it is (W: 11/90). Anxiety suspends us in the interval marked in and by the phrase "beings—and not nothing," such that by way of this manner of speaking we make possible its exposure: there is a pause, a hiatus, and for a moment we are held between being and nothing, in the very question of our own existence: "Da-sein means: being held out into nothing" (W: 12/91). Here we uncover the problem that will now concern Heidegger, for what is the nature of this "holding"? "Who" holds? Furthermore, this manner of thinking has suggested that in some sense to be examined, being and nothing are the "same," which only places more pressure on the manner of our own exposure, our own ek-sistence, or Da-sein. This complex interrelation of being and nothing has a duplicity or ambiguity (*Zweideutigkeit*) that cannot be settled but rather persists as a "turbulence" within our existence and our language (W: 13–14/92). Because of its deeply unsettling nature this anxiety is ignored or "repressed," and this is precisely what has occurred in our ontological inquiries by way of the traditional logical treatment of nothing as negation, for these inquiries can only proceed by excluding the position of the inquirer; "beings only and otherwise—nothing" (W: 14/93). Hence the existence of nothing as that which is both impossible to define and yet also essential to being and language exerts an abyssal pressure on our thinking and speaking, such that it undermines any logic that would seek to marginalize it as simple negation.

Nothing cannot be broached in any ordinary language, but it can exert itself at any time on our existence, for it is by way of this pressure that we are, even if it is a pressure that we cannot bear. Thus our being is traversed by a tension that exceeds it and that exposes itself only by way of the absences of speech and thought that punctuate our existence *as* being, and not nothing. Heidegger is moving toward a theme here that will percolate throughout his later works; that of the significance of what occurs when speech and thinking do not come, and what arrives in their place, and what we can say of the place we thereby hold. For if, as Heidegger remarks here, we are the "placeholder" or lieu-tenant of nothing, then this is a deeply dissymmetrical relation, for it places us under a finitude that makes it impossible to respond to the nothing that grants it (W: 15/93). The question of metaphysics, as the questioning that *is* our existence, insofar as it holds us out into nothing, is thus of the highest seriousness and urgency as it indicates that being itself, because it only manifests itself by way of nothing, is also finite (W: 17/95). Metaphysics is not only the mark of our existence, but also the mark of our existence as transcendence, insofar as we *are* only by way of the nihilation of beings as whole (*meta ta physika*), which means that our existence and our inquiries can only proceed by recognizing nothing as that in which we are abyssally grounded, and that science by suppressing it can only become hopelessly misguided (W: 18/95–96).

Heidegger's use of "metaphysics" and "transcendence" here will disappear in the years to come as both terms become increasingly inadequate for a thinker trying to free himself from traditional modes of thinking. However, the lecture as a whole will remain a constant part of Heidegger's work, as an afterword is added in 1943 and an introduction in 1949, refreshing its position in his thinking and reinstating its significance as a key step of his thought. Indeed when the *Pathmarks* collection is published in 1967, this lecture will be placed at the very beginning of his path of thinking. For by introducing nothing Heidegger has exposed language and thinking to an endless demand, which not only causes him to turn away from scientific modes of thinking, but also to question the grounds of his own thinking in such a way that this questioning *becomes* his thinking as he seeks to find a language in which he can hold himself out into nothing.[7] It is in the face of this demand that in the 1930s he turns to a more poetic and contorted mode of thinking and writing, until he gives to this punctuation of being and nothing the name of *Ereignis*.

This development is already apparent in the current piece, for if our mode of thinking designates its concern as "beings only and otherwise—nothing," then it encounters a fundamental problem, for the delimitation of the object of inquiry occurs *by way of language*, which is itself disregarded. Heidegger is deliberately and provocatively drawing our attention to what is ordinarily treated as transparent and unproblematic: the basis upon which we open our inquiries, which is language. This does not mean that we can simply rephrase the statement as "beings only and otherwise—language," for this is to fail to address the specificity of "nothing." Heidegger does not use this construction casually, nor is he in using it substantivising nothing into something, but in a very real sense, the same sense that enables us to disregard it and overlook its difficulty, language "is" nothing. For it is no thing that we can address ourselves to as we would to any being—which is what Heidegger pursues in the body of the lecture, for language dissolves in the encounter with nothing—instead what is being attempted in this formulation is the task of drawing out the language of our thinking as it is. That is, not to substantivize it into an object of study but to turn our thinking around to its own language, but this also necessarily occurs in thinking by way of language. Hence, the anxiety and difficulty of pursuing this endless turn in which we seek to enter that space designated by the qualification ". . . and otherwise—nothing," which is nothing, but language.

While Carnap found this manner of talking absurd and nonsensical, Ludwig Wittgenstein could "readily think what Heidegger means" by this discussion of anxiety in which we "run up against the limits of language," something he did not feel should simply be consigned to silence, but should be pursued because of its difficulty.[8] Indeed, the ontological shock that occurs when we come face-to-face with the limits of language, with the sheer fact that there is something, rather than nothing, is for Wittgenstein "ethics." Fascinating as this proposal is, he appears not to have followed it through; for Heidegger however, this encounter cannot be turned away from as it is not only the basis of thinking, but also being, by which we can also come to understand the transformations that occur in Heidegger's language over the rest of his career. These include transformations like the development of terms such as *Riß*, *Brauch*, *Geschick*, *Ereignis*, and *Austrag*, which are not so much concepts designating objects of thought as reflexive turns of language, terms that are concerned with their own terms as limits of language and that thereby direct us toward the nature of language as the relation *of* being, as that which locates our inquiry (beings only) by dislocating our inquiring (. . . and otherwise—nothing). Any attempt to read Heidegger must be attentive to this ambivalence in his language, one that is not unconscious but deliberately pursued as the ambi-valence of a language that both is and is not, which provides access to what is, while deferring access to itself.

But if language is that by which we are granted access to what is, how are we to encounter language itself? To encounter language as such, that is, outside its signification or communication, would seem to be impeded by the fact that we must engage in language in order to do so, hence, as that which grants access it is both that which is closest and that which is most distant from thinking, for any attempt to turn thinking around to encounter its own language will find that it has already translated and mediated that language by virtue of its attempt to access it. This problem, which parallels but also moves beyond the phenomenological difficulties encountered in trying to access the coming to presence of phenomena beyond their apparent presence, is what drives Heidegger toward the examination of poetry and its relation to thought. That he finds some sort of solution to this problem in the poetic experience with language is clear, but what becomes disruptive is the need to find a way of translating this poetic solution into the thinking experience with language. It is this need that is behind the transformations in Heidegger's language that take place after 1929, which are thus neither mystical nor nonsensical but that constitute a rigorous experiment in thinking by transforming its language so as to enable an experience with that language.

The question that then arises is whether such an experience is possible, or whether the encounter that Heidegger has found taking place in the poetic experience with language is instead a singular encounter that cannot be translated into another experience. This has been the traditional response to Heidegger's engagement with poetic language: that he has either diminished poetry by presuming to translate its experiences into the language of thinking, or that he has diminished thinking by translating it into the idiom of poetic language. I would dispute such readings by returning to the line from "What Is Metaphysics?," for while Heidegger's use of the rhetorical conclusion ". . . and otherwise—nothing" might seem to be arbitrary or contrived, it is apparent from a closer examination that Heidegger is attempting a very specific dislocation of language that is akin to the mechanisms at work in some poetic experiences with language. Also, as this phrase is examined, it shows itself to be a genuine encounter *with* language; in other words, Heidegger has brought about the experience of nothing that he is discussing. The rhetorical dislocation experienced when the discussion of "beings" becomes the discussion of "beings only and otherwise—nothing," is not just a contrived play on words but a dislocation of the ordinary thinking experience of language into an experience with language itself in its relation to thinking. For the manner in which the object of discussion (beings only) is first qualified and then opened up to a suspension of thought (dis-qualified) is precisely the experience that occurs in the encounter with language, when thinking in turning in on itself, in running up against its own limits, encounters nothing, but language.

As significant as this aspect of Heidegger's thinking is to the development of his later works, it inevitably becomes submerged when he is concerned with other topics: history, technology, politics, and so forth. At these times the poetic experience with language is subverted to these other topics, which brings about its own problems and raises the question of the place of such experiences within thinking; how are we to follow through on the experience with language without abandoning its essential singularity? Perhaps this is what is at issue in Wittgenstein's gnomic affirmation that it is here that we find ethics, and thus also the stakes of our own responses to Heidegger's thought.

. . .

Thus, in order to understand Heidegger's thinking of poetic language we must first locate it within the broader course of his thinking, but with this comes the realization that Heidegger's thinking of poetry is not an arbitrary or eccentric diversion from his early "philosophical" thinking, but is instead the inevitable development arising from the grounds of that earlier thinking. I will begin therefore, by seeking to delimit these grounds in order to understand the basic intuition that guides Heidegger's thinking of poetry, which will thus serve as a basis upon which to assess his later development. An analysis of his early works indicates a persistent concern with the nature of philosophical language and with the specific problem of whether it is capable of responding to the demands of a phenomenological hermeneutics of facticity. The intuition that any approach to facticity requires a phenomenological hermeneutics is the basis upon which the early Heidegger assesses the nature of language and logic, and although these rubrics will fade from his vocabulary by the end of the 1920s, their guiding suppositions about the requirements of any ontology remain. These suppositions take the form of the dimensions within which Heidegger's thinking of language develops, which are its essential relations with finitude, repetition, and truth.

These then become the dimensions through which Heidegger's thinking of poetry develops, and as a result, poetry in turn comes to indicate the logic of language. This necessarily implicates the language of philosophy and thereby issues a radical challenge to any language that would attempt to articulate the meaning of being, that is, to be an ontology. The depth of this challenge is partly illustrated by the fact that Heidegger himself only seemed to become fully aware of it in the 1950s; prior to this, his concern with articulating the historical meaning of being led to a diminution of the role of finitude in favor of a more resolute temporality. An examination of two of Heidegger's major statements on language from the 1930s ("The Origin of the Work of Art" and "As when on a holiday . . ." in chapters 2 and 3, respectively) will indicate this tension and lay out the need for alternative readings. This can be found initially in Hölderlin's writings, which Heidegger studied in this period, but that articulate a very different relation between language and temporality, thus allowing us not only to assess how far Heidegger's thinking has traveled by the 1950s, but also to leave open the possibility that the situation of finitude in language may uncover an unanswerable demand. It is to this problem that the writings of Blanchot seek to respond by interpreting this demand in terms of its alterity, thereby transforming the task of ontology into an ethics and suggesting that insofar as poetry responds to this demand, it not only indicates the logic of language but also unveils itself as a language *of* finitude.

To understand the relation of poetic and philosophical language we need to understand how Heidegger's later writings developed out of his earlier thinking; thus I will be reading the earlier works with a view to what they reveal about Heidegger's changing relation to language. As I will argue, Heidegger's encounter with Hölderlin provokes a rethinking of the finitude of language that paves the way for a new approach to the language of philosophy. Thus themes that guided his early thinking of language find themselves radically reconceived in the later writings by way of what Heidegger has learned from his reading of Hölderlin. While Heidegger's relation with Hölderlin has been extensively researched, it has rarely been placed in the context of his rethinking of the nature of language in his later writings. Equally, the few works that have studied the later language essays have not considered the role of Hölderlin's writings as a constitutive part of the development of Heidegger's thinking in these later works.[9] But it is by way of his reading of Hölderlin that Heidegger comes to see that the repetition of language encounters its own finitude in *writing*, and that repetition is thus the condition of both the possibility and the impossibility of relation, be it logical or ethical.

To understand this, we need to perceive Heidegger's encounter with Hölderlin in terms of its textuality and its rhetorical *praxis* and thus not to see Hölderlin as simply another piece of Heidegger's thinking that needs to be explicated, or as an example of Heidegger's philosophical arrogance in appropriating the language of poetry. The former approach is the traditional understanding of Heidegger's reading of Hölderlin and poetry in general, while the latter, critical approach has become increasingly popular recently.[10] Noticeably, the nature of each approach accounts for their weaknesses, as the exegetical readings spend too little time trying to understand Hölderlin's work on its own terms, and the polemics seek too quickly to damn Heidegger for insensitivity. In both cases the problem is the same, for the relation between the two has been decided beforehand, as either proximal or remote, while the reading itself only takes seriously one side of the relationship. The overall structure of my approach is designed to counter this failing, for we need to take Hölderlin's thinking as seriously as Heidegger's language.

Thus the development of this work involves a number of interrelating strands, including the relation between Heidegger and Hölderlin, poetry and thinking, and language and writing. In developing this combined approach it is possible to see that Heidegger is neither appropriating nor misappropriating Hölderlin's thinking, but is engaged in an exploration of the same problem: that of the *relation* of language. It is this approach that underpins each of their works, and is the most pressing concern of their writing. This brings Heidegger's work into relation with Blanchot, whose work persistently interrogates the very possibility of writing as relation. Here lies the necessity for inquiring into the possibility of poetry *after* Heidegger: for within Heidegger's work, alongside his interlocutors, lies the most far-reaching examination of the relation of language, and what it means to reach the limits of this relation. For at these limits lies the basis of a new kind of writing in the ellipsis exposed by the finitude of language, a writing that could be understood as the *mimēsis* of this ellipsis, the hidden ground and endless repetition of its truth: the only relation left to us.

Part One

The Mark of a Poem

1

Repeat
The Experience of Poetic Language

> At the end we say: *Being is the most said.* For it is said in every word of language, and nevertheless discourse and writing talk for the most part only about beings. This comes to articulation. Even where we actually say the "is" and thus name being, we say the "is" only to assert a being about a being. *Beings are said. Being is kept silent about.* But not by us and on purpose. For we are unable to discover any trace of an intention not to say being. Hence, the keeping silent must indeed come from being itself. Hence, being is a keeping silent about itself, and this is certainly the ground of the possibility of keeping silent and the origin of silence. In this realm of silence, the word first arises each time.
>
> —Heidegger, *Basic Concepts*, 1941

On the last day of his final seminar at Zähringen in September 1973, in the closing minutes after reading and discussing a paper on Parmenides, Heidegger made the following announcement: "I name the thinking here in question tautological thinking. It is the original meaning of phenomenology. Further, this kind of thinking is before any possible distinction between theory and praxis" (S: 399/80). To understand this extraordinary statement we need to return to the very beginning of Heidegger's thinking; as he indicates himself, here at the end of his career, our task is as always to go back and start again. The obscurity and even eccentricity of a "tautological thinking" is only to be made sense of if we can perceive its relation to phenomenology, and this is what I shall proceed with here, for in tautology we find the deepest roots of Heidegger's poetic thinking.

Heidegger's first investigations of phenomenology centered on the attempt to find a language that could respond to the dual problems of intuition and expression; how are we able to access the world without reducing it and how can we bring it to language without objectifying it? These questions had originally been raised by Paul Natorp in response to Husserl's phenomenology and as Husserl's assistant, Heidegger devoted much energy in his first courses after the war to trying to answer them (ZBP: 99–109/83–92). In these courses Heidegger developed his own form of phenomenology by grounding it in an inquiry into the nature of logic that had first arisen in his habilitation of 1915. Here, his study of the relation between the categories and the meanings of being in medieval scholasticism was conducted by way of his readings of the neo-Kantian Lask.[1] The influence of Lask on Heidegger's early work is considerable for Lask interpreted Husserl's work on categorial intuition—by which we are prereflectively absorbed in a world of categories—to mean that this intuition would itself give rise to its own reflexive categories, thus implying that our factical experience was not formless but already meaningful and thereby pregnant with its own logic as a *primal surplus*, in the form of its "formal indication." Lask's response was thus to advocate a dedication (*Hingabe*) to this factical experience, from which a generalized reflexive category of "there being something experienced" arises within language as a simple "there is" (*es gibt*) of presence.

Logic, as the relation between the factical and the reflexive, has thus been grounded in experience rather than in value, but an experience that gives rise to form by way of its material categories. Within his first postwar course in the spring of 1919, "The Idea of Philosophy and the Problem of Worldview," Heidegger moves on from the theoretical position of this earlier reading by addressing the implications of this factical dedication, for if we are immersed in the experience of a "world" rather than of data, then this is a world whose logic already expresses itself by way of our intentional engagements, such that experience is already a prereflective interpretation (ZBP: 70–76/59–64). The language of philosophy needs to come out of this factical logic *of* phenomena, and to do so this phenomeno-logy needs to be revealed by way of a hermeneutics of facticity, that is, an interpretation that is a repetition of the interpretation already present in the formal indications of what is. This interpretation, which is thus a logic *of* logic, is only proposed here and still needs to be worked out, but already Heidegger has, by his elaboration of the implications of factical dedication, shown how this reveals an *event* of "worlding," and one in which the coming about of the meaning of presence—its appearance as a world—occurs by concealing its ground (ZBP: 115–17/97–99). Thus the logic of worlding primarily comes to language as a sheer *es gibt*, in which the presencing of presence is, as Theodore Kisiel observes, both a tautology and a heterology in that it simply repeats itself, "*es*" "*gibt*," and in doing so becomes different, *es gibt*, which thus places pressure on the language through which we come to this experience, as it is both the medium and the meaning of worlding.[2]

Heidegger works over the next few years to develop these initial insights by way of further readings and criticisms of Husserl, Lask, Natorp, Dilthey, and Jaspers, as well as inquiries into the phenomenology of religious experience. A key change that occurs in these years is the awareness that the "dedication" to experience that he had earlier pursued is insufficient, insofar as it is not distinguished from the immersion into everydayness that characterizes the experience of the masses. Already in the last hour of the first 1919 course he had noted that the "immanent historicity of life as such constitutes hermeneutical intuition," but over the next few years this unfolding would become sharpened by his encounter with Jaspers's work on "limit-situations," and by his examination of the religious experience of the "moment" (*kairos*) (ZBP: 219/187). According to Jaspers's work in *Psychology of Worldviews,* our awareness of existence only arises out of certain limit-situations, like death, struggle, guilt, or chance, where we encounter our own finitude. Heidegger's lengthy review of this work indicates how much he appreciated this idea, but also how he felt that it needed to be translated into an ontological problematic. Within this context Heidegger first mentions the role of the "conscience" (*Gewissen*), as that which brings about an experience of the self through an encounter with one's own historicity in a moment of union of past, present, and future.[3]

The significance of these developments is manifold, for the ontological understanding of finitude means that the hermeneutics of existence is first characterized by a distress or insecurity that carries a formal indication of the essence of our being. That is, there is a *logos* here that is uncanny and that needs interpreting, and in doing so it indicates the duplicity of our being as that which is both immersed in historicity and facticity (*da*), and exterior to that immersion, indicating the *logos* of our being (*sein*).[4] The pressure of this duplicity is not only ontological, but also affects our attempts to interpret and articulate, our ontic hermeneutics, as well. This means that Heidegger is in need of refashioning his way of thinking to bring it into accord with this need; thus the unsettling conscience of our existence needs to be translated into a "destructuring" (*Destruktion*) of the philosophical tradition itself by a thinking that is now required to put our own being at the heart of its inquiries. This hermeneutic folding of the ontic and the ontological also implicates Heidegger's thinking into an interrogation of the relations between history and language, and the nature of the language of thinking; if we are to bring to language an understanding of the *logos* of being, then how are we to do so? And what does this entail for our thinking relation with such a language?

Thus it is that, in the summer of 1921, he turns to a reading of Aristotle that will continue unbroken until the winter of 1924.[5] Within this period Heidegger will not only begin work on *Being and Time*, but also will start and then drop book-length projects on Aristotle and Dilthey. These works will give him the opportunity to develop his thinking in private and extend his coursework in more radical directions. In doing so, he will lay the grounds for the work included in *Being and Time*, and also possibilities that will have to be put aside until that project is over. The discoveries of his Aristotle readings not only include the understanding of *alētheia* as unconcealment but also that this unconcealment "is said in many ways," which leads to the interrelated concerns of this speaking or *logos* of *alētheia* as *pathos*, *praxis*, and *phronēsis*. The significance of these developments lies not only in the relation of logic to the movement of *alētheia* as unconcealment, and thus as a finite *kinēsis*, but also, and thereby, to an understanding of the nature of truth as grounded in a temporal moment (*kairos*) of unconcealment and as thus marked by a unique historical unfolding. Thus a logic of the categorial structures of phenomena reveals them to be modes of *alētheuein*, "being-true," that is, "modes in which factical life temporalizes itself, unfolds itself, and *speaks* with itself."[6] The problem of our relation to language is thus given its full ramifications, for as the logic of phenomena it is not only the logic of being, but also *our* logic; the language and the temporality of our own existence.

This understanding is part of Heidegger's move to recover the ontological possibilities of Aristotle's thought, for he finds in book 6 of the *Nicomachean Ethics* that the manifold meaning of being transpires through different modes of *alētheuein*, some of which (*epistemē* and *technē*) refer to the world, while others (*sophia* and *phronēsis*) refer to one's own being. Within this separation there is also a further distinction between those modes that deal with that which is permanent (*epistemē* and *sophia*) and those that deal with that which can be otherwise (*technē* and *phronēsis*). As modes of truth these latter modes are thus liable to ambiguity, for they can either take things as they are or in ways that differ from how they are (*pseudos*); there is thus a "taking-as" (*legein*) in *alētheuein*, such that what is appears as (*apophansis*) it is or as it is not. These modes of *alētheuein* parallel the later distinctions Heidegger makes between the world and one's own being, and the inauthentic and authentic; hence *epistemē* and *technē* govern the worldly spheres of *theoria* and *poiēsis* as those modes that deal with the present-at-hand and the ready-to-hand. With *sophia* and *phronēsis* the latter becomes more important for Heidegger as it is grounded in the finite dealings of *praxis*, that is, with the singular facticity of existence, rather than with the completed and pure understanding (*sophia*) of the *archē*. *Phronēsis* thus has a distinctive relation to time in that it is directed toward the future by virtue of its consideration of how to act well, not in terms of any particular future outcome, but rather to a preservation of the moment of acting well; it is thus both a temporalization of our being as "care" (*Sorge*) and the "doubling" or repetition of this temporalization as "resolution" (*Entschlossenheit*).[7]

Here lies the origin of the dimensions of Heidegger's inquiries into the meaning of being, as it is distinguished from the meaning of our everyday lives, which indicate that in our ontological position we experience the *logos* of *alētheuein* as both *pathos* and *phronēsis*, that is, as that which both affects us in our being by determining our state or disposition and also calls us to care for our being by drawing us into the moment of its ownmost possibility. Thus the meaning of our being is not primarily experienced as *theoria* or *poiēsis*, but as *praxis*; it is not something that we "view" or "make," but live, insofar as it is that which constitutes what we "do" and "how" we are, and that becomes apparent when it is taken to its limits (*peras*), which is the basis for Aristotle's understanding of the definition (*horismos*) of meaning.[8] It is thus from here that in the course of the 1925 summer semester Heidegger can announce that the "uncoveredness (*Entdecktheit*) of Dasein, in particular the disposition (*Befindlichkeit*) of Dasein, can be made manifest by means of words in such a way that certain new possibilities of Dasein's being are set free. Thus discourse (*Rede*), especially *poetry*, can even bring about the release of new possibilities of the being of Dasein. In this way, discourse proves itself positively as a *mode of temporalization* (*Zeitigung*) of Dasein itself."[9]

This would seem to be the first significant mention of poetry as a constitutive part of Heidegger's thinking of the meaning of being, and as such it reappears in very similar forms over the next few years until 1934.[10]

Although its reappearance at this time seems more understandable now that its relations to logic, language, and temporalization have been sketched out, it is more difficult to explain its absence from Heidegger's development until this time. Partly, this is simply due to the variety of concerns that Heidegger is pursuing up until this point, but just as his work throughout is engaged with examining the language of philosophy, so too, especially in the 1920s, is Heidegger interested in the "scientific" status of phenomenology as fundamental ontology. It is only when he abandons this attempt that he begins to open up to a more poetic language, mediated first by an intensive investigation in the early 1930s into the essence of truth and the nature of the work of art.

Central to this change is Heidegger's awareness of finitude, which since his earliest readings of Lask has been present as that inevitable concealment that is equiprimordial with revealing. But the finitude of existence occurs not only as the horizons of our temporality, but also as the hiddenness of the *logos* itself. As we will shortly see, the finitude of the *logos* is initially pursued by Heidegger through a phenomenological hermeneutics, in which the position and status of a phenomenological language develop by way of an analysis of the structure of "explication" (*Auslegung*), by which the initial problems of intuition and expression come together in the hermeneutic circle of existence. That this is not truly a circle, but is rather *elliptical*, is a result of the extreme finitude of explication, as the logic thereby expressed is born from the anticipation (*Vorlaufen*) that enables explication, which not only falls far short of ever finding its way back to the *logos* that it seeks, but also rends itself from the hiddenness it leaves behind. Whether Heidegger's studies of the nature of language and poetry and their relations to thinking find a response to this finitude is the question that motivates this inquiry.

. . . The Turning of *Logos* . . .

The development of Heidegger's understanding of *logos* has thus come up against an internal tension, for although the logic of phenomena is that which allows it to appear as it is, there is also, within the facticity of this appearance, a repetition in which this logic brings its own temporalization, leading to a doubling and finitude of appearance. The *logos apophantikos* leads, as the Aristotelian understanding of *alētheuein* has shown, into a *logos* of *hermeneia* as well, of interpretation as well as appearance.

However, the position of this *logos* within Aristotle is secondary to the apophantic *logos*, which is the primary locus of the constant presence of *ousia*. It is from this latter sense of *logos* that logic as assertion and judgment has originated, with its understanding of truth as fixed and propositional, that is, as a property of being, rather than as part of its event. In his course on logic in the winter of 1925–26 Heidegger explored this need to move to an understanding of logic grounded in temporality rather than in presence, and in doing so proposed a "phenomenological chronology" as a way of bringing the horizons of temporality to language, to find a logic of time, but this faltered and was never followed through.[11] Instead, he perceived the possibility for a "destructuring of Greek ontology and logic" by drawing on the logic of rhetoric and poetics, which because it operated within the singular historicity of a *praxis*, the hermeneutic "as" rather than the fixed apophantic "as" of simple appearance, could find the logic of its own finite temporality.[12]

This aporetic relation of logic to temporality and finitude is a major reason why Heidegger dropped the project begun in *Being and Time*, which found its language becoming inappropriate when it sought to bring the ecstatic nature of temporalization within the terms of a horizonal schematization. Alongside this difficulty is the concomitant problem of the ontological difference, of the relation between being and beings, which is actualized in the temporal ecstases of being. Within the model of a horizonal schematization being is seen as the ground against which our existence becomes temporalized, but this brings too much of a sense of an originary separation of being and beings that does not make possible an understanding of how this differentiation takes place. Instead, the explication of *logos* as *praxis* and *phronēsis* means that the event of temporalization occurs out of a moment of finitude (*Augenblick*) that renders its temporalization singular and factical. Being is thus not a given, not a ground or horizon upon which beings appear by virtue of a logic that is still apophantic, but an occurrence of finitude that exposes our own existence. The language within which the thinking of this event of differentiation (*Ereignis*) can occur must therefore respond to the recurrence of this event, which leaves it endlessly singular and finite, by attempting to speak from out of its opening (*Auslegung*). But in responding to this temporalization language brings its own historical unfolding, so we have to ask whether it is by way of this explication of *logos* that we are exposed to our own temporalization. But if this is the case then how can we speak of this unfolding, if it is always already occurring as our language?

Part of this doubling comes to be taken up by Heidegger's understanding of phenomenology, which by virtue of its parts, *phainō* and *logos*, involves a sense of repetition in which each comes to reflect the other, such that a phenomeno-logy means: "to let what shows itself be seen from itself, just as it shows itself from itself" (SZ: 34/58). Furthermore, this phenomenological hermeneutics parallels the doubling of our factical hermeneutics as *zōon logon echon*, the "life that has speech," thus implicating phenomenology itself as part of the *alētheuein* of existence, such that Dasein *in its being* is both the appearance and the explication of facticity, the *praxis* of its own *logos*. While the problems of intuition and expression have thus become ontological inquiries in that they explicate our very being, they have also become inquiries bounded by the finite hermeneutics of our practical, historical existence, something that differs from the Aristotelian *logos* of constant presence. In this way we can see the beginnings of how Heidegger's understanding of phenomenology can become transformed into a tautological thinking that is prior to and that thereby grounds both *theoria* and *praxis* through the repetition of its *logos*, which renders it both creative and finite and finds its logic through this event.

It is thus significant that Heidegger's only real reference to poetry in *Being and Time* occurs in a discussion of the way in which language expresses itself (*Sichaussprechens*) through Dasein, such that Dasein is thereby ex-pressed through language in its "being-outside," and in doing so poetry is marked (uniquely) as a form of this disclosure of existence, the only example of the disclosive nature of language (SZ: 162/205). The situation of this point belies its apparent casualness, for it comes amid a discussion of language in which its essential dimension is revealed not to be communication or mediation, but hearing. The mention of poetry then occurs just before a description of hearing as the constitutive mode of being open to one's ownmost potentiality-for-being (*Seinkönnen*), which appears like "the voice of the friend whom every Dasein carries with it," a remark that anticipates what will be discussed later as "the call of conscience," which also, if we can open ourselves to hearing it, discloses us to our own existence. Thus language is that which we always find ourselves in a position of responding to, but that we first need to learn to hear.

However, this paragraph also follows Heidegger's examination of explication as an anticipatory mode of understanding, insofar as it projects it into the modes of forehaving (*Vorhabe*), foresight (*Vorsicht*), and foreconception (*Vorgriff*) (SZ: 150/191). For Heidegger this projection itself becomes the ground from which assertions are derived such that, reversing Aristotle, the apophantic *logos* is then grounded in the explication of the hermeneutic *logos*, and understanding is thus possible only on the fragile basis of its projected anticipation (SZ: 152/194). By virtue of this hermeneutic "circle" understanding thereby anticipates itself in the mode of explication, which is precisely how Dasein gains the capacity to hear the call of conscience. This anticipatory doubling would seem to find the *logos* operating in a manner akin to the voice of the friend or the word of poetry: "as one which calls us back in calling us forth," disrupting our everyday existence and exposing us to the ground of our finitude, not by signifying, asserting, or indicating anything, but by way of its silence and emptiness (SZ: 280/326, 273/318).

At this point Heidegger's attempt to find the being of *logos* has uncovered the ground from which logic as we ordinarily understand it is derived, but in so doing has exposed a complexity that is deeply unsettling. The call of conscience repeats itself throughout Heidegger's work, for its voiceless, wordless call indicates the alterity and finitude of our existence by indicating the sheer facticity that grounds it; that which was earlier uncovered as the presencing of the world that simply presents itself as that which is. As such, the factical nature of the call presents us with a limit that can never be appropriated, hence its finitude and alterity, but that also indicates that our existence is always already grounded in this facticity and is thus thrown into the world in its finitude and projected beyond it in an endless alterity. So, while the call of conscience is that which brings about an event of appropriation in which we come to be in this situation, it is also the claim of language and temporality that marks our existence as that which persists *by way of* its repetition in time and language, for it is through these dimensions that we respond to its claim.

Thus, if Dasein is a *phronēsis meta logon*, that is, a "care through speech," as Aristotle insists that all the modes of *alētheuein* are, then the logic of its *praxis* is a tautology, insofar as it calls from itself to itself, and a heterology insofar as this self is never identical (SZ: 275/320). For, as Heidegger remarks, we can no longer refer to this self-explication as hermeneutics in the traditional sense, nor in any manner that understands it as a hermeneutic "circle," for such things derive only partly from the existential structure of meaning-anticipation, which does not in any way return to itself within a circle of substance (SZ: 153/195).[13] It is as such that he then turns to the self-announcing exposure of poetic discourse and to the voice of the friend, thereby explicating the radically noncircular and yet repetitive structure of the call of conscience. Does the *logos* of poetry thereby suggest that it is not a *poiēsis* but a *praxis* arising out of such a *phronēsis*, which Heidegger had felt was the best Aristotelian translation of conscience?[14] Does this also suggest that such an annunciative event in arising "out of" the *phronēsis* of language, is an indicator of the *pathos* of poetry, which radically displaces the poet, rendering him, like the rhapsode in Plato's *Ion*, he who is *ekphron*?

To summarize: Heidegger's path of thinking in these early years is stated concisely by two comments from *Being and Time*, the first is from the end of the introduction, which he finishes with an apology: "With regard to the awkwardness and 'inelegance' of expression in the following analyses, we may remark that it is one thing to report narratively about *beings*, but another to grasp beings in their *being*. For the latter task we lack not only most of the words but, above all, the 'grammar'" (SZ: 38–39/63). Later on, when discussing the nature of language, Heidegger returns to this point to give it its historical and ontological necessity as the "task of *liberating* grammar from logic," insofar as the "logic" with which we come to language is "based upon the ontology of the present-at-hand" in which what takes place in language is understood as a discourse of assertion (SZ: 165/209). Twenty years later, at the beginning of his programmatic letter to Jean Beaufret, this task is restated quite significantly, when, after remarking on the fact that the terms "subject" and "object" are "inappropriate" for thinking as they have "seized control of the interpretation of language" in the form of "logic" and "grammar," he proceeds to claim that the "liberation of language from grammar into a more original essential framework is reserved for thought and poeticizing" (W: 145–46/240).

From logic to grammar to language, it is now possible to see how in 1934 Heidegger could pass from a course on logic to lectures on Hölderlin, for as he later recalls, the title of this course on logic "conceals" the real matter of the course, which is "the conversion of logic into the question of the *essence* of language" (WHD: 100/154). Recalling the same course again two years later he remarks that "it was a meditation on the *logos*" (US: 89/8). While it is not surprising to find Heidegger lecturing on the relation between logic, language, and *logos*, as the course develops the question of logic turns into a questioning of the essence of language, of man, and of history. Then on the very last page we find that these concerns converge into the issue of "poetry as the original language," and it is as such that Heidegger is able to move on in the following course to discuss Hölderlin.[15]

As we can see though, this meditation on the *logos* concerns two further questions: the conversion of logic and the essence of language, which although clearly related have distinct places in Heidegger's thought. On the one hand, the examination of the nature of logic is what concerns Heidegger's early work, insofar as he is inquiring into the ontological basis of logic, the logic of logic, which governs his own attempts to ground phenomenology in the facticity of being. But understanding the being of logic, of the *logos*, not only requires understanding how it exists, but also how we are to gain access to it and bring it to language, and this means moving away from a theoretical approach to one that is the practical explication of the logic of being. Here we begin to see how the two aspects of the *logos* fold into each other, as the being of logic gives way to the logic of being, something explicitly repeated in the later Heidegger's examination of the relation between the essence of language and the language of essence. Thus, there is not only a need for a phenomenological hermeneutics of facticity, but also for a new logic of explication.

If we now turn to Heidegger's reading of poetry by way of this earlier understanding of *logos*, its position within his thought seems to be in no way arbitrary, but is instead the return of an inquiry that has been, as he later remarks, necessarily held in the "background" of his thinking from his student days (US: 88/7). As such, if by poetry we are directed to the original essencing of language, then we should understand the Aristotelian dimensions of the *logos* of poetry as aspects that relate to both *pathos* and *phronēsis*, and thus to the practical temporalizing of its *alētheuein*; its factical, historical, truthing of language, by which it indicates that it is a logic of being.

To do this we have to understand how Heidegger's engagement with poetic language is not limited to his studies of Hölderlin, Rilke, Trakl, Hebel, or George, but extends into the language he adopts to conduct these studies. This approach resulted from the perceived failing of *Being and Time* to develop a language adequate to its concerns, which thus gave rise to the need for an alternative mode of philosophical articulation that could address what had been missed. This in turn led to an examination of the nature of linguistic articulation itself, as it is found in rhetoric, in such a way that during the 1930s Heidegger begins to make explicit use of devices such as tautology, oxymoron, chiasmus, parataxis, and paronomasia, in order to understand how language operates in these modes. As a result, the way in which Heidegger begins to write becomes as important, if not more so, than what he writes; as he remarks himself: "it is advisable to pay attention to the path of thought rather than to its content" (SI: 85/23). Thus it is essential to follow the language of his essays carefully, and of particular interest to this project is the way in which Heidegger uses these rhetorical figures to explore the nature of poetry. That these figures are part of a poem will be obvious, but what complicates this is how Heidegger uses poetic figures to indicate this.

To use poetic figures to explain the work of a poem appears circular but this is by no means an accident, for Heidegger is seeking to approach that which always turns aside; thus circularity is a necessary part of his method, for if this turning cannot be avoided then it must be made explicit, that is, repeated by figures that can explicate it further. It is for this reason that in chapter 2, I will begin with "The Origin of the Work of Art," as this essay more than any other of the period signals the advent of the later Heidegger insofar as its language attempts to render its own turnings and differentiations visible. Part of this new approach comes from Heidegger's renewed analysis of *logos*, taken up this time by stepping back from Aristotle into the works of the Presocratics, principally Anaximander, Parmenides, and Heraclitus, as a means of recapturing the possibility of a *logos* not grounded in presence but that is, as Heraclitus particularly showed, the word for both being and saying. At this point in the development of philosophical language the propositional structuring of presence has not taken priority over its rhetorical expression, and thus there is the possibility of bringing this *logos* to language by taking up its figuring as tautology, the saying of the same as the *logos* of the saying of being, which is the repetition of being by way of language.

In order to read this essay we have to understand first how such figuring *works*; what does it mean for something to "work"? And what kind of "work" does this make it? The ambivalence of "work," as a word that is both verbal and nominal, needs an approach that is double-sided and this leads Heidegger to the use of paronomasia. This is a rhetorical device used to designate the play on words that have a phonetic, graphic, or etymological similarity, and although Heidegger does take advantage of these structures on many occasions, as a method it involves all forms of iteration.[16] Thus, by the repetition of certain words like *alētheia*, *phusis*, *Ereignis*, or *Kehre*, Heidegger is able to develop a multidimensional approach in which the use of one word implies others that are not present. If, when we hear *alētheia*, for example, we also come to hear *phusis* as well, then saying that truth "is" *alētheia* is no longer a simple statement, for the "is" in this statement is no longer the transparent and one-dimensional relation used by predicate logic, but something else entirely. By taking up this method, Heidegger is taking advantage of the facility that paronomasia brings of being able to speak in a way that is not limited to the figures in use, but that also indicates what is obscured by those figures.

What must be recognized is that Heidegger is deliberately putting certain rhetorical figures into play in order to draw attention to them *as* figures and thus to make us aware of the figuration at work in all poetry and philosophy, but even more significantly, to make us aware of the presence of figuration in general. It is the figuration of language that con-figures language and world: it holds them together by saying in a very concrete and particular way how they *are*, that is, *that* they are *as* they are together. Thus, to understand a poem it is first necessary to understand the relation it has to the world, and although this can be done in a number of ways (and much of Heidegger's work of this period is engaged in negotiating the "aesthetic" ideas of Plato, Kant, Schelling, Hegel, and Nietzsche), all are at a risk of reducing that relation to something else. Heidegger's use of rhetorical figures seeks to avoid this trap by using what might be termed a method of indirection where his writing, by configuring itself in such a way as to draw attention to its own figuring, indirectly indicates the figuring of the poem. The demands of this method are very high, as it runs the risk of becoming persuaded by its own configurations and thereby not exposing, but overpowering the poem by its own figuring.

Thus, inherent to Heidegger's need to find a means of approaching the complexity and ambivalence of our relation to being is a realization that philosophy itself may be part of the problem, and that other ways of thinking might be more appropriate. Consequently, what is of interest here is the way of thinking that develops in Heidegger's later works, in which it is not as important to know the precise meaning of *Ereignis*, *phusis*, or *alētheia*, and so forth, or even how these terms relate to each other, as it is to understand the reasons and implications for this way of thinking. To understand why *Ereignis* and *phusis*, for example, say the same thing, at the same time as they say different things, that is, to be both tautological and heterological, is to come closer to that unthought element in Heidegger that remains always out of reach. This is to come closer to what he was driving at, what his thought was on the way to. But if this method is taken up in order to find a way of talking about being, the question then is; what is it about being that leads to such a change in Heidegger's style? Why does he feel that it needs to be approached in this way?

. . . SAYING THE SAME . . .

To understand the reasons for Heidegger's changed approach to language we must look at his understanding of truth. In his early works the essence of truth is understood via the Greek word *alētheia*, which he translates as *Entdecktheit* (uncoveredness), *Erschlossenheit* (disclosedness), or *Unverborgenheit* (unconcealment). In each of these terms Heidegger is focusing on a duplicity that would occupy him from then on, for discovering or disclosing refer both to the action of emerging and to that from which it has emerged. This concealment is hidden in the word itself as the *lēthē* (concealment, forgottenness) in *alētheia*, which Heidegger highlights by writing it *a-lētheia* and this, he suggests, was what the ancient Greeks heard when using this word. That is, they were hearing both the active and privative senses of the word, as the revealing and un-concealing that make up the essence of truth, rather than our more common understanding of truth as correctness or adequation, which stems from the Latin translation of *alētheia* as *adequatio*. In support of this, Heidegger cites Heraclitus' fragment 1 that speaks of the hiddenness of the *logos* as that which needs to be actively attended to in order to draw out its essence (SZ: 219/262). *Alētheia* is thus an effort, and one akin to theft in that it needs to be appropriated carefully and surreptitiously from its more basic concealment, toward which it always naturally tends (SZ: 222/265).

There are several immediate problems with this: firstly, the nature of etymological translation is not so straightforward that this rephrasing of *alētheia as* unconcealment can be accepted uncritically; translation is never pure or simple and etymology is itself an historical science with its own perspective on the nature of linguistic change; *etymos*, after all, means "real" or "true," which would mean that it is only the "original" meanings of words that are "true." Secondly, the suggestion that this was the original hidden meaning of *alētheia* that the ancient Greeks heard but did not know is not only speculative but also suggests a certain hidden original "truth" *to alētheia*, which is ascribed to it in terms of its apparent "meaning" *as* unconcealment. Thirdly, the need for this new translation is espoused on the basis of it not being adequate to the original Greek experience, but this is to use a sense of adequation that we are told is derivative and thus not true to the original. Fourthly, "unconcealment" itself is an arbitrary translation that imposes its own parsed structure of privileged and unexamined meaning: what is "hidden" here and why can it only be understood negatively?[17] Fifthly, what are we to make of an attempt to ground philosophy in the hidden original meaning of a long forgotten word that is only now being shown to us in its true form; isn't this the oldest and most suspect mechanism of metaphysical thinking?

The point to remember with these issues is that Heidegger is not offering "unconcealment" as a new "translation" of *alētheia*, but is instead using it quite deliberately to unsettle our traditional understanding of "truth" and also to set in motion a whole sequence of movements, as the questions I have just raised demonstrate, which seek to unsettle what we might understand as the meaning of any particular word.[18] While Heidegger did come to realize the limitations of "unconcealment" as a translation of *alētheia*, in that it had, contrary to his earlier thoughts, no basis in Greek experience, what was retained from this translation was the openness it unleashed. This was an openness given to thought by language, language rethought in translation *as relation*, which thus provided the possibility for a rethinking. By way of this rethinking, the relation of thought and word is brought into focus through the vicissitudes of translation, and the groundlessness of this relation is revealed as the basis for a radical openness and responsibility. It is not that the use of rhetorical or poetic figures provides an allegorical description of the world, but that the figuring of language in such modes reveals the relation of language and world as open and ungrounded. This lack of ground does not simply mean the freedom of arbitrary meaning, as it carries with it an endless demand; even if *alētheia* calls for thinking it will never be given, for it is always to come.

At this point we come across one of Heidegger's most troubling formulations, that of the oblivion of being (*Seinsvergessenheit*), by which he refers to the forgetting of the forgetting of being, the withdrawal of its withdrawal, such that even the traces of being's concealment have over time become lost and thus its question has become forgotten. On the surface this seems to be an inevitable consequence of his thinking of *alētheia*, but if this forgetting or withdrawal—and we must emphasize both insofar as each are translations of *lēthē*—is itself forgotten or withdrawn, then this doesn't mean that it has simply vanished, for this would be to misread what takes place in forgetting. What is forgotten may not be available to be recalled but this lack *punctuates* thought and thus leaves a mark *of* forgetting which itself cannot be forgotten, even if it cannot be recalled. As this inapparence, forgetting occurs in a manifold of ways and so the oblivion of being, which for Heidegger is our modernity, is anything but a simple double occlusion. While he came to realize in the early 1960s that there had been no decay of truth in which its withdrawal had also withdrawn, and thus no epochal movement into oblivion, there is still a hint of simplicity in the manner in which the formulation of "the forgetting of forgetting" is deployed. Although it may be the case that the *alētheuein* of being means that it takes place in a manifold of ways, this can, indeed must, also be the case for the withdrawal and forgetting of being as well, for it is this concealment that lets unconcealment occur. It is to this abyssal retreat that the repetition of language directs us and that this work will attempt to sketch out, as the manifold of inapparence brings an entirely different imbrication of concealment and unconcealment to Heidegger's thinking, one that deflects his understanding of the relation of time and language into an other relation, an *inordinate* relation.

This moment is marked quite distinctively in "The Origin of the Work of Art" at precisely the point where Heidegger first has to negotiate the relation of "work" and "truth." As he does so, it becomes apparent that the truth of a work relates to its essence, but that its essence relates to its truth: "A curious entanglement shows itself here. Is it only a curiosity or even the empty hair-splitting of a conceptual game, or is it—an abyss?" (H: 37/28). At this time Heidegger steps back from the abyss but, as I will show, his later works persistently return to its depths, for its groundlessness indicates that if there is no basis upon which we can determine words like truth or essence, then there is only the endless, fragmentary echoing of their depths, which we know as the unanswerable demand of language. So, even though Heidegger reads *alētheia* not as a word or concept, but as a way of thinking *through* language that forces a rethinking of the relation between thought, being, and word, the risk is ever present that this understanding will start to treat this ungrounding of words as being itself a ground. Thus this ungrounding requires an inversion of the traditional method of phenomenology, for it is not the appearance of things that is of concern here, but what is not apparent. But, as we have seen, this relation of appearance and nonappearance is at the heart of Heidegger's understanding of the tautological logic of phenomena, something that is finally given explicit form in his remarks at the very end of his last seminar in September 1973, which pertain to exactly this necessity of finding "a phenomenology of the inapparent" or "nonappearing" (*Unscheinbaren*, also, "inconspicuous" or "insignificant") (S: 399/80).

In this seminar Heidegger returned to the main problem of his early thinking, the relation between phenomenology and *alētheia*, to re-examine it from the position he had reached at the end of his career. This retrospective attitude had always been present in Heidegger's thinking but had been explicitly addressed a decade earlier when he had insisted that to understand *alētheia* as "truth," as he had done in *Being and Time*, was "inadequate" and "misleading." Rather, he suggested, we should focus on concealment, or *lēthē*, "as the heart of *alētheia*," which indicates that *alētheia* is not engaged in truth as much as "the clearing of presence concealing itself" (ZSD: 77–79/70–71). However, this dynamic revision of being as "clearing and presence" did not go far enough and in the 1973 seminar he returned to consider this point again. On the last day of the seminar Heidegger read out a brief paper he had written the previous winter entitled "*Aletheies eukukleos atremes etor*" (The well-rounded untrembling heart of truth), named after fragment 1.29 of Parmenides' poem on truth, but before doing so he stated that the understanding of *lēthē* as the heart of *alētheia* does not follow from what is said in Parmenides' poem (S: 395/78).[19]

Thus, in his paper, Heidegger begins by retranslating this fragment on truth, such that "well-rounded" becomes "fitting encircling" (*schicklich umkreisend*), which by *not* referring to any movement of unconcealment indicates that the "untrembling heart" of *alētheia* must refer to something other than concealment. As Heidegger goes on to explain, what Parmenides is referring to is answered in fragment 8.1–2, where, in passing along the way of *alētheia*, "there still remains one saying of the way, which leads forth to there . . . (that shows): *os estin* 'that it is'" (*monos d' eti mythos hodoio / leipetai os estin*). If *alētheia* shows "that it is," this leads us to the question of what "is," and Heidegger finds Parmenides' response in fragment 6.1, "(it) is: namely being" (*esti gar einai*). Rather than reading this as saying that it is *something* that "is," that is, *a* being, Heidegger proposes to think *einai* "in a Greek manner" as *anwesen* (presencing or emerging), leading to a rereading of the entire phrase as saying that what "is," "presences, as presencing" (*anwest nämlich anwesen*) (S: 404–5/95). If we ask *how* presencing presences, *then* the answer, Heidegger claims, is "in unconcealment," but this can only be the case if we now understand presencing (*eon*) as "the heart" of *alētheia*. But this leads to the baffling conclusion that *alētheia* itself should then be understood as "presencing: presencing itself" (*anwesend: anwesen selbst*), that is to say, the presencing of presencing (S: 405–6/96).

This would appear to be a tautology, but instead of shying away from this Heidegger insists that tautology is a thinking of the sameness of appearance (what appears is what appears), which is the meaning of

Parmenides' thinking of *alētheia*: "We stand before an obvious tautology. Certainly, and before a genuine one too. It does not count the identical twice. Rather it names the same, and it itself, once" (S: 405/95). It is only by way of its repetition that tautology can say the same for the first time, but in doing so the hiddenness of *lēthē* disappears and is replaced by the sameness of presencing, presencing itself. In disappearing from being hidden *lēthē* is essentially obscured, but this is not a loss; it is the way it should be, the way most proper to it. This inapparence is marked in the statement by the hiatus or interval of the colon that allows the repetition of presencing to appear as repetition, and that separates it from itself. This absence cannot be brought to the light of thought as it is that which never appears, since it is the very event of appearing. The displacement of *alētheia* away from unconcealment into presencing is partly due, as Heidegger admits, to the impossibility of maintaining the idea that the nature of *alētheia* has changed: Nowhere did the ancient Greeks ever experience *alētheia* as unconcealment; it was always already understood as adequation, which means that there was no decay of truth into oblivion, no forgetting (ZSD: 78/70).[20] What is hidden was always so; the origin of presencing is forever concealed.

But even if concealment itself was never experienced, it is evident that the presencing of presencing involves a thinking of ambiguity that although unmarked, has now been *re-marked* by Heidegger in his rereading. This remarking (*Bemerkung*) is necessary as it is perhaps the only possibility for thinking tautology, and thereby presencing, from out of itself (S: 407/97). For there remains an ever-present danger of simplifying *alētheia* by thinking of presencing as a dialectical movement of concealing and revealing. This arises from the Heraclitean thinking of *polemos* and *phusis* that Heidegger originally used to understand *alētheia*, but, as he remarks in response to a question from Beaufret, "if one is able to read Heraclitus on the basis of the Parmenidean tautology, he himself then appears in the closest vicinity to that same tautology," for "tautology is the only possibility for thinking what dialectic can only veil" (S: 400/81). This enables Heidegger to make the radical pronouncement, half a century after his first investigations into the language of phenomenology, that such "tautological thinking" would be "a phenomenology of the inapparent." Such thinking would be neither theory nor praxis but would open up the path from which the two would emerge, for tautology, understood as the re-marking, or saying of the same, *to autos logos*, is that which speaks of presencing in its presencing, and this, Heidegger concludes, "is the original meaning of phenomenology" (S: 399/80). But this is to say that it both speaks out of presencing and as presencing, and can thus also be read as an autology, or saying from the same, out of itself.

While this use of tautology recalls the rhetorical formulations of Heidegger's essays on language, which will be discussed in chapter 5, it also introduces something entirely new by elevating this rhetoric to the position of an ur-phenomenology. This is not just an admission of the centrality of language to a thinking of being, and particularly the poetic language that uses these rhetorical modes, but also a suggestion that in such a language being is given as it is, *in its presencing*. But if this is the case, then there is seemingly no room for difference in this saying of the same, insofar as there is no ontological difference as there is no being of beings; now there is only presencing.[21] The appearance of things in themselves has, through tautology, become the appearance of things as repetition, the same in its differentiation of itself, which, as we will see, is grounded in the event of *mimēsis*, understood as neither imitation nor production but as a sheer dissembling, which is itself to be understood only by way of the finitude of language.

As Heidegger stated in 1962, such a thinking of being in itself, outside of beings or the difference between being and beings, is the only way "to think being without regard to metaphysics," and this is necessary if we are to have any possibility of "bringing into view the being of what *is* today" (ZSD: 25/24, 2/2). This abandonment of difference entails a change in our understanding of the same, and of the relation between being, language, and thinking. For if language does not refer to the difference of being and beings, then it must partake of a sameness that we have not reckoned, a sameness that is not equivalent or identical but is that of an infinite proximity or intimacy. This rethinking of the same arises from Heidegger's reading of fragment 3 of Parmenides' poem; "thinking and being are the same," which he reads as meaning "belonging together," rather than as implying any sense of identity (SI: 90/27–28). It is only later, in metaphysical thinking, that the notion of identity emerges and as it does it obscures that which preceded it by drawing out only part of the essence of the same: the "together" of "belonging together" (SI: 92/30). But as "*belonging* together," a thinking of the same of being yields the possibility of saying thinking and being together in such a way that their belonging together is not articulated in any way, but is a simple *belonging* together, that is, thinking: being.

If this is an example of tautological thinking, then each is the same as the other in a way that does not determine how that sameness is to be, but simply reiterates that sameness *as* difference. In coming to this point, Heidegger has moved away from the use of poetic figures as a means of reading appearance as unconcealment, toward a tautology that reveals what is *by way of* its iteration, its saying again. In doing so, tautology lets the inapparent appear as inapparent, as that which does not appear, for this inapparence cannot be brought to language as it is the inapparence *of* language itself, since that which brings to language cannot itself ever be brought to language. All we can say is that there is presencing, never presence, and so while there is no difference in the sense that there is no being of beings, in another sense there is nothing but difference, in that presencing is simply differentiation. This is the abyss that Heidegger had noticed in the relation of essence and truth in the work of art (the essence of truth: the truth of essence), which indicates that tautology is not just the ground of language as relation, but also its ungrounding.

. . . The Limit of Writing . . .

To discover how Heidegger was able to reach this radical dislocation of language we must return to his encounter with poetry, and to enable us to situate this encounter I will first examine Hölderlin's hymn, "As when on a holiday . . ." Before doing so I will make a detour into Blanchot's reading of Heidegger's encounter with Hölderlin, for in this reading Blanchot makes clear the conditions of the encounter of philosophy with poetry. We can never approach "poetry" or "philosophy" directly, let alone the field of their encounter, for this is a field that we are already entirely implicated within. The history and the language of this encounter is the history and the language within which we think and write, and thus seeking to approach this encounter (again) we must take account of the demands that it already places upon us, even before we begin. The depth of this implication already claims the language we use to explicate it and so before we even read Heidegger or Hölderlin we are already involved in a negotiation, not with, but of language. So we need to enter this encounter by way of language; to become aware of how language intervenes in our negotiation with poetry or philosophy and thereby becomes the condition of that encounter's possibility and impossibility.

Blanchot discussed Heidegger's reading of "As when on a holiday . . ." in 1946 in a short article entitled "The 'Sacred' Speech of Hölderlin." Although Heidegger's essay had only recently been translated into French, Blanchot's remarks betray a familiarity with both Heidegger's and Hölderlin's work that far exceeds their context. This makes for an article whose brevity belies its depth, rendering its comments elliptical in what may well have been a deliberate maneuver, as Blanchot's awareness of Hölderlin's work outside of Heidegger's reading, and Heidegger's work outside his engagement with poetry, make this occasion a unique chance for Blanchot to bring together a number of concerns that he will never address again quite so directly. Given that Heidegger's own reading of Hölderlin is also intriguingly unique and pivotal, as it is the first time he devotes an essay to a single poem (one he considered to be "the purest poem on the essence of poetry"), and yet it is also an essay that he will shortly after declare to be a "disaster" (EHD: 44/61). Given as well, that Hölderlin's hymn is also the locus of a particular and tragic failure within the development of his poetry, then we find that Blanchot's essay, even before we start to read it, is in palimpsest with a singular convergence of traits.

This layered implication of poetry and philosophy will guide the course of our inquiry and as we proceed from Heidegger to Hölderlin the concern will initially be with uncovering the sources of their respective failures. For in their singularity, and because of their failings, these encounters reveal both the stakes and the inevitability of failure. This will enable us to approach the abyss onto which these failures open by moving on, in part two of the study, to the ways in which Hölderlin, Heidegger, and Blanchot each seek to come to terms with the inevitable disaster of writing.

While the title of his essay raises the matter that concerns and divides Heidegger and Hölderlin, Blanchot begins "The 'Sacred' Speech of Hölderlin" with a note of what he will not discuss, which are those "questions that concern Heidegger himself." But as Blanchot proceeds the possibility of this exclusion becomes complicated for, as he informs us, although Heidegger's method of reading Hölderlin is "careful" and "detailed," its legitimacy is never addressed and thus will not concern Blanchot, except to remark on its apparent strangeness (PF: 118/111). This is rather disingenuous, for although it is true that Blanchot never inquires into the legitimacy of Heidegger's method, he never ceases to inquire into its possibility, and this indirectly involves those questions that concern Heidegger himself; the very possibility of Heidegger's thought as it is exposed by way of its encounter with Hölderlin. I will cite the whole passage to indicate the care with which Blanchot approaches this problem:

> Heidegger's interrogation interrogates each word, each comma and demands from all the isolated elements, taken one after the other, an answer complete and also isolable. The impression is often very strange. However, in the final analysis, there is in it more of appearance than of reality; for if the question has indeed the exorbitant aspect of a question that asks of each particle of the poem its account and forces it to justify itself analytically, Heidegger's analysis, progressing according to the circular procedure that is characteristic of him, ends up finally, not by reconstructing the general meaning beginning from all the particular meanings it specifies, but by finding again in each moment the passage of the poem's totality beneath the form where it has momentarily settled and paused. (PF: 118–19/111–12)

Heidegger's method of reading is not being given here the legitimacy it fails to provide for itself, but in Blanchot's explication it emerges as a maneuver that removes one level of strangeness only to replace it with another. The exorbitant nature of Heidegger's questioning does not lead to the analysis and subsequent synthesis of meaning that is common to some forms of literary inquiry, where the "general meaning" of a piece is revealed by adding together all of the particular meanings it contains, but instead works in the opposite direction. Here each instant is not a part of the whole, but a *mark* of its totality in the form in which it has momentarily settled. Such a proposition can only work for a language whose meaning is not drawn from the combination of its words, but somehow resides beneath each word, which reveals it by a temporary image of its total movement. Notice that it is not a general meaning that is hereby discovered, but the shape in which the poem has come to rest. Thus the nature of the poem itself and the relation it has to the words is not revealed by this method, but through the words we are provided with a means of accessing the poem through what *remains* of its movement. The poem in itself is absent, but the words, as images of its passage, allow us a glimpse of what it was in its passing. This distinctive tension between a poem and its words, which is both constitutive and preventative of our understanding, is thoroughly in accord with Heidegger at this point, but the attention Blanchot is bringing to it is a signal that it can never be avoided or settled.

Thus Blanchot has not provided any judgment on Heidegger's method here; instead he is for the moment only concerned in bringing out its conditions, but in doing so he has brought out the problematic status of this approach as the key to what follows. As he discreetly suggests, we can "wonder if a meeting is possible between the vocabulary of an autonomous philosophical reflection and a poetic language, which came into our world almost a century and a half ago." The dimensions of this encounter are two very distinct forms of language separated by time; not philosophy and poetry in general, but a particular conjugation of a present vocabulary and a past language. Again, the relation of a language's parts to its whole is being flagged as a sign of its relation to presence (in terms of both its temporality and autonomy), and this, as Blanchot quickly moves on to specify, is precisely what occurs in a poem: "a poem is not without date, but despite its date it is always to come (*à venir*), it speaks itself in a 'present' that does not answer to historical markers. It is foreboding (*pressentiment*), and designates itself as that which is not yet, demanding of the reader the same foreboding to make an existence for it that has not yet come" (PF: 119/112). Despite the historical age of Hölderlin's poem, and the fact that its words speak of what has passed, it is still to come. By marking its words as the traces of what is no longer, a poem retreats into an absence in which it is itself also marked as not yet. There is no present that can satisfy its conditions for speaking, so its speaking must always be deferred; hence its distance from us is not a question of age, but of a different relation to time and language. Thus for us to read a poem, to make an existence for that which does not yet exist, we have to become that which is not yet, and the implication is that this foreboding cannot be achieved if we only focus on the parts of a poem in terms of the vocabulary of an autonomous reflection.

A poem such as this has the same effect on the reader as it has on the poet; for as that which is to come it renders all contact imminent and thus not present, absent. Heidegger's reading is thus placed under an immense demand: to respond to this foreboding as foreboding, something Blanchot seems to be saying is impossible. But only as such is the strangeness of a poem preserved, a strangeness that comes not from its age but from its exteriority from history and words, its excess, which means that it will never be present *in* time or language, but will always be on the way. A poem emerges as this foreboding when the poet seeks to respond to its demand, which places its appearance in an excessive imminence. The language of a poem withholds itself and thereby draws the reader with it, for its imminence means "being ahead of itself and of distinguishing, beneath the word that has worked, the word that shines, reserved for what is not yet expressed" (PF: 119/112).

Thus if the words instantiate the movement of a poem then they do so only insofar as they instantiate it as absent, as coming but not yet arriving. An examination of a poem's words is thus the only means of accessing it, even if in doing so access is only granted on the basis of this imminence. Thus Heidegger's attention to words cannot suffice, if in doing so he is following a path that believes that words "carry in themselves a hidden truth that a well-conducted interrogation could make appear." In place of this archaeological approach, which Heidegger favors in his examination of each word and etymology, Blanchot obliquely refers to the "rhythm" that is the "superior truth" of Hölderlin's words. In doing so, he draws attention to the manner in which Hölderlin himself negotiated this tension between a poem and its words, not by making the words the containers of a poem's truth, but by responding to the *fact* of a poem's existence as the *question* from which it is born. This is to say that the occurrence of a poem does not have the certainty of a present thing, but only the doubtfulness of that which has not yet arrived, and yet this doubtfulness is also that which first gives rise to a poem; it comes about through the imminence of its own question in such a way that the poet is also drawn into its deferral as that which always succeeds it, that which only arises out of, and in response to, a poem. In this way, Hölderlin's poetry led to "a poetic existence so strong that, once its essence is unveiled, it was able to make itself the proof that it was impossibility and to extend itself out into nothingness and emptiness, without ceasing to accomplish itself" (PF: 121/114). This "rhythm" of occurrence and deferral seems to refer to the movement by which the words both reveal and conceal a poem's existence, but by rendering this movement in terms of impossibility Blanchot is indicating that as close as Heidegger's examination comes, it fails to appreciate the extent to which the lack of presence of a poem affects the poet's own existence.

This means that a poet is in the impossible but necessary position of being both the speaker of a poem and what is spoken by the poem. For Blanchot, this contradiction "is the heart of the poetic existence, it is its essence and its law; there would be no poet, if he did not have to live out this same, endlessly present, impossibility." The consequence being that "the poet must exist as a foreboding of himself, as the future of his existence." In Blanchot's eyes this is the *dürftiger Zeit* (needy, destitute, or distressing time) that Hölderlin speaks of in his elegy "Bread and Wine," the time of "not yet" in which the poet must reside, waiting, never present to himself (PF: 124/117). In the poverty and misery of this time without time the poet enters the foreboding of the poem, which is itself the very condition of there being a time to come, as it is an "affirmation of something that is beyond itself" (PF: 125/118). It is only through this double movement of coming but not arriving that a poem emerges, for in seeking to respond to the imminence of its word the poem recedes into its own imminence, such that the poem's approach only occurs while this approach is still being sought.

This transformation inflects the language of a poem by rendering it double, as Blanchot observes in referring to a phrase from Hölderlin's elegy "The Walk to the Country / To Landauer" ("Der Gang aufs Land / An Landauer"), which reads, "And to the opened glance the shining will be open" (*Und dem offenen Blik offen der Leuchtende seyn*): "The double repetition of the word *offen*, open, answers exactly to the double movement that 'the Open' signifies: to open up to that which opens up" (PF: 119–20/113).[22] Referring to this movement as a "double repetition" reminds us that repetition is never unitary, but proliferates, such that the opening *of* the shining is, by virtue of its ambiguous genitive, already double, by which ambiguity it responds to the similarly ambiguous opening of the glance. To open is always a movement that involves both an opening and an opening up, a repetition of itself that in repeating doubles itself. This doubled opening brings forth the language of a poem in such a way that it also both opens and is opened, thereby placing itself in an endlessly occurring imminence: it is always to come. In opening it sets out the conditions for its own opening, thus deferring the opening while also preparing it, so that the opening occurs but is never present; it comes but never arrives. This attention to the rhythmic movement of the words passes by Heidegger's interest in the words themselves to focus on what arises out of their inscription, which is to answer to the poet's own demand to seek not what was in the poem, but what was being attempted by way of it. In doing so, Blanchot is drawing the inquiry away from Hölderlin's words toward their *writing* as the basis of their foreboding, and this is a distinct move away from Heidegger.

Tentatively, but persistently, Blanchot is indicating how Heidegger's interrogation of the poet's words, however careful and revealing, has failed to reveal the extremity out of which they came to be written. Although he refers us to the importance of the poet's experience, Blanchot is not deferring to a psychological inquiry for he fully agrees with the starting point that Heidegger adopts, which is the poem itself; what he wishes to assert is the claim that a poem makes on the poet when he writes it. This is the claim of language that the poet is seeking to respond to in his writing of a poem, a claim that is the essence of the inquiry each poem makes into itself. Such an assertion adds to Heidegger's inquiry by pointing out how the ambiguous status of a poem's words cannot be engaged without involving the poet as well, something that will have extraordinary effects on our attempts to understand a poem as a work. These effects have already been indicated by Blanchot in the repetition of the time of a poem as that which is not yet and that which is to come, that which in not being present to itself is always absent. Such a thing can never be a work for Blanchot, for its imminence both resists and evades its possibility of becoming a work; rather this exteriority and estrangement unworks a poem, bringing about a "worklessness" (*désoeuvrement*, as Blanchot will call it later) that destabilizes and decenters it, leaving it eccentric and impossible.

In exposing this lacuna in Heidegger's inquiry into Hölderlin's poem, Blanchot is showing up a blind spot in the encounter of philosophy with poetry, a blind spot that coincides with its language. For the encounter only occurs in and through language and as such already asserts its tacit claim on the movement of thinking, a claim that can only be responded to if thinking turns back on itself, doubling its inquiry, so that in addressing poetry it comes to address itself. But within this address there is a tension between language and that which it seeks to address, as Blanchot announces in the title of "The 'Sacred' Speech of Hölderlin," which means that although they may co-respond they can never coincide. But this failure of language is the mark of its persistence; it is what allows a poem to occur without ever taking place; it is not just the event of poetry as Heidegger would read it, but an event that perpetually recedes from our ability to think it even as it constitutes our sole ability to think it, disabling the possibility of poetry even as it enables it. To Heidegger's claim that the agitation of this inappropriable finitude is led to stillness in the speech of the poet, Blanchot states quite unforgivingly; "Speaking, this is necessary, it is this, this alone that will do. And yet speaking is impossible" (PF: 133/127).

What Blanchot has drawn our attention to in his response to Heidegger is the curious status of a literary work, and in particular, a poem. On one side a poem is pre-eminently the trace of a singular encounter; its existence rests in this singularity, the utterly unique and irreducible moment of which it is the record. However, a poem is inhibited from becoming this singular mark by virtue of the fact that it is a work of language, which exists only by way of its endless repetition. By drawing our attention to the experience of the poet in trying to negotiate this double bind, Blanchot is indicating that a poem does not exist outside of these conditions, whose combination renders it impossible. While Heidegger's reading is sensitive to the poem as both the source and the result of this double bind, he fails to see how this necessarily implicates the poet's own experience. For Blanchot, the poet's relation to language exposes him to impossibility in the form of this singular mark, a rupture he marks quite explicitly: "Impossible, the reconciliation of the Sacred with speech demanded that the poet's existence come nearest to nonexistence" (PF: 135/131). By way of a poem the poet is exposed to the impossible combination of the singular and the repeated, a combination exterior to thought for it requires coming to terms with language as both finite and infinite, and past and imminent. This is the demand that language lays before us, and to respond to it is to find a way to address that which is never present, that which is inherently ambiguous and unstable to the point of impossibility.

As a result, the status of the literary work cannot be addressed within a thought that does not also place itself within this ambiguity and instability. Blanchot's insight was to realize that this impossibility is both the source and the failure of poetry; the conditions under which it endlessly strives and by which it fundamentally unsettles the poet's existence. But in doing so he directly questioned the nature of Heidegger's readings, for the implications of this impossibility affect the very language by which we seek to approach poetry. If this radical repetition is of the essence of language, then its ambiguity and instability cannot be limited to poetic language but are always already present in the language we use to approach poetry. Thus the language we use must change if we are to attempt to encounter poetry; we must become aware of how our thinking is already engaged in an encounter with poetry by virtue of its language, and that as a corollary it is never "thinking" that encounters "poetry," but an (impossible) engagement of language with itself in an endless presencing and deferral that draws our existence up to the very limits of being, up to the finitude that is the utter absence of time and language.

. . . AGAIN, ANEW . . .

Pursuing this problem in more concrete terms I will now turn to Hölderlin's hymn "As when on a holiday . . ." which he first conceived in prose in 1799 and then tried, in his one and only attempt, to convert it into strict Pindaric verse.[23] This meant following the strophe-antistrophe-epode structure that he felt was the key to what he was trying to say, which was a public celebration and demonstration of the poet's vocation. By alternating between strophe and antistrophe the Pindaric verse achieves a distended harmony common to hymns that were sung or performed, which is in turn punctuated by an epode in which each strophe is summarized. While Hölderlin achieves the systematic balance of strophe and antistrophe it is in the final epode that he fails, that is, it is precisely where the strict form of the verse requires a resolution and culmination that he struggled. The significance of this means that we have no authorized version of this poem: as is the case for the majority of Hölderlin's later writings it was never given a finished form and thus the question of its editing for publication raises profound problems. The versions published to date that have received the widest circulation have been those edited by Norbert von Hellingrath and, latterly, Friedrich Beißner, from whose edition the standard English translation has been drawn.[24] In both cases the poems have been extracted from the palimpsest of Hölderlin's manuscripts in order to present them *as* poems, that is, in some more or less conclusive form. However, as the recent edition of Hölderlin's works by Dieter Sattler has demonstrated (and what has emerged from greater analysis of Hölderlin's theoretical writings), the idea of a conclusive form seems to be foreign to Hölderlin's understanding of poetry.

As will become apparent, particularly in chapters 3 and 4, Hölderlin's writing practice is the essential opening for any understanding of what he approached in his poems. This means that we have to return to his manuscripts and try to read them without the guiding hand of poetic editing. The difficulty of this is unavoidable for it is impossible to *read* a palimpsest; hence some form of editing is always going to be present. However, the necessity of trying to do this arises from the fact that what Hölderlin was attempting appears to be related to this impossibility. Thus, the version of the poem that I include here attempts to follow some of the lines of overwriting and underwriting that make up its manuscript, but any sense of finding a complete understanding is inappropriate.[25]

As when on a holiday, to see the field
A countryman goes out, at morning, when,
Out of the hot night the cooling lightning had fallen
The whole time and the thunder still sounds in the distance,
The river trips into its banks once more,
And the fresh ground becomes green
And with the gladdening rain from heaven
The grapevine drips, and gleaming
In quiet sunlight stand the trees of the grove:

So in favourable weather they stand,
Whom no master alone, but wonderfully
[All-present] [Now] she educates in a light embrace
The powerful, divinely beautiful nature.
So when she seems to be sleeping at times of the year
Up in the heavens or among plants or the peoples
The poets' faces also are mourning,
They seem to be alone, yet are always divining.
For divining too she herself is resting.

But now day breaks! I waited and saw it come,
And what I saw, may the holy be my word.
For she, she herself, who is older than the ages
And above the gods of Occident and Orient,
Nature is now awakening with the clang of arms,
And from high ether down to the abyss
According to firm law, as once, begotten out of holy chaos,
Inspiration, the all-creative,
Again feels herself anew.

And as a fire gleams in the eye of the man,
Who has conceived a lofty design; so
Once more by the signs, the deeds of the world now
A fire has been kindled in the souls of the poets.

And what came to pass before, though scarcely felt,
Only now is manifest,
And they who smiling tended our fields for us,
In the form of servants, they are known,
The all-living, the powers of the gods.

Do you ask about them? In the song their spirit blows
[When from the sun of day and warm earth]
[That also the sun, like flowers, and darkest earth]
[It awakens] [Grows], and storms that are in the air, and others
That more prepared in the depths of time,
And more full of meaning, and more perceptible to us
Drift on between heaven and earth and among the peoples
The thoughts of the communal spirit they are,
Quietly ending in the soul of the poet.

So that quickly struck, for a long time known
To the infinite, it quakes
With recollection, and kindled by the holy ray
Its fruit conceived in love, the work of gods and men
The song, so that it may bear witness to both, succeeds.
So, as poets say, when she desired to see
The god, visible, his lightning fell on Semele's house
And ashes [mortally] [divinely] struck gave birth,
To the fruit of the thunderstorm, to holy Bacchus.

And hence the sons of earth now drink
Heavenly fire without danger.
Yet us it behoves, you poets! to stand
Bareheaded beneath God's thunderstorms,
To grasp the father's ray, itself, with our own hands
And to offer to the people
The heavenly gift wrapped in song
For only if we are pure in heart,
Like children, are our hands innocent

[The father's ray, the pure, does not sear it]
[Then the pure does not kill it, does not sear it]

The [higher]	And deeply shaken, sharing the suffering
sphere	Of the stronger, remaining in the [down-rushing]
that is	[unstoppable] storms of
higher than	God when he nears, the heart still holds.
that of man	But oh my shame! (when of
that is	a self-inflicted wound my heart is bleeding, and
the god	deeply lost is peace and freely-modest contentment,
	and unrest and lack drive me to the abundance
	of the gods' tables, when round about me)

[My shame!]
and let me say at once,
That I approached to see the heavenly,
And they themselves cast me down below the living
The false priest that I am, into the dark
To sing for those who can learn the warning song.
There

A holiday is of course a holy day or festival, when the union of nature, gods, and man is celebrated by a time of shared joy and feasting, but it is also a time of private contemplation and restraint when the absence of nature and the gods is pondered.[26] This paradox is at the heart of Hölderlin's exploration in this poem, and as such is something that is not simply the subject of the poem but also its mode as well; it does not just depict the presence and absence of the gods, but enacts this in its own passage from communion to separation. As a result the structure of the poem is essential to its development, which breaks down into three sections that repeat a pattern of slow discovery. The first section covers stanzas 1 to 3, in which the idyllic morning that follows the storm finds the countryman surveying the aftereffects of the union of heaven and earth. All about him nature yields up the fruits of this union, and amid them "stand the trees of the grove" that bravely withstood the thunder and lightning and now appear as the sole witnesses to the event, passing on their fruits to the countryman. These trees are privileged in their position, for although they appear to exist in a state of waiting and calm persistence, it is on these holy mornings that they come forth as touched with "a light embrace, [by] / The powerful, divinely beautiful nature."

It is as such that they are figures of the poets, for although they seem "to be sleeping" they "are always divining." Here the poet makes his first discovery, for in setting up the holiday in his poem he is brought to a point of realizing that his writing has effected the very same configuration that he has described. In setting forth in the first few lines he has accomplished the same passage as the countryman, which is to find the figures of the witnesses, but these are not the witnesses of the storm but of the poem itself. His own writing, in seeking to approach the appearance of nature in the gladdening rain of heaven, has itself become the source of this gladdening rain, which has left exposed the witness of this event as himself: the poet. This parallel, which is set up by the opening allegory, comes to its point of realization in the last lines of the second stanza, for if the poets "are always divining" so is nature even while she is resting. The poet, in writing of nature's awakening, has reached a point of sharing in this event, such that he can now say, "But now day breaks!" This line is no longer describing something that has occurred; instead the reserved and distant voice of the first two stanzas is now suddenly interrupted with the poet's realization of his own position.

But as soon as it is said, it disappears. The explosive moment passes, and the poet is left with only his memories and desires of the passage: "I waited and saw it come, / And what I saw, may the holy be my word." The reverberations of this moment echo on into the rest of this stanza, but the time to begin again has arrived. The next three stanzas step back from the thunderstorm and follow the fire that "has been kindled in the souls of the poets." This fire has been sparked by that which "came to pass before, though scarcely felt," the transient communion that left only a memory. If we ask where this memory resides, then we are told that it lives on in song, which passes through the "thoughts of the communal spirit . . . / Quietly ending in the soul of the poet." Here the word of nature's event "quakes / With recollection," as it will not lie dormant forever but surges forth as nature "feels herself anew." So too, the poet cannot allow his memory to remain a memory, and in recalling the story of Semele he awakens the thunderstorm again and the kindling power of its "holy ray." He too desires "to see / The god, visible," to reanimate the holy word, that "fruit conceived in love, the work of gods and men," but this cannot be done with impunity.

This second attempt is weaker than the first, and only brings out its danger. This time the lightning only falls on Semele, and although this brings forth the "holy Bacchus," from whose grapevines the "sons of the earth" may now drink the "Heavenly fire" without harm, Semele has been destroyed. For her impertinent desire she has been punished, and this fate now befalls those poets too who wish to renew "the deeds of the world now" by offering "to the people / The heavenly gift wrapped in song." But this can not be done. The last two stanzas trail off into disintegration, the lines becoming more chaotic before eventually fading away. The section in parentheses at the end of stanza 8 is drawn from Hölderlin's notes and is included to suggest how it may have developed, but it must be stated that this is only a sketch and that ultimately the hymn remains incomplete despite several attempts to finish it. The use of the personal pronoun here is possibly an attempt to return us to its earlier appearance in the aftereffects of nature's event: "I approached to see the heavenly, / And they themselves cast me down," but the moment is past and cannot be reconceived.

The possibility that drives Hölderlin's poetry is the same one that renders any realization of it a failure: seeking to give an account of the communion of man, gods, and nature is the very thing that destroys that communion, and so the poets are caught in an impossible position in which what they are driven to, their very vocation, is bound to fail. They cannot cease to try, but they can never succeed. But in their failure is found their poetry; it is born of their ruins and while it consistently fails to reach the poet's criteria, its success is tied to this failure: it is from this failure that a poem speaks most completely. This does not turn failure back into success as this activity cannot be adumbrated, for in its writing there are no ends that can be substituted for means, and this is something that poetry and philosophy must confront. Writing turns all possibilities into impossibilities and yet this turning is itself an opening, perhaps the only one available to us.

2

Hiding
Figures of Cryptophilia in the Work of Art

> Language is charged with the task of making beings manifest and preserving them as such—in the linguistic work. Language gives expression to what is most pure and most concealed, as well as to what is confused and common . . . The word as word never offers any immediate guarantee as to whether it is an essential word or a deception. On the contrary—an essential word, in its simplicity, often looks like an inessential one. And on the other hand, what shows itself in its finery in the appearance of the essential is often merely something recited and repeated by rote. Thus language must constantly place itself into the illusion which it engenders by itself, and so endanger what is most its own, genuine utterance.
>
> —Heidegger, "Hölderlin and the Essence of Poetry," 2nd April 1936

Heidegger started making notes on the origin of the work of art in 1931; further notes followed in 1934 and the first public lecture was given in November 1935, before the essay as we now know it was delivered as a series of three public lectures in Frankfurt am Main in November and December 1936.[1] But Heidegger was never completely satisfied with this essay as is evinced by the epilogue and addendum that were added to it over the next twenty years, the latter coinciding with his concession that the whole work now needed a "second part" if it was to take account of certain developments in modern art, notably the work of Klee and Cézanne.[2] In his later years the question of art and its current direction would continue to attract him, leading to some six further lectures between 1956 and 1970. The lectures of 1936 thus come out of a stream of thinking that persisted for much of his career and so in reading them we have to be aware of their provenance. The first lecture, in Freiburg 1935, is a continuation of the inquiry begun in his course of the previous semester, *Introduction to Metaphysics*, where his examination of the changing relation between *phusis* and *logos* since Heraclitus was punctuated by a long analysis of the second choral ode from Sophocles' *Antigone*. For Heidegger, the poet's word exposes us to the uncanniness of our existence, which is persistently unsettled by the "strife" or *polemos* between *phusis* and *logos*. His understanding of the work of art in the Freiburg lecture pursues this Heraclitean line, emphasizing the violence with which the *logos* of art, as a *technē logos*, emerges, but a year later this has changed.

The significance of this transition lies in the fact that it indicates a greater change at work in Heidegger's thinking in the 1930s, a change that will lead directly into the project of his later years. The sources of this transition are numerous but we can begin to enumerate them by considering what occurs in the year between the first and the final lectures. To begin with, Heidegger's lecture courses following on from *Introduction to Metaphysics* cover Kant's first critique, in an analysis of the nature and spatiality of a thing, then Schelling's treatise on the essence of human freedom, which not only covers the abyssal ground of freedom but the relation of good and evil to this ungrounding, and then Nietzsche's notes on the will to power as art. Furthermore, 1936 also sees Heidegger condensing his 1934–35 lectures on Hölderlin's hymns into a public lecture given in Rome, and the beginning of his private meditations on the nature of *Ereignis*. Just as important is the increasing unease Heidegger is feeling in relation to the direction of the National Socialist regime, which has not only begun to make his academic life more difficult as he is put under surveillance for possible subversion, but also, as the Four Year Plan announced in September 1936 indicates, seems to be heading toward the total technological mobilization of the country.

Each of these developments bring a greater caution and subtlety to Heidegger's lectures at the end of 1936, for the nature of a thing and the event of its being place the *polemos* of his earlier reading under pressure. To highlight this change, I will explore "The Origin of the Work of Art" through three Heraclitean terms (*phusis*, *polemos*, and *logos*) that form Heidegger's figures of *earth*, *draw-ing* (*Riß*), and *poetry*, but in doing so I will pursue the Parmenidean caveat from chapter 1: that we read Heraclitus' fragments on the struggle of opposites from the perspective of a tautology of presencing, that is, not as a dialectic but as a repetition of the same in its difference. In doing so, the *polemos* of a *technē logos* unravels to indicate a deeper and more ambiguous dimension of presencing, which not only alters Heidegger's understanding of the origin of the work of art, but also affects the nature of his approach to language. We should also note how, in adopting these figures, Heidegger is revisiting issues that have concerned him from the beginning; the relation between factical and categorial presencing that gives rise to the material and temporal dimensions of our existence (earth and world); the related hermeneutic problems of intuition and expression that give rise to a doubling of meaning as both passed and imminent (draw-ing); and the moment of coming to be in the truth of this finitude and repetition as the *praxis* of *zōon logon echon* (poetry).

It is out of this Aristotelian analysis of the modes of *alētheuein* that Heidegger is first drawn to the work of art as a mode of the truthing of being, but in the intervening years he has begun to rethink the *logos* of such truthing. Within the Aristotelian understanding of the apophantic *logos*, the experience of truth occurred by way of its appearances, "as" its various modes, but such a model proved to be incapable of responding to the excessive finitude and repetition of existence, in which the appearance of truth is always an event in which we are already implicated by way of our being part of its logic. It is thus that Heidegger turns to an understanding of *logos* drawn from Heraclitus, as the movement of both being and saying, which does not separate the meaning of language from its *praxis*, and as a result is able to see how the work of art is an event of truthing within our existence (*Ereignis*). Thus Heidegger's inquiry into the work of art does not proceed from the point of viewing art as an object, but as an event, so he is not concerned with the beauty or representation or morality of the object, nor is he interested in the sensations that accompany art and that refer to the feelings of a subject. As these approaches exist within the "aesthetic" framework of subjective representation, they require "overcoming" if we are to escape from the "metaphysical" conception of being they derive from: "The question of the origin of the work of art . . . is most intimately connected with the task of overcoming aesthetics and this means simultaneously with overcoming a certain conception of beings as what is objectively representable. Overcoming aesthetics results necessarily from the historical encounter with metaphysics" (BPE: 503/354).

Consequently, it is clear that Heidegger's concern is not with any general idea of art, but with its *origin* (where it arises from and how) and its *work* (how it is and what this does), and this perhaps hints at his own attention to this essay as a work that needed to be reworked, since he continued to add notes to it right up until his death. This emphasis on art as a work signals Heidegger's desire to view it both in its concrete facticity and as a thing that has been *worked*, for unlike other things artworks occupy a peculiar ontological position as they are neither natural objects nor tools. The "work" of art is thus not easy to discern, for it is defined neither by its material nor by its purpose, but by its relation to truth as unconcealment, and so rather than trying to dismiss this ambiguity it is precisely here, in the background to the National Socialists' denigration of "degenerate (*Entartete*) art" and the massive technologization of the Four Year Plan that had begun with the remilitarization of the Rhineland, that Heidegger begins, by organizing his discussion around a painting by Vincent van Gogh and an ancient Greek temple.

Heidegger's efforts to uncover what kind of a thing a work of art might be proceeds by a lengthy examination of the history of our conceptualization of things: as "the bearer of traits, the unity of a sensory manifold, and as formed matter" (H: 15/11–12). Each of these approaches is grounded in the presupposition that the reality of a thing lies outside what it is for us: that there is some kind of pure materiality or substance that precedes our interaction with it, which is then molded into the thing as it is for us. But such a presupposition assumes that we can understand a thing without having a relation to it, and so denies that we are always already in a relation with the things about us, a relation that does not engage with these things primarily as objects or tools but, as Heidegger calls it, as *Zeuges* (stuff or gear), that is, as extensions of our own existence in the world. To assess the essence of such stuff Heidegger turns to a pair of shoes, not to an actual pair but to a painting by van Gogh, in order to uncover what the painting can indicate about the essence of stuff.

For Heidegger, the painting is able to expose the essence of a thing by the manner in which it works it, and its work is precisely this exposure of the stuff-being of stuff, that which makes it "stuff." Thus, in the work of art there is an event in which the truth of stuff is brought to appear, and this is the "work" of art. Not, as Heidegger is quick to point out, as any kind of imitation or depiction, for the painting does not show something that already is; the stuff-being of stuff *first* comes to be through the work of art. Thus the work of art stands in an essential relation to the nature of things, such that if we are to come to an understanding of the thing we must first pass by way of its working, which is what allows its truth to appear. In other words, the nature of the thing becomes a possibility through its working as a *work* of art; it does not exist as an object or value to be found but is only discovered through the *praxis* of its working. Paradoxically, art takes us closer to things as they are through the way in which it works them, and thus we can see how Heidegger's approach here has arisen from but, as we shall see, also subtly altered his earlier attempts to access and bring to language the logic of phenomena. But if the *work* of art is this unconcealment in which things appear, then art itself is no thing, but simply the event of truth, thus the question must turn to the nature and origin of this event; but how can this be brought to appear when it is inapparent?

It is thus that Heidegger turns to poetry, whose role in this essay is considerable if not immediately apparent, for although he briefly mentions a poem by C. F. Meyer the discussion of poetry itself is left until the last few pages when it is suddenly introduced *as* the essence of art. To understand this development we must look to the rhetorical nature of this essay to realize how Heidegger uses the maneuvers of his own language as a means of bringing the event of art to language, and this means understanding the status of the poetic figures that guide the essay, particularly earth and draw-ing. These figures cannot be described as concepts or models in the traditional sense, as they are not seeking to apprehend the work of art in any definite form; nor are they simply metaphors that seek to approximate the unfamiliar through familiarity, for their role is pivotal instead of contingent and their effect is to estrange rather than to familiarize. As such, they are being used as "poetic" figures to lead us away from direct representation toward an indirect indication, which immediately suggests something about the understanding of poetry that is emerging here. Heidegger is using these figures because although they are of language they are also about language and thus can direct us toward the workings of language *itself* as it seeks to approach the work of art. It is in this way that the essay attempts to draw close to the work of art: by indirectly drawing attention to its own workings, a trait that is pre-eminently that of a work of art.

While this may prove to be the case, it does not mean that there is no disfiguring of the work that also occurs, for the ability of a figure to achieve a specific configuration entails a necessary disfiguration or obscuring of other aspects of the work. Only by recognizing this inevitable loss, which is an essential part of the action of figurality, can we come close to the work. While Heidegger had long been aware of the tension between the figuring and disfiguring of truth, the depth of its disfiguring was only recognized during the early 1930s when he uncovered the role of "untruth" as the "concealment of beings as a whole," which "is older than every openedness" (W: 89/148).[3] It is this primordial concealment that is at the heart of what Heidegger calls the "earth," which places it in the context of his study of "nothing" in "What Is Metaphysics?" as that which exposes us to the radical and necessary finitude of being. But the meaning that Heidegger takes up most directly comes from Heraclitus' fragment 123, which states that "nature (*phusis*) loves to hide" (Kahn: 33). To understand nature as *phusis* is not to understand it in opposition to science or culture, but in its essence, which is that aspect of the being of a thing by which it emerges and comes to stand out. But what Heraclitus is saying about *phusis* indicates that this emergence is coupled with another movement that goes in the other direction: into hiding. This brings the understanding of the work into an understanding of the essential *cryptophilia* of presencing.

What first assails us about a work and remains after all else about it has been said is that it *is*. This is to recognize the fact that its nature as a work is centered on its coming to be something that has this presence; that it stands out from what is *not*. *Phusis* is an event of differentiation in which the work is exposed as *a-lētheia*: "arising from the concealed and thus enabling the concealed to take its stand for the first time" (EM: 17/16). *Phusis* is double-sided and this is shown most clearly in the way in which Heidegger retranslated Heraclitus' fragment 123 as "Being (emerging appearance) intrinsically inclines toward self-concealment" (EM: 122/121). In this lies the essence of what Heidegger is trying to say in discussing the work of art through the "earth."

. . . EARTH AND *PHUSIS*: DRAW-ING AND *POLEMOS*: POETRY AND *LOGOS* . . .

In describing art through an analysis of the artwork Heidegger is making an explicit shift away from the artist as creator or the audience as experiencer. Only by doing so, he insists, can we come to an understanding of what the "work" of art is. Art *works* for Heidegger in a very real and physical way, and what it works toward is the "setting up" (*Aufstellung*) of a world: "the work opens up a *world* and keeps it abidingly in force." This is not the world as "the mere collection of things," nor as an "imaginary framework added by our representation to the sum of things"; instead Heidegger states, following a strand of thinking that goes back to his first postwar course in 1919 where he uncovered the factical tautology of presence, the "*world worlds*" (Welt weltet) (H: 30/22–23; ZBP: 73/61). In this tautology we are given a repetition that indicates its movement, its mode of appearance, for by this verbalization the meaning or logic of the "world" is temporalized into the history that surrounds and enables the art to work. For art to work in this way is to initiate or bring about the advent of history through its appearance as repetition, its recurrence. This sets up a very specific relationship between time and the work that Heidegger has already announced in the title of his essay.

Within this relationship is found the play of history, as the work makes history possible by setting up or installing a certain historical *configuration* of truth, an epoch, which was not available before. In emerging, the work stands out into the world, which is thereby exposed *as* a world *in* time. History itself, as a particular determination of truth, becomes a possibility with the advent of the work and as a result, the role of history in the play of decisions becomes available: "art in its essence is an origin: a distinctive way in which truth comes into being, i.e., becomes historical" (H: 66/49). This is a point of considerable weight as it indicates Heidegger's own (historical) determination of the work in relation to politics and it is significant that his language should be especially strong on this issue. For if art "grounds history," such that when it happens "a thrust (*Stoß*) enters history" and it "begins or starts again," then the ground is thereby laid for Heidegger to describe history as "the removal (*Entrückung*) of a people into its appointed task (*Aufgegebenes*) as entry (*Einrückung*) into its endowment (*Mitgegebenes*)" (H: 65/49).

Here the role of art as "the setting-into-work (*Ins-Werk-Setzen*) of truth" is revealed as what is destinal for a people. It is of note then that three months after the triumphalist celebrations of the Berlin Olympics Heidegger should, while addressing the Freies Deutsches Hochstift in Frankfurt am Main, turn to an ancient Greek temple: "It is the temple-work that first fits together and at the same time gathers around itself the unity of those paths and relations . . . [that] acquire the *Gestalt* (shape or figure) of destiny for human being" (H: 27–28/20–21). Through the work a people is able to see itself in history for the first time and thus as having an historical bearing; time is made to matter to it through the opening of history in the work. In turn the being of the people is held in place (*epochē*) by the particular configuration of world and history that is set up, as the "work holds open the open of a world" (H: 31/23). Heidegger's use of a language of "setting up," "holding open," or "fitting together" is not accidental, for what "is here called *Gestalt* is always to be thought out of the *particular* placing (*Stellen*) and framing (*Ge-stell*) as which the *work* essences (*west*) when it sets itself up and sets itself forth (*herstellt*)" (H: 51/38).

Art works to bring about the origin of history by first making such a thing apparent as a possibility, but in doing so it also necessarily brings about its own origin. But if this is the case, then the work always precedes the advent of its own history as it initiates its own origin; thus in itself the work has no origin as it is that which makes such a thing possible. We have here the beginnings of a tension that Heidegger will exploit further on, and that will undermine any possibility of configuring this origin as politically destinal, as we are faced with the situation of trying to discern what kind of event the origin of a work can be. If in emerging it sets up its own conditions for emergence, then in one sense it precedes itself in an unconditioned manner, as nothing, but in another sense its advent as a work is what conditions it, after the fact, *as* such a thing. Together these imply that the work is something that "demands" its own emergence; it "is something that sets up" (H: 30/22).

However, this also implies that the presence of the work is not without ambiguity; it is never present without also marking that presence with an inextricable absence, which indicates that it "is" only insofar as it is also to some extent *not*. That is, the presence of the work only comes about through an absence, a lack of presence. Inescapably, the identity of the work rests on a difference from itself, since it arises out of "the nothing that we scarcely know." Art is what exposes us to this nothing, in such a way that in "the midst of beings as a whole an open place arises (*west*)" (H: 40/30). This is the event in which the spacing or gaping *of* the origin takes place for the first time as the clearing, which *is* the work of art, so that the presence of the work is always by way of an absence that empties it of any stability. But as a result, if the world emerges through art then it does so at the expense of the work, for the appearance of the world comes about by its configuration of the work *as* an origin, which elides the fact that the work of art has no origin insofar as it is simply the opening of a demand "to be" that in opening initiates its own origin. However, as the worlding of the work is the advent of history, then it is apparent that the work resists or in some other way does not fully participate in this, for otherwise it would be unrecognizable as a work.

Thus the work is marked with a partiality as it is not completely of the world, for within it lies another tendency that acts counter to the world. Just as the work of art sets up a world it is also involved in a more latent traffic that necessarily appears as the shadow of the world; that which enables the appearance of what appears but is also obscured by it: the *earth.* The earth is that element that can never be totally used up (*verbraucht*) in the setting up of a world, it is that density that holds itself back, such that using it "does not let the material disappear, but allows it to come forth for the very first time." Earth and world are tied together through the work of art, for in "setting up a world, the work sets forth the earth," as Heidegger describes in the work of a temple:

> The rock comes to bear and rest and so first becomes rock; the metal comes to glitter and shimmer, the colors to glow, the tone to ring, the word to say (*Sagen*).[4] All this comes forth as the work sets itself back into the massiveness and heaviness of stones, into the firmness and pliancy of wood, into the hardness and luster of ores, into the lightening and darkening of color, into the ringing of tones, and into the naming power of words.

In being set up the world holds open the openness of being and in the same movement the work, in setting up the world, is set back into the earth in a self-precedence that supports and shelters the world. But in doing so the work also sets forth the earth, that is, it "moves the earth itself into the open of a world and holds it there. *The work lets the earth be an earth*" (H: 32/24). If the world worlds as the opening of being to history, then what is the earth?

The earth is set forth in the work in a countermovement that emerges *as* hidden beneath the movement of the work as it "sets itself back (*zurückstellt*) into the earth" (H: 34/25). The work then becomes that which indirectly reveals the earth in *its* own manner, as that which "shows itself only when it remains undisclosed and unexplained" (H: 33/25). Heidegger talks of the earth as withdrawing or escaping from us; it refuses our attempts to open it up and remains dumb, opaque. As the groundless ground of history the earth is that which remains outside of history: hidden, immemorial, and unworlded; however, this is not simply pure materiality but rather concealment as the *refusal* (*Versagen*) to presence. But in an added twist, this refusal is itself obscured by the fact that when the earth is made present it does not appear as itself but as something "other than it is" (H: 40/30). This is not simply a representation of the earth in its refusal, but an occlusion of this refusal whose essence is found in the presentation of an endless *dissembling* (*Verstellen*), which *is* the earth. The earth is not simply hidden from us; it also obscures this hiddenness by way of its cryptophilia, as Heraclitus pointed out; this hiddenness is its constant and active pursuit: the earth *loves* to hide.

As it is also of the essence of earth to be set forth it is thus intrinsically double-sided: it is constantly engaged in both emerging and submerging. But it is the submerging that allows the emerging *to* emerge, because the earth does not simply imply a static concealment but an active inclination toward concealment; it is the condition for what is set up to *be* set up, by submerging itself. It is because the setting forth of the earth remains hidden in the setting up of a world and is also concealed in itself through its dissembling, that it is that which allows the world to world. The importance of this is that the earth *appears as* doubly self-concealed; it is that residue that remains of things in their thingness, but it only appears as such through its essential dissembling. Hence, it is not uniform in its self-seclusion but "unfolds itself in an inexhaustible richness of simple modes and shapes" (H: 34/25). In contrast to the construction of tools where the material is apparently fully used up in the worldly stuff of the thing, the work of art initiates an other relation of *Brauch* (usage), one that is based in a lack of use, or uselessness, which brings forth the thing in a way that lets us see it in its self-concealing thingness. As such, it not only presents itself through the nonappearing of refusal and dissembling, which is the way most true to its thingness, but in doing so the earth also "delimits everything that presences (*Anwesende*) into its presence (*Anwesen*)"; its material refraction is the very condition of appearance (H: 33/25).

It would be circumspect to pause here briefly to make this point a little clearer, for it is key to Heidegger's understanding of the work of art that its duplicity is of the essence of presencing as such. In other words, the refusal and dissembling at work in the thing is not limited to art but is at the essence of all things: the double concealment of refusal and dissembling is the condition for all presencing. Without dissembling there could be no semblances; without refusal there could be no granting; together they collect the double-sidedness of presencing as figure and ground (H: 40/30). But it is the priority of concealment that is at stake, for by claiming this Heidegger is claiming that the earth grounds the world, but not vice versa. This is immediately complicated even further by insisting that the grounding of the world is achieved by refusal and dissembling, in which the ground is itself forever absent and incognito.

It is this dissembling of the refusal to presence, this disguising of the absence of ground, which *is* the setting forth of the earth that occurs in the work of art as it sets up the world. Hence, the configuring that occurs in the worlding of the world is not *of* anything although it leads *to* the configuring of history. What the work of art reveals is that the world is not so much grounded by the earth as ungrounded, and if this is the case then if there is a truth in art it can only be grounded in something that, like the earth, also refuses and dissembles, something that can only be called "untruth." By this term Heidegger indicates how he has uncovered the ontological significance of his earlier concern with the resistance and doubling of facticity, for this evasion exposes the finitude of being, rather than just existence. Thus untruth is not the negative or inverse of truth, but that which precedes truth and that is older than every disclosure; the hidden or concealed as it is, the darkness of nothing that Heidegger calls "the mystery." This leads him to term this ungrounding *un-geheuer*, "monstrous," but more literally, "not ordinary (*geheuer*)," which suggests that a richer and more accurate translation might be "inordinate," "enormous," or "immense," if we recall that these words indicate that which is without class (*ordo*), rule (*norma*), or measure (*mensura*) (H: 41/31). This inevitably places pressure on the event of grounding that occurs in the work of art, for if the setting up of the world is grounded in an endlessly dissembling refusal of ground, if this configuring is inevitably disfiguring, what can be the nature or effect of this setting up?

In indicating the step beyond the world, Heidegger uses the earth as a means to show the finitude of this step. This finitude can be viewed in two ways; firstly, from within the openness of being, which it opens up; the worlding of the world is always accompanied by a refusal or withdrawal, an inherent hiddenness that can neither be spoken nor dismissed. This limit is to be found in art, poetry, language, and being itself; furthermore, this hiddenness is neither a lack nor a fault but is essential for the world to world. While it remains irreducible and unmasterable it yet indicates, by virtue of that very intractability, what is tractable and thereby opens up the world and allows it to be the ground of decisions, by bringing into proximity the historical and essential dimensions of being. The work of art brings these possibilities into presence, into the openness in the midst of being in which the work is, but through the earth this "clearing (*Lichtung*) in which beings stand is itself at the same time concealment" (H: 40/30).

This is the second view of finitude: from the perspective of itself as it withdraws, in which the earth is not just the limit or ground of world, but is instead that which directs us toward the relation of being to truth, which is essentially grounded in untruth. For the work of art to engage in the dissembling of refusal that is the earth setting itself forth, is for it to configure an absence in which its figuring is not derived from anything but is instead a pure (non)originary repetition. In other words, it is simply figurality itself, which reveals the condition of figuration in general *as* the dissembling of refusal. This is of course the figuration that makes the artwork itself possible; in opening onto the groundless ground of figurality the work of art opens onto its own impossible conditions, and thereby most truly becomes itself. Hence, if the work of art can make its own conditions of presencing present it does so for the first time, but as a repetition, and thus, like the ancient Greek temple, it "portrays (*bildet*) nothing" (H: 27/20).

By this move Heidegger is distinguishing his understanding of the work of art from "the view, now fortunately superseded, that art is an imitation (*Nachahmung*) and depiction of reality" (H: 22/16). This understanding of art as *mimēsis* is dependent on an idea of truth as adequation and, as such, is inappropriate to Heidegger's work. But such an imitation of reality would require the work to be a likeness of what is, not as a simple copy of its appearance, but as that which reopens the possibility of the world in its appearing, its originality. Thus the work can only be an imitation if it is also original, and as such it is not an imitation of the world of presence, but of what grants it and does not appear, which is the ground of nothing that enables the world to world. So while the Greek temple seems to be distant from any sense of *mimēsis* as we commonly view it, at another level it is mimetic in that it "*portrays* nothing."[5] This twist is not one that Heidegger makes (although it could be suggested that his thinking of *Ereignis* over the following years comes to take its place) nor does he seem aware of its significance, for it is part of the work of art in the modern age, with which he is not concerned. While he later comes to appreciate Cézanne and Klee, the possibility of an art that portrays nothing but itself, Duchamp's readymades for instance, seems to be impossible for him. Although this could be due to the historical perspective that Heidegger pursues, it is of significance precisely because of what the modern work of art contests in terms of the possibility of origination, of being a work of truth, or history, or art, or of being a work at all.

For earth and world to come together in the work of art it must be open to the essence of truth as the figuring of an abyssal untruth, which both ungrounds the world and brings the earth into the open as refusal and dissembling. In being grounded in this way, the work takes up an ontological tension that holds it together only insofar as it is drawn apart, for in doing so its origin is endlessly deferred by its work, just as its work is erased by its origin. Ultimately, our inquiries into the work of art can only lead to the dumbness or refractory nature of the earth as it is set forth in the opacity and dissembling of stone, paint, or language that emerges when these things break down. But this dumbness is the very dumbness of being *resembling and thereby concealing itself*, which lies at the essence of what is: the withdrawal into forgottenness of the essential mystery of being, "that it *is*" (H: 53/40). In describing van Gogh's painting of some shoes and Meyer's poem about a fountain, Heidegger indicates this non-appearance: "The more simply and essentially the footgear (*Schuhzeug*) is engrossed in its essence, the more plainly and purely the fountain is engrossed in its essence, the more immediately and engagingly do all beings become more in being (*seiender*) along with them. That is how self-concealing being is illuminated" (H: 43/32).[6] In the work of art the truth of being is only indirectly apparent. This is the dissembling untruth at the heart of truth, the concealed hiddenness of being that can never be removed or overcome because it is that which enables us to be and to speak, for as the essence of figuration in general it is the very condition of appearance. Without errancy there can be no way; without dissembling there can be no semblance; if "beings did not simulate (*verstellen*) one another, we could not make mistakes or act mistakenly in regard to beings, we could not go astray and transgress and especially never overreach (*vermessen*) ourselves" (H: 40/30).

. . . EARTH AND *PHUSIS*: **DRAW-ING AND *POLEMOS***: POETRY AND *LOGOS* . . .

In setting up the relationship of earth and world Heidegger makes use of Heraclitus' fragment 53, which starts by claiming that "war (*polemos*) is father of all and king of all" (H: 29/22; Kahn: 67). Translating *polemos* as *Auseinandersetzung* (confrontation or struggle), Heidegger is able to read Heraclitus as saying that "confrontation is indeed for all (that comes to presence) the sire (who lets emerge), but (also) for all the preserver that holds sway" (EM: 66/65). In doing so, he is able to say that through the artwork the earth and world reveal their essence as perpetual conflict in which their mutual striving occurs in opposing directions. This provides a model for unity that is neither static nor homogeneous, as each element is brought to its utmost pitch in striving against the other and, as each side provides the conditions for the other, they are bound together through their perpetual striving into a "continually self-overreaching gathering" (H: 36/27).

To bring this out Heidegger uses what I am taking as the second figure of his later works: the idea of a cut or difference that unites. Here the term used is *Riß*, which means a "rift," "tear," or "crack," but is also found in the terms sketch (*Aufriß*), outline (*Umriß*), and design (*Grundriß*). Together this emphasizes the fact that in separating the world from the earth we draw out its configuration, and in sketching this out we set apart its ground. The sketch and the tear are two sides of the same line. Heidegger's use of *Riß* is central to the project of his late writings but the multiplicity of its meanings has become lost through its standardized translation as "rift," as a result I would like to propose a specific retranslation in order to reactivate this multiplicity. While it is obvious that part of Heidegger's use of this term does relate to its conventional and geological meaning as a rift, this is perhaps the least interesting aspect of its meaning. Furthermore, it also feeds too closely into the thematics of soil and earth, which while significant for Heidegger's work of the 1930s, is no longer the case for his later writings. My own interest here in rewriting *Riß* is not so much to erase this early aspect of its meaning but to expose those meanings that enable Heidegger to continue using it in the 1950s, meanings that are necessarily already apparent in the earlier period but that are obscured by their more immediate meaning. In doing so I am also taking up Heidegger's own concern with the need to keep returning to certain key words, to reread and rewrite them in order to preserve them from familiarity. Only in doing so can we understand them.

The problem with translating *Riß* as "rift" is its simplicity; it seems obvious and natural; however, the word "rift" has few of the connotations that *Riß* has for a German speaker. On the one hand *Riß* refers to the verb *reißen* meaning "to tear," and on the other hand as we have noted, it also refers to the family of terms that relate to the practice of sketching or designing. The use of "rift" as a translation here maintains a fidelity to one of the meanings, the most obvious, while losing the others. Thus in order to retrieve this sense of multiplicity we would need to turn away from this obvious meaning, despite its accuracy, and seek a word that can link these ulterior and complex meanings. A word that combines both the sense of tearing and marking, that is both a cut and a line, is *drawing*, from which we have both the sense of drawing blood or teeth, and the sense of it as *a* drawing; a sketch or outline. The impact of this retranslation will become stronger in our readings of Heidegger's later works on language, where he uses *Riß* as a basis for exposing the essence of language in terms of its material, written basis. For now, the link between art and drawing notwithstanding, the significance of this rereading lies partly in this projection into Heidegger's later works, but also in the implicit graphology we find in a term that combines marking and tearing, drawing together and drawing out, and resistance and indication.

For these reasons I find that I cannot use the translation "rift" any longer; as a word it has become yet another opaque unit of Heideggerian doctrine, not a word as such, with ambiguity and variability, but a fixed point that obstructs understanding. The use of "drawing" is, I admit, a rather extreme alternative, losing as it does the obvious meaning of *Riß*, but the need to pursue the texture of Heidegger's thought as much as its contents sometimes requires such extremity, and what is gained in this case far outweighs what has been lost.[7] I will hyphenate it, so that its meaning does not also become fixed as a drawing, and this will help to focus our reading on its oscillation between the two senses of tearing and marking. (As will be explored later, this relation between poetry, thinking, writing, and translation is central to the work of both Hölderlin and Heidegger, forming as it does the matrix of their work. The reasons for this lie in the necessity of bringing the matter of language into focus and holding it there, for only as such can poetry or thinking develop, and in doing so this attention to words through rereading and rewriting itself becomes the work.)

To return: The draw-ing activated in the work of art is the line between earth and world, which sets each against the other and in doing so holds them together while drawing them into further striving (H: 51/38). But more than simply striving, the earth and world are brought together by the draw-ing as the work of truth, or *a-lētheia*, and for truth to work in this manner is for it to bring forth the open in a singular event that clears it and makes it anew: "The more solitarily the work, configured in the figure, stands in itself, the more purely it seems to cut all ties to human beings, then the more simply does the thrust come into the open that such a work *is*, and the more essentially is the inordinate (*Ungeheure*) thrust to the surface and the previously ordinary (*bislang geheuer*) thrust down." This opening is being, which is opened by the work in a way that has never come before and that will never be again, and only as such "does it move (*rückt*) us into this openness and thus at the same time out of the realm of the usual" (H: 54/40).[8] But for us to accomplish this dislocation, displacement, or derangement (*Verrückung*) is to surrender all previous ways, and only by maintaining this restraint from what is usual can the work remain, and we remain with it.

This surrender and restraint is an aspect of the work that Heidegger calls "preservation" (*Bewahrung*), and that he accords equal status with the createdness of a work, the fact that it is, in bringing out what is essential to it, its truth (*Wahrheit*). This is highly significant for our understanding of the nature of a poem, but for now we should note the paradox that the solitary status of the work is only possible by way of our involvement. Even though the work sets itself into the open that it itself is, it cannot remain there without our collaboration, but as the open in which the work is, is also the open that we most essentially are, then it is not the case that we can ever be fully absent from it, even if we are not currently present in it. While the work needs us in order to be, its presencing is a waiting for those preservers who are to come and this waiting is enough on its own for the work to remain in the open, for even "the oblivion into which the work can fall is not nothing; it is still a preserving" (H: 54/41).

Not just the origin of the work is shrouded in obscurity, but so, it would seem, is its whole temporality. As well as calling to us from a time before the past, before its own origin, the work also speaks to another time beyond the future, beyond its waiting for its own preservation to be fulfilled. This absence from worldly time leaves the work standing on its own, cut off from human ties, for it has neither beginning nor end, and yet it is also already over and done with, begun and finished, immaculately wrapped up in its own self-enclosing time without time. Both of these paradoxes arise from the ground of history, which in its essential withdrawal is beyond the time of history, in another time unmarked by presence, immemorial and forgotten, but still and always to come. While this time of the earth is thus the ruin of history, its refusal to presence is also that which, in withdrawing, grounds history. Hence, the withdrawal of the earth is itself never complete because its absence is marked as absence through its dissembling as the work. The nonrelation of the earth and world, their radical separation and difference, becomes a relation through the work, whose existence as such a relation is undermined by the work's inability to fully presence, such that it becomes a relation of nonrelation. This paradox repeats that of the appearance of the nonappearance of the earth that goes on in the work, and inevitably affects the relation between ourselves and the work, both as artists and nonartists.

On each occasion, whether it is in terms of its materiality or temporality, we are told that what makes the work of art is also what places it beyond us. Its very success as a work simultaneously removes it from our ability to apprehend it as such. The work exists at/as the limits of its own repetition, in a time outside time, in a materiality outside materiality; it needs us to exist but this need does not require us to be present; indeed it is most fully itself when it is removed from all human ties. A draw-ing thus occurs between the work and us; we appear to be configured in oppositional terms such that properly speaking we have no relation to it. But this nonrelation is not a complete lack of relation; instead it exposes the essence of the truth of what is: that truth is grounded in an abyssal untruth and this grounding is the setting up of being in the open. It is as a result of this complexity that the work of art becomes turned toward itself in a concern with its own impossible origins, with the very question of itself, and thereby comes to resemble nothing, but itself, thus opening up the possibility that Heidegger's thought in this essay could come to terms with the work of modern art, as that art that is essentially concerned with itself.[9]

If, by turning toward its own origin as its essential question, the work find itself in the position of preceding its own source, then the work in opening itself and becoming a work is that which brings the earth and world into the open for the first time. That which is its origin is then in the paradoxical position of being on the way; it is to come, in the future, ahead of or after the work, and thus only present as imminent. The draw-ing that holds apart the earth and world and thereby joins them originarily is marked by the absence of that which would make it present; thus the work is rendered hollow and incomplete for it can never be fully present. The draw-ing is the mark of this absence, which inscribes the work with a trace that is the remains of the origin as it withdraws into what is to come. This withdrawal of presence cannot help marking itself as such with the trace of its absence, even as it erases itself through the appearance of the work, for this self-erasing mark is the mark of the work as it seeks to confront its own origin. Doing so destabilizes its position in space and time, which is what grants it the singularity of a work while placing it in fragmentation. It will appear, but will never be complete; its origin will always recede into an impossible retrograde imminence in which it will have been forever marked as coming; it will thus open a question that can never be closed as its conditions of closure will never be present. In doing so, it places itself outside human relations while still requiring our industry; within all this we find the struggle of diverging tendencies that somehow through their conflict create an impossible harmony.

This aspect of the draw-ing is the *work* that Heidegger is engaged in in this essay, and as such it figures the relation of poetry and thinking for him. The draw-ing as a term is the very draw-ing of the essay itself as a work, in that it marks it with an imminence of meaning brought about by the rhetorical struggle between the thinking and poeticizing of the work of art. The essay itself emerges as a work that then figures this struggle, as what Heidegger will only later be able to call a "neighboring." In seeking to question the origin of the work of art, Heidegger is drawn into an inquiry that requires him to question the origins of his own work. The extended life of this essay reflects this incompleteness in that it repeatedly exposes its abyssal origin in language while figuring this absence with the earth and draw-ing. As figures they do not so much configure an absent meaning, as figure themselves as the traces of this absence, which in being used only recede from meaning into language itself. In doing so, Heidegger's writing has become a work insofar as it has converged on its own way, exposing its work of writing through the indirection of the *polemos*, which cannot make present its own conditions but that can only re-stage them, for in "the bringing forth of the work there lies this offering 'that it be'" (H: 53/40).[10]

The inserted phrase, as a self-citation, is the very deferred presentation Heidegger is referring to, which exposes the peculiar facility of language to defer itself by opening onto itself, something his later work will pursue at length, as we will see in chapter 5. But it is also as such that the work is a repetition and figure of nothing, but itself, and why, if it has any relation to truth, it is on the condition that its truth is grounded in the abyssal untruth of that which never appears, but is always to come, the inordinate sign of which is never anything but a sign, for the nature of truth "is dominated throughout by a denial (*Verweigerung*)" (H: 41/31). This denial is the double nature of concealment as refusal and dissembling, whose "primal conflict" (*Urstreit*) is the event of the work, for while refusal "is the constant provenance (*Herkunft*) of all clearing," dissembling "metes out to all clearing the indefeasible severity of error" (H: 41–42/31).

The strife (*Streit*) of earth and world exposed by the work is thus not a simple opposition or dialectic, but the sketching or spacing out of a between that persistently destabilizes the work by refiguring its absent origin. This inner distantiation nears its origin through this refiguring, in which the work and its origin are held together *through* the endless dissembling of the earth as it withdraws. The appearance of the world thus occurs out of the withdrawal of the earth into itself and this withdrawal makes the earth what it is by separating it from the world, and so the draw-ing is primary for without it earth and world could not appear. The draw-ing is thus present in the work as a relation of nonrelation that separates earth and world and that projects them into their essential outline, by only bringing them together in the *imminence* of the figure, as a "joining (*Gefüge*), in which the draw-ing joins itself (*sich fügt*)" (H: 51/38).

Thus, this joining is never complete for if the structure is only configured as imminent, it is always waiting for the arrival of its figure. This trace is the remains left by its withdrawal, which projects its nonrelation (its refusal) *as* a relation, that is, as a work (of dissembling). The work thus comprises an abyssal absence, which by hollowing out what is set up as the world, allows it to be so set up, but prevents it from ever being fully set up. The work is an aporia; we cannot get beyond it because it is that which configures the world as it is, but also exposes it as forever disfigured, of only ever being *just* a figure. Although it would be true to say that this configuration was prefigured within the earth as its demand, this can never be rendered distinct from its own disfiguring. While the draw-ing is nothing, as it is effaced by that which it brings about, it is also all that there is, as it is the figure that *is* earth and world. In drawing out the active configuration of earth and world that is the work of art, the work also projects the outline of the striving that is prefigured in this configuration; that of the striving within *alētheia*. What we find in the work of art is the projection of its own repetition, as found in the struggle between concealing and revealing, which can only be revealed in retrospect by the way in which the earth and world refigure this. Thus the work of art exists as a site where *alētheia* occurs in a way that opens us to it. Earth and world, by their striving in the work of art, draw us into an intimacy with an older, more basic tension, which is that within presencing.

This can only happen through the earth; only by attending to how the earth secludes itself in jutting up into the open and dissembles this seclusion as the work, can the intimacy that is both striving and joining take place. The draw-ing that is this drawing together "must set itself back into the dragging weight of stones, into the dumb hardness of wood, into the dark glow of colors. As the earth takes the draw-ing back into itself, the draw-ing is first set forth into the open and thus placed, i.e., set, into that which rises up into the open as self-closing and protecting" (H: 51/38). Thus it is through the self-closing of the earth that "the openness of the open finds the greatest resistance and thereby the site of its constant stand, where the figure must become fixed in place" (H: 57/42). By drawing out the work of art we enter the striving that joins it together, only insofar as that drawing out is also a stepping back into that which refuses this drawing out. Only in doing so are we transported into the openness of *a-lētheia*. The draw-ing works both to draw us in and draw us out; indeed the movement is the same, for what it does is to draw "the opposition of measure and boundary into a common outline (*Umriß*)," that is, into the limit of truth as figure (H: 51/38).

It is not surprising, considering how the draw-ing has been developed, that it recurs quite explicitly in Heidegger's later works on language while the earth appears to be left behind (US: 24/204, 185/90, 240–41/121). *Phusis* continues to preoccupy Heidegger but not in terms of the earth, and while the earth is taken up again in the idea of the *Geviert*, or "fourfold," this is very different from what has been studied here. Rather than being set forth in the setting up of a world and thereby refusing and dissembling this setting-up, the earth in the 1950s is configured alongside the sky, gods, and mortals in a mutually appropriating expropriation in which the coming together of the *Geviert*, which is the world, sends each of the four horizons into its "own." The darkness and muteness of the earth does not arise here; instead it is simply the "bearer" and "nourisher," which lies under the sky supporting the dwelling of mortals and remaining before the gods (VA2: 23/149, 50–51/178). It is as though, in discussing the earth so directly in "The Origin of the Work of Art," there were too much risk involved, that it was too easy for the earth to be taken as naming the ground and, despite everything that has been said, of thereby fixing it as such.

Instead, the draw-ing takes up a more central position, and this would seem to follow for, as he has pointed out here, the thinking of the drawing is primary whereas the earth cannot be thought in itself, but has to be found indirectly. The draw-ing does however experience a transformation in Heidegger's later works, becoming the "dimension," "region," or "neighborhood" in which difference is gathered, and it also persists in a more tacit form, in the way in which the Heraclitean idea of *polemos* is continually reformulated in Heidegger's thought. While the explicit use of Heraclitus in "The Origin of the Work of Art" is limited to one passing reference his influence is everywhere, and his ideas on *logos*, *phusis*, *alētheia*, and *polemos* are decisive for all of Heidegger's later work. The structure of *logos* as a "laying that gathers," *phusis* as an "emerging that abides," and *alētheia* as a "revealing that conceals," exposes the *polemos* in the heart of each, as a mutual striving between opposites, a division that binds together. The sounding of this tension constitutes a large part of Heidegger's method, as we have seen from the paronomasia of such terms as *Wahrheit* (truth) and *Bewahrung* (preserving), *Gefüge* (structure) and *fügen* (to join or fit).

In these turns of phrase Heidegger is not engaging in mere wordplay, but is rotating the terms to set them against themselves, thereby joining their divergent meanings together in their figuring of the text and in doing so exposing an inner tension within each word that holds a countertone or echo. While avoiding a dialectic of image and reversal that might obtain from this countering, Heidegger makes the further move of indicating it as an originary draw-ing within the word. Thus the figuring of the word is the draw-ing turning on and joining itself, not to resolve or defuse its tension, but to layer it with a veiling that admits of its concealment without exposing it. This leads to the conjecture that this veiled tension is indicative of the relation of man to language, a relation in which man and language are each needed or used in the saying that they are. This relation calls each to the other and is what must be heard in saying if it is to be approached.

. . . EARTH AND *PHUSIS*: DRAW-ING AND *POLEMOS*: POETRY AND *LOGOS* . . .

By working through his ideas of earth and draw-ing, Heidegger's study of the work of art reaches a point where he can say that the work of art is both the "*becoming and happening of truth*," and in saying as much he can conclude that all art is "*in essence poetry*" (H: 59/44). The transition between these two statements is focused by the following line, which says that truth "appears in becoming poeticized (*gedichtet*)." This term, *gedichtet*, refers to a dense problem that recurs in most of Heidegger's writings on poetry, and while it refers to both poem (*Gedicht*) and compose (*dichten*), there is also the more cumbersome construction of "what has been composed" (*Gedichtete*), which refers to the ground and origin of poetry. This is an essential part of any understanding of what a poem is, but it is also what is perpetually obscured by the presence of the poem itself. In this light there is a further meaning to *gedichtet* that is relevant here, for *gedichtet* also means "sealed."

Here the term *dicht*, meaning "thick" or "dense," is being emphasized as a way of bringing poetry and truth together in their essencing.[11] If the appearance of truth is one of thickness or density then it is not a transparent appearance, but is in some sense "sealed" in a simultaneously inapparent appearance or concealment. That this thickness is also that of the composure of a poem is what justifies the subsequent statement that all art is essentially poetry (*Dichtung*). In this we hear nothing as much as a "thickening" or "condensation" (*Verdichtung*) of appearance, as the appearance of appearance, which must now be thought in terms of the *Lichtung* as lightening, in both of its meanings. However, as he points out in a footnote, this understanding of the relation of *Lichtung* and *Dichtung* is still "inadequate." Before this relation can be thought through the question of poetry "as the need and use of saying" (*als Brauch der Sage*) must first be addressed. For Heidegger it is saying that is basic, and so the usage of poetry for and by saying is itself still "questionable" until the relation of saying and poetry is understood (H: 59n/44n).

What can be said here is that "poetry" has nothing to do with imagination or *poiēsis* understood as simple creativity, nor is it simply that region of literature associated with poems. This latter sense Heidegger accepts is part of what he means by "poetry," but it is as such only because it brings about a particular variety of what is understood to be a more originary ontological poetry. It is important to realize that Heidegger's use of "poetry" does not imply any poietic productivity; rather poetry works negatively, to unsettle or displace. As we have seen, the work of art is only brought about by the setting back of the work into the earth. This setting back brings the earth into the open as self-secluding, and in this opening "everything is other than it was . . . everything ordinary and hitherto existing becomes an unbeing (*Unseienden*). This unbeing has lost the capacity to give and to preserve being as measure." The notion of measure is associated with the world and is part of what is lost in the preservation of the work, so to lose it is to step back into the refusal of the earth. By bringing us face-to-face with the earth we become displaced from any sense of being but this is not an "effect" of the work for "the work does not consist in a taking effect (*wirken*)"; it is in this sense ineffectual, *workless* (H:

59–60/45). Thus the work of poetry is not production, but rather the refusal or evasion of meaning by which we come up against the utter ungrounding of meaning in the earth, in such a way that the word "only now becomes and remains truly a word" (H: 34/25).

By doing so, poetry speaks in its most essential manner and thus names beings *in* their being, which calls or projects them into the open. Projecting is "the releasing of a throw as which unconcealment sends (*schickt*) itself into beings as such. This projective announcement forthwith becomes a renunciation (*Absage*) of all the dim confusion in which beings veil and withdraw themselves" (H: 61/46). The language here is very strong: the appearance of truth in the poetic word is not mild or benign, but a shocking and sudden event that ruptures what is and "projects ahead into the draw-ing of the figure," in such a way that the open is only now brought forth (H: 60/45). This makes poetry "the founding of truth," which Heidegger insists we should understand as a self-establishing projection that involves "bestowing," "grounding," and "beginning" (H: 63/47). There is something excessive about this overdetermination of the projective power of poetic naming, as Heidegger admits by describing it as an "overflow" but this is necessary; for the origin (*Ursprung*) of the work is an "originary leap" (*Ur-Sprung*) in which history "starts again" (H: 65/49).

The excessive and discontinuous nature of naming as a founding of truth can be dangerously overemphasized, as is passed over in the mention Heidegger gives to the founding nature of political, religious, and philosophical acts (H: 49/37). But this is only possible if we forget the essential dissembling of figurality that lies at the heart of its overflowing and that leads to it becoming a figure of nothing, like the ancient Greek temple. By casting itself into the "draw-ing of the figure," poetic naming reinstates this radical dissembling by figuring itself in terms of the complex self-erasure of the draw-ing. As Heidegger notes, the projection that sends truth into what is and renounces the confusion in which it veils itself should not be understood as a projection *into*, or even *of*, the clearing, but as a "projection of draw-ings." Only by understanding naming as the subtle complication of figuring and disfiguring can we understand the nature of founding, for the essence of poetic naming lies in presencing: in calling beings into the open by announcing them *as* being. The difficulty and fragility of this act lies in its double-sidedness for "the preparation of the sayable at the same time brings the unsayable as such into a world" (H: 61–62/46).

The secret of the poetic word that enables it to bring the unsayable into a world as such lies in its naming power "in which announcement is made of what beings come into the open as." To name is to call, and this is to bring forth obscurity into illumination, but to do so it is first necessary to attend to this obscurity, to what lies beyond the open in order to bring it forth into the open. Naming thus implies a listening, for only in restraint can we hear what lies beyond, and to hear in such a way is to find ourselves called by that which is beyond. In calling then, we too are called forth into the open, and so in naming it is not we who name but the beyond itself which does so through us. What finally is this call, but the call of being to itself that was earlier called the call of conscience: "naming nominates beings *to* their being *from out of* their being" (H: 61/46).

This double-sidedness of poetry as the saying of the said and the unsaid enacts the movement of *a-lētheia* as a "poeticizing projection of truth that sets itself into work as figure" (H: 63/47). In other words, the oscillation and reciprocity within poetic naming is the oscillation and reciprocity of being as it opens out and holds together both hiddenness and revealing, which in turn sets itself up as earth and world. This to-and-fro dynamic is what holds open the openness that is being, alongside the withdrawing of the hiddenness that gives rise to this opening. This gives us a clue as to what this hiddenness is: for it is the very limits of what poetry seeks to say in trying to speak its other, which is the earth as the ground of the open: "Poeticizing projection comes out of nothing in this respect," the same nothing that the work exposes us to and toward which it always tends as a figure of absence. But only insofar as it is a genuinely poetic word is its saying able to converge on this nothing, because as such it is a "beginning [that] already contains the end concealed within itself" (H: 64/48). In this movement, poetry is seeking to say the earth by reaching beyond the limit of its language and saying its other, but this means that to say the earth is to unsay poetry, for in seeking its own limits poetry is trying to speak its own ground, to be its own closure and origin, to be whole and thus sealed up in muteness. But this closure is what is always lacking from poetry by virtue of its finitude; it can never travel far enough to reach its own origin, which remains separated from it by an abyss.

But this finitude is also the source of the openness that is being, because it is the hiddenness of withdrawing that gives rise not just to being, but also to the vagrant ways of poetry. In this we need to be careful to play out the full extent of this reciprocity and realize that just as poetry belongs to the earth, which is poetry's source and ground, so too does the earth need poetry as its saying. However, as its (un)grounding the earth is precisely what prevents poetry from ever fully achieving this saying, but this failure is the sign of its genuine convergence upon the earth, for the saying of the earth as earth is a saying of muteness. To understand this we need to recall that the opening of being needs beings in order to be, that is, it gives rise to its own other, but in doing so it loses itself in the manifold dissembling of beings. However, this dissembling *is* the voice of the earth as it seeks to find a way to its own naming, such that it can be, and it is this voice that poetry's failing echoes in its impossible attempt to say the earth.

To take stock of this point, we can say that a poem enacts the impossible situation of the work of art to an extreme. It finds itself caught between speaking and silence at the precise point where sound emerges into word. But this is an ontological rather than physiological point; it is the nature of speaking as annunciation and configuration that is at issue, which is the very movement of *a-lētheia.* The poetic word hovers on this brink of emergence midway between the said and the unsaid and thereby speaks the very opening of being as it is. But the status of the poetic word is always in jeopardy for the same reasons of materiality and temporality that were part of the work of art in general; it speaks its own end and thereby seals itself up before it is even uttered. It is lost and unobtainable because it does not exist in a time or a form in which we can speak it; there is no way to it, no moment right for it, no means of finding it. Yet it still speaks from this very absence and from this point outside, for it is of the outside, its lostness is its voice. Thus, recalling Heidegger's early work on Aristotle, we can say that poetry experiences the *pathos* of the *logos* in its exposure to its own finitude, but in doing so responds by way of *phronēsis* in seeking to preserve the moment of this exposure, which indicates its double-sidedness, as poetry is caught between the *pathos* and the *praxis* of its own *logos,* thereby doubling or thickening (*verdichten*) it into the *logos* of *logos.*

Heidegger has long pursued this duplicity and ambiguity of the *logos,* but it finds its most concise formulation in his explication of Heraclitus' fragment 50: "If you have heard not me, but *logos,* then it is wise to say accordingly: all is *one*" (EM: 137/135–36). Within this brief statement Heidegger reveals the density of Heraclitus' thoughts. To begin with, we are told that the *logos* is something we can hear, but that this hearing should not be confused with what is heard in speech. Therefore, the *logos* lies hidden in some way beneath the sounds of speaking, but even if we can somehow hear this unspoken sound, this is not all, for the wisdom of the *logos* comes with its saying. However, this saying is only wise when it is in accord with the *logos* that has been heard, that is, with what has been heard beneath what has been said; with the unspoken. To reiterate: the *logos* requires this speaking in order to fully be, but this speaking can only be the *logos* if it is in accord with what is unspoken.

Here lies the paradox at the heart of all Heraclitus' thought: to be most fully is to be in accord with what is essential, but what is essential is what is most foreign and elusive; therefore to be is to always be vagrant, absent. This is the voice of poetry as the voice of silence and darkness in which accord takes place as the other of speech and words, as its unthought, unspoken side. Thus, speaking enacts the same meaning as the *logos*: "all is one," for what is laid out in speaking is gathered together in the speaking of it, but this is not the same as the *logos* itself for speaking can not coincide with what is, since the *logos* is exactly that which is not said but is. But through this speaking the meaning of *logos* and its action are the same, as to hear (*hören*) the *logos* is to belong (*gehören*) to it; to be in accord with it by way of the resonance of its echoing, and to speak it is to enact the same, to echo it further.

This is the riddle that Heraclitus presents, for if saying is hidden but essential, it does not coincide with the words we hear, but resides beneath them, and so we will only "get closer to these riddles if we step back before them" (VA3: 4/60). In speaking we have to coincide with that underside; we have to say what is always unsaid; we have to unsay, and in doing so, and only in doing so, can we really say at all. Heidegger in talking of poetry is carrying over all of these complications into an understanding of the way in which the open is called forth in saying. Only in this light can we think the ungrounding of earth and world and the projecting-fissuring of the draw-ing. We are not drawn into the openness of *alētheia from* anywhere; nor is this openness grounded *in* anything, because it is none other than the openness in which we already are, but that is hidden from us. To speak of this paradoxical intimacy of obscurity and illumination, nearness and remoteness, and strife and release, we have to find a way to say this unsaid as unsaid. Combining three of Heraclitus' fragments here (54, 51, 32) we might say that because "the hidden harmony is stronger than the apparent," then "a thing agrees at variance with itself," such that it is "unwilling and willing to be spoken of" (Kahn: 65, 83). We find here the concealment of *phusis*, the tension of *polemos*, and the evasiveness of *logos*; the opening of *a-lētheia* brings about all of these and is brought about by them.

Although this is all that Heidegger says about poetry here, the significance of it should not be underestimated, as the position it holds in the conclusion of "The Origin of the Work of Art" alludes to its pivotal but as yet unworked-out role. This is further supported by the extensive footnotes that were added to this section, more than for any other, and Heidegger's repeated warnings that we have still not fully thought through the nature of poetry or its relation to language. In a footnote added later he questions whether language itself should rather be understood as "saying and renouncing" (*Sage und Entsagen*), which would thus imply a need to negotiate the relation of "language and body (sound and writing)" (*Sprache und Leib [Laut und Schrift]*) (H: 62n/47n).[12] By this he seems to be introducing a crucial and rare mention of the physical dimension of saying, the body (as sound and writing? or just writing?), as being that of renouncing or unsaying. This physical aspect of language will be dealt with in greater length in chapter 4 where I will discuss Hölderlin's understanding of translation, and in chapter 5 where Heidegger comes to understand the essence of language as being itself revealed in some way by way of "writing."

. . . *THESIS*: STELLEN: *PERAS* . . .

We have to ask, after all this, what it means, as it seems unlikely that anything could be taken up from this account and actually used in an understanding of a particular painting, sculpture, symphony, or poem. But this was not Heidegger's intention, for such an approach is at risk of ignoring the ontological status of the work, which looks to art as a means to understand being. So, while Heidegger's use of a van Gogh painting and an ancient Greek temple might remain too brief and too general to really help our understanding of particular arts, instead they cast light on the relationship between art and being, *by which each is indirectly illuminated in themselves*. This is perhaps the place then to ask about the limits of this essay.

Following the line of Heidegger's thought we can say this: The origin of the work of art is art itself, which has no origin because it is the advent of truth. As an event, art takes place in the history of being, and as historical, art, or as Heidegger insists, "great art," it is epoch-making (H: 26/19). This occurs through the fact that the advent of great art brings with it a particular appearance of truth, which through its greatness is constitutive of that particular historical phase of being. In Heidegger's words, it is "destinal" (*geschicklich*); by making not just an historical advent of truth, but an epochal one, great art is active in bringing to bear a decisive appearance of truth that cannot be turned away from, as it is that which surrounds and grounds all others in that epoch. Great art is decisive then for the very nature of the historical dimension of being, and thus for the historical becoming of beings like ourselves (H: 65/49). Given the metaphysical turn that has guided the history of being since Plato, art too has suffered from an increasingly technological framework that has become dominant in the modern age. This framework gives to the "world" its greatest determination by fostering the seed of world-making at the expense of the earth, and thus this gives to the earth-world strife its greatest polemic.

This is the key point that Heidegger himself felt was "unsuitably conceived," as he wrote in the addendum that was added to "The Origin of the Work of Art" in 1956 (H: 74/55). By emphasizing the "*setting*-into-work" of truth, too much weight is given to the technical-historical worlding of each epoch as decisive of the relation between being and beings. This reading is intrinsically polemic as it follows the striving that comes from the advent of each epoch and does not pay enough attention to the ruination and refusal of this history that is given by the earth, which would deny any moment for such a decision to take place. Heidegger attempted to contain this refusal through the way in which the strife of earth and world was "fixed in place in the work's figure" (H: 57/43). But the risk here is that this "fixing" or "setting" is interpreted as static and willed, so, as Heidegger cautions, it is only if we understand how this word has developed from the Greek word *thesis* that we can avoid this risk, for doing so reveals that "the 'fix' in 'fix in place' can never have the sense of rigid, motionless, and secure" (H: 71/53). Rather, he insists, we should follow the meaning of *thesis* as a "letting lie forth," and see the sense of "fixing" as that of bringing something into its outline (*peras*), which sets it free into the unconcealed.

Moreover, the problem with these phrases is also due to the way in which they configure *truth* before this term has itself been adequately negotiated. Although we might now have a better idea of the relation of *thesis* and *peras*, the "use of the name 'truth' for the still-withheld clearing and the cleared" is itself "inappropriate" (H: 1n/1n). This note was placed at the very beginning of the essay and suggests that the whole thematics of truth, as a means of approaching the clearing, is misguided. If we recall the relation between *alētheia* and presence that is problematized in Heidegger's late thoughts on tautology, we can only assume that here too Heidegger is indicating that we should look at the language of presencing that is at work. This means that it is to language that we should look to understand the presencing of a work, for it is in language that we find the *work* of art. We need only recall the paronomasia around the root *stellen* (to place) to see this in action, for from it Heidegger took up a whole network of ideas with which to pattern his argument from *Gestell* (frame) to *Gestalt* (figure), *aufstellen* (to set up) to *verstellen* (to adjust, misplace, obstruct, or disguise) to *herstellen* (to produce) and *darstellen* (to present).

While this root is related to the term *stele* (a standing block), the more important point is that *stellen* is the German translation of *thesis.* Through paronomasia this root phrase is held up in such a way that it can be turned around by its different cognates so that we can view its different sides, and in doing so *stellen* becomes something multidimensional and changeable. By combining the various cognates together we cannot hear one without also involving the others and consequently, the possibility of each term having only one meaning is erased. *Aufstellen* is also *verstellen,* to fix is to place, which is to release into place. Each word's meaning is no longer fixed in place but is open to variability, which is to say that its meaning is exposed to presencing. By watching it change we are party to its hidden sides that are indirectly involved but never revealed in that change: those that allow it to change. This is Heidegger's *thesis,* which would suggest that alongside an examination of the work of art as a mode of *technē,* there is also the beginnings of a *topological* approach that seeks to uncover the way in which art works to open up places in which such setting-up is first possible.[13]

This follows the strategy that Heidegger has taken up from Heraclitus of focusing on a word and seeing what work it does. In this strategy the phrases of Heraclitus are not to be read as sentences or epigrams so much as single words, or rather, as fragments before which we need to step back in order to approach them. For in this manner we are forced to release the word to itself in order to see what work it does. *Phusis,* for example, becomes exposed in this manner as what Heidegger calls a "guideword" (*Leitwort*): its meaning cannot be immediately ascertained but can only be taken up as a companion to thought that over time reveals different aspects of its meaning as it is used. The importance of *phusis* in particular reveals this fact, for in the use of this word lies the emergence of form that it actually states. The same can be also said for *polemos* as it does not describe so much as indicate an opening that can be pursued. This method is recapitulated by Heidegger in the way in which he structures this essay through guidewords of his own, such as the tautology: "the world worlds"; or the oxymoron: "truth is untruth." These words *are* Heidegger's thesis; they *are* what he puts into place, which lets the things of which he speaks come forth into their essential outline. By undermining the specific manner in which meaning is delivered through simple predications, Heidegger is able to show not just other ways in which meaning emerges, but something more significant: the possibility of meaning itself as the *way* of language. This is the *work* of language, which is Heidegger's overriding concern in this and in other essays from his later period.

Despite this we cannot avoid taking up the question of whether Heidegger's concerns in "The Origin of the Work of Art" are worked out in the light of his desire to "correct" certain false impressions that may have arisen from it. This is a critical question for it would seem that despite his late attempt to redirect our reading of this essay, this cannot make up for the way in which the essay was written, which is the irreducibly refractive dimension of his saying. It seems that even if we take up his points about the reading of the verb "to fix," that this does not fully accommodate how the strife between earth and world is configured. A number of different tensions are at work here for Heidegger's account of the world does not seem to take up what was said in his account of the earth, which in turn does not seem to tie in fully to what he was saying about the nature of the *polemos* between them, which finally leads to a configuration of the work of art that has the weaknesses he noted, but not for the same reasons. My point is that his reading fails to fully take up the demands of the obscure materiality and temporality of the work, which refuses the setting up of the world more powerfully than he recognized. For if we are to take seriously the obscurity of the earth then we have to take seriously the nature of our encounter with this refusal. This does not mean that we would have to contend with the complete absence of the work, for such a thing is, as we have seen, not possible for its absence could never avoid being configured as such. Instead we have to understand that the refusal of the work presents us with an utter evasion of relation, an absolute lacuna, which permeates and fractures our every attempt to pursue relation.

Such a work would barely merit the name for it would suspend its relation to the world; it would be in no place and would lie in a state that suspended presencing. Having no relation and no place it would resemble nothing and would exist in some way outside the openness of being: it is the enigma of finitude in itself, which is an endless mystery, uncontained by being. This seems incredible but it is a possibility that lies within the terms that Heidegger has set out. This is the path taken by Blanchot in his reading of Heidegger's essay, for he insists that art "originally represents the foreboding and the scandal of absolute error, of something not true, but whose 'not' does not have the decisive character of a limit, for it is rather the full and endless indeterminacy within which the true can find no path (*ne peut frayer*)" (not even a *Holzweg*, Blanchot seems to be suggesting).[14] That being the case we have to make room for such a possibility within our understanding of the nature of work. From this insight we will attempt to draw out another reading of the work of art that works from the absence of presence and relation, and even of work, and that consequently does not give rise to an overarching polemic of technical and historical striving. This is the relation in which, by setting itself back into the earth *as* earth, being is taken up into its ahistorical ground and its withdrawal from mastery. What this means for a poem is hard to grasp, but is nevertheless essential if we are to find the language of this hiding.

3

Beyond

The Limits of the Word in Heidegger and Blanchot

> You are right, this writing is a "disaster." *Being and Time* was also a disastrous accident. And every immediate presentation of my thinking would be today the greatest disaster. Perhaps this is a first testimony to the fact that my attempts sometimes come into the proximity of genuine *thinking*. All direct thinking is in contrast to that of the poet a disastrous accident in its immediate effect. In this way you can see that I can *not* anywhere identify myself with Hölderlin. Here the encounter of thinking with a poet is under way, where the en-counter first poses what is opposed. Is this arbitrariness or supreme liberty?
>
> —Heidegger, letter to Max Kommerell, 4 August 1942

At the heart of the work of language for Heidegger there is the annunciation of being; language is what makes it possible to articulate the meaning of being, by bringing it to language. Poetry has a privileged position in Heidegger's thinking precisely because it is the means by which the word of language can itself be articulated; it is as we have seen, the *logos* of *logos.* But, as we have also noted, the coming to language of being is an event marked by an irreducible finitude, both in the sense that it is through finitude that the experience of being comes to language, but also because this coming to language is itself marked as being singular and finite. If the word comes, then it is always outside the event; thus its relation to being is attenuated to the point of its disappearance. This is the point of Blanchot's reading of "The Origin of the Work of Art"; that the work always contains the possibility of losing itself and this is also what is at stake in the poetry of Hölderlin. The finitude of the word is thus central to the *practice* of poetry, to its *writing*, and this is a key development in Heidegger's thinking of language, but one that arises only indirectly, as a result of his failure to turn the word of Hölderlin into an event of historical renewal. Thus the significance of Heidegger's essay on Hölderlin's hymn "As when on a holiday . . ." is that it indicates the general dimensions of the transition that takes place in the decades after *Being and Time*, and it does so because it is a failure. In it we find a turning from history to language that draws its cue not from Hölderlin directly, but from Heidegger's experience of the failing of language in the face of the demand of poetry, which is in itself the very experience of Hölderlin's poetry.

Heidegger's study of "As when on a holiday . . ." was originally delivered as a private lecture on several occasions in 1939 and 1940 before being published in 1941.[1] The poem and Heidegger's commentary on it both inquire into the relationship between what Hölderlin calls "nature" and the poet; how is the poet able to respond to nature, Hölderlin asks, what makes poetry possible? In examining this, Heidegger is drawn into a similar territory to that explored in the earlier essay on the work of art, inasmuch as the same questions are being asked about the relation of language to the world. It is for this reason that he has chosen "As when on a holiday . . ."—the first time that he has dedicated an essay to a single poem—for it is "the purest poem on the essence of poetry" (EHD: 44/61). Immediately we can see that Heidegger is only interested in Hölderlin's poem, and by extension it would seem any poem, insofar as it concerns what he considers the essence of poetry. This essence is that which makes a poem what it is, but it is also that which makes anything what it is: its figurality, which is itself unconfigured. That this essence is distinct from poetry but still part of it suggests that it can be revealed if the poem is made to converge on itself, that is, by figuring its own figurality it is able to undo its own configuration and in doing so it becomes essential poetry: that which reveals the essence of poetry.

The word that Heidegger uses here is *Dichtung*, which although ordinarily meaning "poetry," or in a broader sense, literary or fictional works (*Erdichten*), that is, those areas that are by definition distant from truth, is itself a word of complex and ambiguous meaning. Given Heidegger's interest in etymologically unraveling words it is surprising, considering the significance it has for him, that he does not perform this operation on *Dichtung*. Instead, he seems to follow a more indirect route, for while the popular but inaccurate linkage of *Dichtung* and *dicht* is not, to my knowledge, explicitly denied by Heidegger it is, as noted in chapter 2, consistently deployed. Equally, on the few occasions that he does indicate the meaning of *dichten* he gives very different readings, for in 1954 he states that *dichten* derives from *tihton*, which says the same as the Greek *tikto*, "to bring forth" (US: 135/46). While twelve years earlier he had stated that *dichten*, because it is the same as *dictare*, thus referring us to the Latin rather than to the Greek root, "means to write down (*niederschreiben*), to fore-tell something to be written down," that is, to say (*dicere*) *by way of* letters (*litera*: "smudges" or "smears").[2]

The Latin *dicere* itself comes from the Greek *deiknumi* (to show), indicating that the roots of *Dichtung* are double, being derived from both *tikto* and *deiknumi*. This also indicates that in the translation from Greek to German via Latin the meaning of showing and bringing-forth has itself been doubled or smudged by the additional layer(s) of writing. Evidence of this is to be found in the link between the two meanings, which Heidegger referred to in 1934, for *tihton* in Old High German means "to draft (*abfassen*) in writing," which also derives from *dictare*.[3] So the repetition of showing and bringing-forth in writing leads in the opposite direction of occluding and disguising, which is itself a showing and bringing-forth of something else. Thus *Dichtung* would appear to be that which is *both* a showing and a bringing-forth *and* a showing and a bringing-forth in writing, *and* a showing in occluding and an occluding in showing, and so on; its repetition is endless and is thus both *phusis* and *technē*, but neither separately.

This suggests that the meaning of *Dichtung* oscillates between showing, bringing-forth, and occluding. This in turn suggests that *Dichtung* as such is reducible to none of these aspects separately, but engages all of them, and as a result it cannot be *phusis* or *technē* that is at the heart of this ambiguity, but rather an implicit reading of *mimēsis as* figuring, production, and repetition. That *Dichtung* should concern the realm of letters means that we should perhaps understand the distance from truth that is marked in literature as being found in the very distance marked out by its writing, a distance found *in* its movement of figuring, production, and repetition. Consequently, Heidegger's use of an implicit but ersatz etymology through his linking of *Dichtung* and *Verdichtung* could perhaps be seen as part of the repetition and dissembling that is at the heart of writing and *dichten*, as its showing and bringing-forth of something other. The essence of *Dichtung* would seem to lie in the ambiguity of being neither a concept nor an object, as it is only in a partial or derivative sense that it indicates the notions of creation and representation that are found in the common use of the terms *poiēsis* and "poetics."[4] Properly speaking, *Dichtung* is not, as it is not a thing that "is"; rather it is the horizon of language as that which gives it *as* language, that which enables it to appear but obscures itself in doing so, thereby appearing by way of this obscuring, and so on. It could thus be the essence of language, as it is that which enables us to take things "as" they are, but that in itself cannot be taken "as" anything. *Dichtung* does not indicate a theory or doctrine in Heidegger's thought, but a limit: it cannot be generalized or represented but only taken up as that which allows language to presence, but is in itself always absent or withdrawn.

In reading Hölderlin then, Heidegger is not seeking to describe or interpret his poetry, but to allow the presencing of its language to appear as such. It is, as his title (*Erläuterungen*) to the collection of Hölderlin essays indicates, an "elucidation" that can only make the poems clearer by listening to the sound (*Laut*) of their language, which is *Dichtung.* A subtle displacement has occurred through the choice of this word, for it signals a move away from the phenomenological approach to language as an "appearing" to one that seeks to operate from within the movement of language's own presencing as a "sounding" (*Erläuterung*). In addition, this signals the different approach to reading that Heidegger is adopting, one that focuses on the presencing of words in poetry in terms of their physicality and textuality, that is, their appearance *as* words. To allow the presencing of Hölderlin's language to take place *as* presencing in his own language, Heidegger must take up a position of such proximity to Hölderlin's *Dichtung* that it can repeat itself in his language as itself. Paronomasia is one of the devices Heidegger uses to try and achieve this, along with tautology, oxymoron, chiasmus, and parataxis (as in such later examples as, "the essence of language: the language of essence"), for in these modes language is broken up and made to repeat itself (US: 166/72). This repetition forces us to listen in a way that is no longer attendant to the words as terms, but rather to the essential turning of language that enables these words to sound but that is itself hidden, that is, to the echoing of *Dichtung.* As a result of this rhetorical maneuver, Heidegger's reading effectively effaces itself to make way for the sounding of words as a presencing of the limits of language.

As such, Heidegger is clearly remaining in the ontological vein of "The Origin of the Work of Art," in which the work of art is considered insofar as it relates to being as that which sends being into its limit. In pursuing our own inquiry this essay on Hölderlin is crucial, for in it Heidegger focuses on one poem and asks what it is. That this is also Hölderlin's concern, allows us to bring out the differing ways in which the poet and the thinker approach this question. In doing so, it will be necessary to attend to the *materiality* and *temporality* of the poem, which draws us into the work of the poem, which in turn centers on the *word.* The work of the word does not lack those dimensions that characterize other works, but it is complicated insofar as it is a work within a work, because of the way in which language itself works. The work of a poem, its poeticizing (*dichten*), is always already doubled or thickened (*verdichtet*) by this fact, which means for the poet or the thinker that they must approach this doubling itself in order to take up the work of the word. While the *work* of art was complicated in being both nominal and verbal, the work of the word laminates this with a further layer by being both the *mimēsis* and the tautology of that work; the inappropriable dissembling event and singular factical speech of its figuring.

The work of the word not only says the way; it is the event of that way itself; thus it operates at the very limits of its own existence, which means that it operates at the limits of its own possibility *and* impossibility. In examining the poet's word both Hölderlin and Heidegger find their own words under pressure from this doubling, for the work of the word has the possibility of either effacing or succumbing to its own impossibility, which is to say what cannot be said—its origin and limit; nature—by unsaying what is said. The duplicity of the word as both present and absent is the key that Heidegger wishes to turn in this essay on Hölderlin. Just as the poem (*Gedicht*) reveals its essence, that which has been put into the poem (*Gedichtete*), by folding in (*gedichten*) on itself, so too does Heidegger want to take up this method for thinking and make his own philosophical method the topic of concern. The use of rhetoric is the key to Heidegger's later thought, especially in his treatment of poetry, for it forces us to recognize the complicity between the matter and the manner of thinking as the presence of figurality itself, as the folding or thickening of the limits of language.

That part of Heidegger's insight into this emerges from his study of "As when on a holiday . . ." is surprising, but as a result is also highly revealing, considering that he makes very little mention of the singular features of this poem. Although he notes that it is incomplete and that there are other "fragments from an earlier draft," these points are not included in his discussion. He even goes so far as to say that the text of the poem he is using for his lecture "has been repeatedly checked against the original manuscripts," although doing so would surely have indicated the specific nature of Hölderlin's writing in this hymn (EHD: 51/74). However, the publication of Sattler's "historical-critical" edition of Hölderlin's works has to some extent vindicated the selective nature of Heidegger's reading of "As when on a holiday . . ." in that it places his selection on equal terms with later readings, which have ostensibly delivered a more comprehensive and accurate analysis of Hölderlin's manuscripts. This has come about because Sattler's edition has indicated how the earlier Beißner edition was as selective as the first edition by Hellingrath, from which Heidegger worked.

When Beißner published his version of "As when on a holiday . . ." in 1951, the inclusion of the fragmented last strophe seemed to indicate to many readers that this was now the definitive edition of the poem. This in turn cast doubt on Heidegger's reading, which although based on the truncated Hellingrath edition had also, as he himself pointed out, been "checked against the original manuscripts." That Heidegger did not include the last strophe, which was now presented in a conclusive form in the Beißner edition, seemed clear evidence of Heidegger's "selective" reading. However, the Sattler edition has now demonstrated that Beißner also delivered a misleading version of the poem, which suggests that contemporary readings based on this edition, as most are, are just as deceived as to the nature of Hölderlin's work as those readings based on the earlier Hellingrath edition. In such cases we are hardly justified in calling Heidegger's reading "selective" if we are only basing our own reading of Hölderlin's poem on the Beißner edition.

What has been indicated by the publication of the Sattler edition is how Hölderlin continually struggled and failed to get this poem into any definitive form. The manuscript shows layers of rewriting in which lines, words, and phrases accumulate alongside each other in such a way that any *single* reading seems impossible. This is characteristic of Hölderlin's mature work in which his writing practice was primarily *rewriting*, such that his poems *are* in palimpsest, for he rewrote in such a manner that earlier attempts were rarely discarded in favor of new ones but were allowed to remain alongside them. This is not just a stylistic tic or a contingency arising from his failure to get many of his poems published, but a practice Hölderlin deliberately pursued, stemming as it does from his understanding of the nature and role of *translation*. This layering of text not only allows for accidents of juxtaposition to emerge, but also and more importantly, it allows Hölderlin's writing to maintain a poetic matrix or generative network that actively resists closure. In many cases it seems as though Hölderlin was attracted to the opening of possibilities through writing, over and above the composition of completed poems. Thus, writing for Hölderlin appears to consist of this practice of maintaining the midpoint of transition between beginning and ending, in order to bring his writing closer to the opening that is the origin of poetry. But this maintenance is excessive; only more writing can hold it open, a fact to which Hölderlin's mature poetry seems particularly drawn.

As a result, this makes it exceedingly difficult to read much of Hölderlin's later works, for just as every reading will necessarily be selective, it will also be reductive and misleading. Thus Heidegger's reading can be no more inadequate than any other; however, his admission that he had consulted the original manuscripts means that he cannot simply hide behind the selective editing of Hellingrath. Instead, his reading has not only omitted the fragmentary last strophe, but also completely elided the entire question of Hölderlin's practice and the palimpsest this creates. This is not simply misleading, but deceptive, and the same must also be said for the Beißner edition, for in both cases a definitive article is presented, the poem, which to some extent does not actually exist in Hölderlin's works. Although the Beißner edition does indicate the incompleteness apparent in the last strophe of "As when on a holiday . . ." and thus is not quite as deceptive as Heidegger's presentation of the text, this doesn't detract from the way in which each presents the poem without indicating the variable and irreducibly ambiguous nature of its last lines, and Hölderlin's writing practice as a whole.

Despite this, it would be wrong to suggest that Heidegger is demonstrating an insensitivity to poetry in the way that he appropriates it to philosophy, for it would be more apposite to suggest that it is the very *impossibility* of poetry's appropriation that Heidegger wishes to take up.[5] Rather than seeking and failing to appropriate poetry to philosophy, Heidegger is instead engaged in an exploration of the limits of poetry and philosophy. This is precisely what is at issue in his discussion of *Dichtung*, which as the horizon of language is that which cannot be appropriated, because it is that which appropriates. By raising this horizonality of language, there is a possibility of appropriating its resistance as a means of approaching the limits of language. By finding a way of speaking at the limits of language, at the limits thereby of any kind of meaning, we are also engaged in the limits of being as that which gives being to *be* said. This finitude is also the relation that brings about the very possibility of poetry and philosophy. Although we have to be aware of the different ways in which poetry and philosophy speak, we cannot confuse this with that which gives the possibility of speaking itself.

To discern this maneuver as it develops we need to focus on the transformation of Heidegger's language from the 1930s onward, and in particular on his rhetorical and grammatical experiments by which he develops a way that does not so much appropriate poetry, as *expropriate philosophy.* In this transformation what is proper to poetry, and what Heidegger focuses on, is precisely its refusal of appropriation, or *impropriety.* As such, his lack of sensitivity to the singularity of the poet's experience is due to his interest in what is proper to the work, that is, poetry, in the sense of its essential limits and ground. This property is also the property of philosophy, not in terms of identity, but as that which gives philosophy *its* limits and ground. That which gives this property, whether to poetry or philosophy, is what interests Heidegger in his study of poetry because it is also that which gives being. In trying to follow this we have to tread a fine line between the poet and the poet's word, and between the saying and the said, in order to discern the limits of the work as that which gives it to be said. However, at issue in this is the possibility that the event of such a saying is such that it is destabilizing for any thought that attempts to turn it to any present use.

. . . The Reading of the Word . . .

Although "As when on a holiday . . ." begins as a hymn in which nature is celebrated in its bounty and majesty, Hölderlin complicates this by incorporating the poet's composition of the hymn into the celebration of the poem. Thus, it is no longer simply a poem celebrating nature, but a poem celebrating the act of composing a poem about nature, and while this would seem to put the poet at a further remove from nature, it is also the case that the former celebration would be incomplete without the latter. This doubling is also necessary as Hölderlin felt doubtful about the possibilities of simply writing about nature directly; instead the hymn could only work if it focused on itself. By doing so, nature would speak through the hymn as that which makes the writing of a hymn possible, but this speaking would be essentially elusive. This poses a serious challenge to Hölderlin, for a failure of the hymn would mean that nature had also failed to speak and thus his presence as a poet and as a person would be undermined by the loss of his language, but a success would mean that nature would speak through him in such a way that his presence would be utterly displaced. The pressure of this challenge falls squarely on the poet's word that cannot speak of nature, but must rather speak of itself as nature; but what words can a poet use to speak of that which is there but that is essentially elusive?

Hölderlin begins with nature, which is described as "powerful, divinely beautiful," for through these qualities nature makes itself present in a way that simultaneously withdraws and holds itself back, thereby taking hold of the poet who it teaches in a "light embrace." As Heidegger notes this embrace, because it holds and withdraws, "captivates and enraptures" (*berückt und entrückt*) the poets: "They are drawn into this embrace. This inclusion transposes the poets into the fundamental characteristic (*Grundzug*) of their essence. Such transposition is education" (EHD: 54/76–77). Although nature grants this education it is in itself the "unapproachable" (*Un-nahbare*), for it "renders every immediate intrusion of the mediated in vain. The holy confronts all experience with something to which it is unaccustomed, and so deprives it of its ground. Un-settled (*ent-setzend*) in this way, the holy is the unsettling (*Entsetzliche*) itself" (EHD: 63/85). For Heidegger this is evidence of what Hölderlin calls, in a translation of one of Pindar's fragments, "the law," which is that nature mediates to all things what they are through their connections to each other, but in this, nature is never mediated itself as it is that which mediates, that is: the immediate (EHD: 62/84). This presents two problems in that there is no connection between the immediate and that which is mediated, for such things are only ever connected to other mediated things; thus the immediate is in itself utterly inaccessible. If this is so, how can we have poetry? How can a word, which is the mediated, speak of nature, which is the immediate? Furthermore, why would such a thing even be necessary? If all things are connected, why is there a need for poetry?

The answer to both of these questions resides in the relation between the mediate and the immediate, wherein we also find Leibniz's question of why there are beings at all and not simply nothing. This nothing, while immediate, would also be without communication or distinction, for it has no limits. But this limitlessness, according to Blanchot, itself becomes a limit insofar as the immediate rejects all immediate contact, even with itself, and thereby ejects itself from itself such that distinction comes about. The immediate "needs to be mediated" and this is what the poem provides, not just as distinction but also as being, as persistence; the poem enables the immediate to *be,* it is how nature awakes (PF: 129/124). Before this, Heidegger tells us, nature is "at rest," but this is not a passive or stagnant state; rather, nature is "at one with herself, thinking ahead to her own coming" (EHD: 55/78). In this is an explanation for both why the poem is necessary and how it emerges, for this "thinking ahead" (*vordenken*), like the earlier study of the hermeneutic *logos* of being and saying, is both a projection and a repetition, a sup-position, by which both nature and the poem emerge. This doubled emergence is apparent in the ways in which Heidegger and Hölderlin treat the appearance of the word. Hölderlin is cautious, emphasizing the distinction between nature and its name:

> But now day breaks! I waited and saw it come,
> And what I saw, may the holy be my word.

Heidegger reading these lines provides the following commentary: "The exclamation 'But now day breaks!' sounds like a calling of nature. On its own the call calls to what is coming. The poet's word is the pure calling of what those poets who are always divining wait and long for. The poetic naming says what the called itself, from its essence, compels the poet to say. Thus compelled, Hölderlin names nature 'the holy'" (EHD: 57–58/80). There is a complex temporality in Hölderlin's lines that is followed by Heidegger in his commentary until the final sentence, where it seems to have been ignored. Hölderlin carefully fills out his saying with a temporal manifold in which the arrival of daybreak (present), gives way to the recollection of the poet as he waited for it to come (past) and waiting, desired to say its word (future). Hölderlin does not "name" nature in the present; instead "the holy" is designated as the word he would *like* to say but cannot use directly as this would extinguish it. In doing so, by saying "*may* the holy be my word," Hölderlin is able to say it *in its coming,* in its imminence and its nonarrival; only as such can he name nature. Furthermore, this nonarrival is aided by the way in which the saying is given a specific balance by the breaks that occur in the middle of each line, which each provide a pause or interruption. For Blanchot, these interruptions allow the absence of nature to present itself as the speaking of a silent voice, which Hölderlin is drawn to but can only echo with his desire to name (EI: 55–56/39).

The traditional complaint in this, here voiced by Hans-Jost Frey, is that Heidegger fails to notice this point, which suggests that there is a confusion in his commentary between what the word *is* and what it *says.*

According to Frey, "Heidegger reads as if Hölderlin says: 'the holy *is* my word,'" because he "fails to consider the temporal structure of Hölderlin's verses," which leads to a position in which the "word is, for Heidegger, what it says in that it says what it is." More specifically, Frey argues that Heidegger "ignores the subjunctive" in Hölderlin's verse "*may* the holy be my word" and thus "sees the named as being present on account of its being named." As he then goes on to state, the "phrase 'the essence of what is named unveils itself in the word' expresses this precisely. It is unimportant for Heidegger to distinguish between *being* and *naming*, because to him the word *named* by the word *is* in the word."[6] What Frey has missed is the differentiation between saying and naming for after writing that "the essence of what is named unveils itself in the word," Heidegger goes on to say that this naming means that "the word separates essence from non-essence" (EHD: 58/81).

What this means is that while the holy unveils itself *in* the word it does not do so in a manner that would make it present *as* the *saying* of the word. This is because its essence is to be coming, so in becoming separated from its nonessence as what is present, poetic naming names what is *as* what is coming, that is, what is *not* present. Thus the essence of nature, the holy, unveils itself not by becoming apparent in the saying of its name but in unveiling itself *as* the inapparence of the word, its imminence. In this way, although the word says what it is (the word of nature) this does not imply that the reverse is true, that it is what it says (the holy itself), for that would imply a complete coincidence, symmetry, and reciprocity between saying and being that goes against what Heidegger says, for while the holy as the immediate is that which mediates, it is not possible for anything mediated to approach the immediate as such. Despite Frey's reading on this point, Heidegger is rigorously faithful to Hölderlin here as he clearly states that "nothing mediated, be it a god or a man, is ever capable of directly attaining the immediate" (EHD: 61/83). The use of "directly" in this line is key for it means that the poet names the holy by *not* saying it; because the "manner of its presence is to be coming" the holy only presences in the "stillness" of the poet's silence, in which it "is quietly present as what is coming" (EHD: 67/89).

Despite the inaccuracy of this particular criticism Frey's general point is significant as it exposes a stylistic weakness in Heidegger's writing of this essay that ultimately leads to its failure. As we now know, Heidegger himself admitted in a letter to the literary critic Max Kommerell that this essay was a "disaster" (see the epigraph in this chapter), and the reason he gave for this was the "immediate presentation" of its language, which in turn arose from his "direct thinking."[7] Examples of this are widespread and are particularly focused in his manner of reading Hölderlin's words by paraphrasing them as ontological statements, such as, "beauty is all-presence," "the open itself is the immediate," "chaos is the holy itself," or "the holy is the unsettling itself" (EHD: 54/76, 61/83, 63/85). All of these phrases refer to nature, which Heidegger wants to read as *phusis* so that he can inscribe his own thoughts into the other beginning of this poetic thinking, and this urges him to combine all of Hölderlin's names for nature (the "wonderful," "powerful," "all-creative," "all-living," etc.) together, despite the lack of any synonymy of this kind in Hölderlin. Considering how his reading also opts to repunctuate Hölderlin's hymn by omitting the additional fragments that made up the eighth stanza, inserting an "intervening thought" to make up for the missing ninth line of the fifth stanza, adding a period to the last line of the seventh stanza, and deciding that the "incompleteness" of the hymn "demands a concise conclusion," it is clear that this essay suffers heavily under the mark of direct thinking (EHD: 51/74, 67/89, 72/94, 75/97).

But if we consider the fact that Heidegger consented to the unrevised publication of this essay and to its inclusion within his collected works, then this suggests that he felt that its failings were either marginal or symptomatic of something more interesting. The former is evidently not appropriate given that he termed his "writing" in this essay a disaster, so it is not surprising that he should then comment: "Perhaps this is a first testimony to the fact that my attempts sometimes come into the proximity of genuine *thinking*." This is what those critics who are keen on dismissing Heidegger's readings of poetry often forget; that the failings of these readings were first noticed by Heidegger himself and that as failings they constitute a deeply significant encounter. The key to this encounter is precisely that of the directness of language, which had haunted Heidegger's work for years, and that now found its most compelling explication in his encounter with poetry.

This situation is made all the more unavoidable by the fact that it is the same problem that Hölderlin himself came up against when trying to respond to nature. If we return to the "law of mediatedness," as Hölderlin terms it, the problem is that of relation; how can beings as mediated approach the immediacy of nature? As we have seen, Hölderlin uses a complex deferral of saying to accomplish this (non)relation, which although

Heidegger is aware of, he is unable to fully apply in his own writing at this time. While he manages to avoid this trap when discussing Hölderlin's lines, as soon as he steps back to think through the poet's words he seems to slip. Hence, the failing of his language arises when he says that "beauty *is* all-presence" rather than the supposition and deferral ("may be") Hölderlin uses, for in doing so he is bringing beauty and all-presence into the terms of an ontological equation that renders them as things that are, that is, beings rather than being. This is not simply to translate Hölderlin's words into Heidegger's thoughts but to make the immediacy of nature mediate, to make it appear as present, rather than as presencing.

This problem emerges explicitly in the last pages of the essay as Heidegger tries to make sense of Hölderlin's law. As his efforts to repunctuate the last lines of the hymn indicate, Heidegger seems unable to accept their collapse and ruin on their own terms. Instead he tries to turn the poem back to what he sees as its essential "word"; the "final word of this poem must return to the holy," which as its origin must be preserved (EHD: 72/94). For Hölderlin, the experience of the poem is such that despite his attempts to speak within the limits of the law the outcome is always failure, for the immediate is always already engaged in its own destruction by virtue of its excession as the mediated: the origin cannot be preserved for it is already lost through its originating. As such, his words both in and as the poem are precisely that which lead to his ruin; the law is always being broken and that is how it is constituted. But for Heidegger, the necessity to maintain a hold on this saying in its saying requires him to ignore this ruination and to try to show that the origin cannot be harmed by its originating, that it remains pure, that "what sprang from the origin cannot do anything against the origin" (EHD: 74/96). He draws evidence for this from a piece of marginalia that is highly ambiguous, and in doing so his own attempts to assert some kind of control over Hölderlin's text by way of his thought are exposed and he retreats from his reading into a familiar discussion of history and nation.

What is exposed by way of this is what Hölderlin also discovered; that writing has a resistance that arises *out of* its ruination, out of its refusal or evasion, and that this evasion *is* the very relation by which language approaches nature. An awareness of this is perhaps what led Heidegger to preserve this essay despite its failings; in fact we could argue that it is because of its failings that it was preserved, for Heidegger possibly saw in its problems a way of speaking which, albeit implicit, laid the path to what would emerge in his later lectures on language. Doing so will require him to leave behind his desire to keep the origin pure, which will in turn affect the language that is then used to speak of this origin. In this essay, Hölderlin's many terms for nature are gathered into one so that they can be displaced by Heidegger's more "proper" term: *phusis.* This is necessary to prevent the origin from becoming translated by what is subsequent to it, which would replace "that which is proper to the beginning with something alien to it" (EHD: 56/79). Later, this whole idea that one can find a way around this position of subsequence and discover the origin in itself will be revised, as Heidegger will suggest that language has no origin other than itself, in which case it is a question of entering into this language to find its essence.

In light of this, Heidegger's final remark in his analysis of his disastrous writing proves to be the most revealing point, as his encounter with poetry is phrased as a countering of thought to poetry whose ultimate provenance cannot be decided. This may well be the heart of the relation of thought to poetry: that it can never know whether its decisions (and this would seem to include the whole range of Heidegger's selective readings) are made from a position of liberty or are simply arbitrary. Is it arbitrary to read a poem in a certain way, or is it the "supreme liberty" of the thinker to do so? It is as such that Heidegger's own thought is compelled to languish, in that its decision is unknowable and any attempt to force this decision, whether it be in the publication of *Being and Time* or the figuring of the poet (or thinker) as an historical event, is bound to be disastrous. But what is the mediacy or indirectness that could prevent this? Is it the deferral of an unforced decision, which would be the sign of genuine thinking, but what would this mean, what shape could deferred thinking ever take? For if this is the case, then how could this deferral ever cease, or is the moment for such a decision an impossibility? The implication is surely that we can never know whether our thinking is too direct, for we have no way of knowing anything of that which our thinking is called to and hence we are always writing in the face of disaster.

This would suggest that deferral is also the nature of the thinker's relation to the poet, which would mean that thought cannot translate poetry by somehow approximating it, no matter how violently this is attempted, for there is no position of immediacy to be gained here that could achieve this. Instead translation must defer its relation so that it marks its own appearance as such even as those marks are erased. As a result, "poetry" will always appear for the thinker as a name that indicates an impossibility, just as "nature" does for the poet and "nothing" is for being, a bridge that obscures and defers that which it attempts to reach.

But in this deferral a relation is possible if in its endless return we recognize that which is imminent, which Heidegger hints at in borrowing Hölderlin's lines: "In awakening, nature comes to herself. Inspired, she feels herself anew" (EHD: 60/82). In their own inspiration, the poets participate in this return in the imminent coming of the word, so that nature in awakening speaks through them in their songs as the "quaking" of the immediate. But the imminence of this awakening carries a risk for the poets, as the "richness of the primordial grants to their word such an excess of meaning as can scarcely be uttered" (EHD: 66/88). For Heidegger, this quaking and excess is "preserved and made quiet" in the "stillness" of the poet's soul, in his waiting for the deferred return. Instead of being given to speech where it could be "represented and grasped as an object," nature is quieted by being unspoken, because the "manner of its presence is to be coming" (EHD: 67/89). As such, it can only be awaited and in the stillness of the poet's waiting the awakening nature comes:

> Now when the holy ray strikes the poet, he is not carried away into the blaze of the ray, but is fully turned toward the holy. The poet's soul "quakes," to be sure, and so lets the quiet shaking awaken within itself; but it quakes with recollection, that is to say, with the expectation of that which happened before; this is the opening up of the holy. The quaking breaks the peace of silence. The word comes to be. The word-work that originates in this way lets the belonging together of god and man appear. The song bears witness to the ground of their belonging together, bears witness to the holy. (EHD: 69/91)

As we will see in chapter 4, this moment of bearing witness to the union of gods and men is for Hölderlin the essence of the tragic as it is a moment riven by its inevitable loss, which brings about a radical temporal displacement away from what is present into what is not, for the poet quakes with recollection as the expectation (future) of what has happened (past). The poet's word is drawn into the imminence of nature, which is to come *as* that which is returning; thus the presence of the word in the poem leads into an absence that makes it a sign; a marker of absence and imminent presence. Likewise, in entering nature's light embrace, the poets also find themselves displaced by this doubling and deferral into a liminality in which they "must leave to the immediate its immediacy, and yet also take upon themselves its mediation as their only task" (EHD: 71/93). For on the one hand, the *presence* of the poet's word is always a mourning for the absence of nature and hence a saying of its absence in its absence. But on the other hand, the *saying* of the poet is also a recollection and expectation of its deferred return, for in its saying it echoes the opening of nature as that which is to come and that which is returning: "the divining of what is coming is both a fore-thinking and a thinking-back" (EHD: 55/77).

The poem thus only becomes a poem by being doubled or thickened, *verdichtet*, by the repetition in which its language, by turning back on itself, is both obscured and deferred. But for the poets to reach this is to let nature speak through them and thereby expropriate them into the suffering of nature, which "suffers from its essential beginning (*Wesensanfang*)," where suffering means "remaining steadfast in the beginning" (EHD: 75/96). However, this is not to begin at all, for a beginning that remained a beginning would have to endlessly defer its opening by which it begins. Despite this, for Heidegger, the poem remains an event whose word is "another beginning of another history" (EHD: 76/97). But the possibility of another history arising from the poet's word would require an end to the endless deferral within which nature's return is awaited. This would seem impossible for the poet, for if the poetic saying is that which gives the poet, and if the poem "is, as what is coming," then the poet is never present to the poem as he who could draw its waiting to an end and thereby release another beginning (EHD: 55/77). Instead by his waiting, the poet enters the deferral of the word, but not as himself, from which he has been removed by the saying of the word.

In being removed, the poet enters the time of the poem, which is a time without present, a time without time, as the opening of the poem onto the imminence of the word draws the poet into a time that is always to come. He is *interrupted by the poem*, exposed to the endlessness of the wait for that which is always to come.[8] Heidegger had touched upon this wait in his discussion of the oblivion in which the preservers of the work of art subsist, but had not recognized the level of its disturbance. For this abyssal opening utterly ungrounds Heidegger's attempt to draw the poet into the history of being, as it opens onto the imminence of a poetic language that removes any possible decision into deferral. In this deferral, just as with the draw-ing of the work of art, the word holds the poet to the between in which the turning of the word is the repetition of nature, which constitutes its deferral by this repetition. If this word speaks of what is to come then it is not only, as Heidegger believed, "as the gathering (*logos*) at the extremes (*eschaton*)," which would reveal it as the language of "eschatology" (what is to come as the last things, ends), but also as a *teratology* (what is to come in its coming to us as signs of its coming) (H: 327–28/246–47).

The event of nature cannot be made present in language, but it can be intimated through the signs of its imminence; these signs of what is to come (*teras, monstrum*) do not present what is, but what is to come. These signs emerge within the words of Hölderlin and it is Heidegger who attempts to read them, to bring their augury, their saying of what is to come in the signs of what is to come, into the thinking of being. In doing so he most properly makes this a teratology by combining these signs with the gathering of *logos*. From this comes the monstrous element, for these signs make present nothing that is, but rather what is not, and this suggests that there is something monstrous involved in any reading. For if these signs emerge within and as the words we use, then they are already present in Heidegger's own words as he brings them to a reading of Hölderlin. Perhaps in this there is the enforced hybridization of monstrosity that we are more familiar with, in that using signs to read signs brings about the misshapen progeny of an overly determined language, where signs cannot speak themselves because they are being forced to speak through other signs.

Only by following the double emergence of nature and word that occurs in the repetition of nature can our language remain with the language of nature. That is, the word has to be treated as the sign that it already is, the imminence that it entails, by not reading it as much as deferring it by way of its own dissembling repetition. There can be no phenomenology *of* language for language is its own phenomenology, its own speaking *and* appearing, and so it is only by following language that phenomenology can achieve its aim of speaking of things as they are: in their appearance and inapparence. Thus, teratology, the speaking of the sign, is the mark of being and language, of being *as* language, for in it the conditions of possibility of saying are found at precisely that point or limit where they become impossible, where they intimate what is not.[9] It is only insofar as the poet's word exists as the impossibility of the poet, that the poet exists; only at the limit of this saying does the turning of impossibility to possibility take place.

. . . The Writing of the Word . . .

While Blanchot follows Heidegger for much of the way in his reading of Hölderlin, it is over this last critical point that he diverges; as for him there is no way of evading the impossibility that marks the relation of nature to the poet. While he does not dispute that the shaking of nature becomes stilled in the poet's word, what he wishes to raise are the conditions of this, which are those of impossibility. In doing so, Blanchot is directing us away from the role and position of Hölderlin's poetry, as Heidegger perceived them, to the difficulties of its practice in the writing of the word, in which the "language of the poem is nothing but the retention, the transmission of its own impossibility, it is the reminder that all worldly language . . . has as its origin an event that cannot take place" (PF: 131/126). Thus, in terms of the work of art as considered in chapter 2, Heidegger has moved too quickly into a discussion of the historical worlding of Hölderlin's work, without giving due consideration to the earthly resistance and dissembling of the actual practice of his work and, as a result, has not paid sufficient attention to the effects that this resistance has on the poet in his attempt to speak these words of nature, which it is impossible to speak.

In raising this point, Blanchot is not opposing Heidegger as much as pursuing a divergent path that is still true to Hölderlin's work. As we saw, Heidegger is not insensitive to the demands placed upon the poet, but there is nevertheless still room for another voice to emerge here to speak of this demand. This voice Blanchot introduces, not to repeat or refute Heidegger, but to follow up on the errancy of nature's demand, which remains unsaid by Heidegger solely by virtue of its inexhaustibility.[10] A significant moment of such divergence is exposed when Heidegger mentions those lines of the hymn in which Hölderlin recalls the tragic fate of Semele, who was destroyed after looking on Zeus in all his glory, since for Heidegger this is only a "countertheme" (*Gegenspiel*) within the poem that reveals what happens when it does not succeed (EHD: 70/92). But for Blanchot the possible failure of the poem cannot be so easily accepted, as it reminds us that the immediate can *never* be mediated or appropriated, despite the demand that it must, for when the poet speaks he becomes lost, "suspended in emptiness itself," his existence in time and language interrupted if not destroyed (PF: 134/129).

As such, the risk and the demand of poetry is of a writing of the word that does not appropriate but expropriates. Or rather, neither, for without appropriation there can be no expropriation: there is nothing "proper" about the immediate, and so its word must be likewise. It is Hölderlin's last stanzas that suggest this, which show the poet falling, which Heidegger did not include (while he notes that Zinkernagel's edition includes some of these final lines, and had himself checked the original manuscripts of this poem, it seems that Heidegger only became aware of the current standard version when he saw Beißner's edition of 1951, and as his essay had already been published in the second, expanded edition of the *Elucidations*, he again appears to have chosen to leave his commentary intact rather than to change it):

[The father's ray, the pure, does not sear it]
[Then the pure does not kill it, does not sear it]
And deeply shaken, sharing the suffering
Of the stronger, remaining in the [down-rushing]
[unstoppable] storms of
God when he nears, the heart still holds.
But oh my shame! (when of
a self-inflicted wound my heart is bleeding, and
deeply lost is peace and freely-modest contentment,
and unrest and lack drive me to the abundance
of the gods' tables, when round about me)

The [higher]
sphere
that is
higher than
that of man
that is
the god

[My shame!]
and let me say at once,
That I approached to see the heavenly,
And they themselves cast me down below the living
The false priest that I am, into the dark
To sing for those who can learn the warning song.
There

These lines are pieced together from the original manuscripts and would seem to indicate the drama of Hölderlin's struggle to complete the hymn. After this attempt he would not try such a form again, and although we cannot simply take these lines as "speaking" of their own failure, there is more than enough here to attend to.[11] It could be suggested that this failure arose from a combination of the public form of Pindaric verse and the personal experience that Hölderlin was undergoing as he wrote, in that his separation from Susette Gontard was a trauma that the public nature of the verse could not contain.[12] But the breakup of this hymn is not so much a biographical allegory as a break in the very heart of Hölderlin's existence as a poet. For in being ruptured so catastrophically, his poetry exposes its own limits and thus the destruction of its ability to demonstrate its own vocation, which would thereby indicate the failure of his language as a possibility of saying. However, that the loss of his beloved is implicated in this failure might suggest why the mention of Semele is so pertinent here: Personal suffering and interpersonal rupture occurs hand in hand with the saying of the holy, which means that the breakup of this hymn does not simply indicate a failure to complete it but a ruin at the very heart of it; sometimes the suffering is too great and the words cannot be written; sometimes there is only destruction and failure.

If we examine the manuscript of "As when on a holiday . . ." as Heidegger claims to have done, this loss becomes more apparent, for immediately prior to writing the hymn Hölderlin worked on a translation of the opening scene of *The Bacchae*, in which Dionysus discussed the nature of his birth and his need to vindicate his mother and himself. Dionysus was born of the monstrous and catastrophic union of the human and the divine; Semele's irresistible and exorbitant desire to see Zeus led to her immolation, but out of her ashes Dionysus the half-god arose. Looking closely at the manner in which Hölderlin's hymn develops it appears that this scene of transgression, destruction, and birth is the core around which his writing worked. Thus the implication arises that the central scene of the hymn is *not* the invocation of nature that occurs at the beginning of stanza 3, which Heidegger proposes as the hymn's essential word, *but* the point at which Hölderlin articulates the tragic position of the poet at the end of stanza 6 and at the beginning of stanza 7. But such an interpretation would seem to rely on discerning a point of origin in Hölderlin's manuscript, which the writing as a whole seems to deny, for this "origin" only arises retrospectively, and then only out of the translation and rewriting of a scene in which the possibility of origin is only found through destruction. So, insofar as Heidegger's reading of the source of the hymn focuses on the naming power of the poet's word, its authentication *as* the poet's word, this is to the extent that it passes over the fact that the word itself arises not from a point of origin but from out of its own destruction, which is to say that the word "is" only in ruins, not in its naming.

By drawing out the fate of the poet in the figure of Semele, Hölderlin makes plain the danger and unavoidability of this transgression, and just as Dionysus' divine origin can only be made visible in destruction, so the hymn in seeking to celebrate its own origin also enters a ruinous collapse. In both cases the tension between the immediate and the mediate is made extreme, for the mediate (the poet and the poem) cannot bear the presence of the immediate, although it is its source and legitimation. All of this would seem to undermine the claim that Semele "is *only* introduced into the poem as a countertheme," but we have to take what is meant by "counter" here carefully. As we can recall from the Kommerell letter, Heidegger's understanding of countering is far from simple, for the encounter with poetry proceeds only insofar as thinking "first poses what is opposed." Within this movement we find the relation to the work of art in which it is sheltered and preserved, as countering is constitutive of the work for Heidegger, since in its strife the draw-ing of *polemos* finds "the site of its constant stand," as the re-marking and self-erasing basis of its encounter. It is thus highly revealing that the figure of Semele is a "countertheme" for Heidegger, which is only introduced to indicate what happens when the authenticating presence of the holy is absent, as this suggests that it is to be incorporated into the work as part of its strife, while the actual experience of its rupture, which exposes the work to destruction and impossibility, has been missed.

For as the last stanza of Hölderlin's hymn shows, the experience of this absence of the word is unavoidably *tragic*: its evident pain and disruption; the rejection of the poet as unworthy to approach the gods and receive their word; the resulting fall into the darkness that precedes the word as a formless chaos that knows no dawn; the vain hope that even here his song might still be heard as a warning to those to come, vain because the voice of darkness does not ever know words and so can only be heard by those who can hear beyond them, into the unannounced and unspoken. "There," lies the poet's fate, and there also appears to lie Heidegger's limit, for in attending so closely to the saying of the word to thinking he is unavoidably led away from the demand of the word itself, of its endless finitude and repetition. As he noted in the year following the Kommerell letter, the nature of the difference between thinking and poetry lies in the different ways in which they experience the *word*:

> The saying of the thinker comes from a long-protected speechlessness and from the careful clarifying of the realm thus cleared. Of like provenance (*Herkunft*) is the naming of the poet. Yet because that which is like is so only as difference allows, and because poeticizing and thinking are most purely alike in their carefulness (*Sorgsamkeit*) toward the word, they are at the same time farthest separated in their essence. The thinker says being. The poet names the holy. (W: 107/237)

Thus if poetry is the same as thinking *by way of* its difference, then this is mediated by their different modes of caring (*phronēsis*) for the word. This suggests why Heidegger is led to focus on the quieting of the word, which is its mediation into language, instead of what Hölderlin himself seems to have attempted, which is to approach the immediate in its mediacy as the word, before it becomes mediated. In construing the question of poetry in terms of ontology, Heidegger makes the poet the essential mediation of the immediacy of nature, and by virtue of this places the emphasis clearly on the *relation* of the word. Thus, by reading the saying of the poet in terms of a thinking of being he prioritizes the ontological unity of this mediation as language, and thereby elides the singular experience of this mediation that places it under conditions of impossibility. There is also a hint of phenomenology here, for Heidegger is focusing on the appearing or lighting up of beings as they come into the light, hence his concentration on the moment that day breaks and the word that says this, while Hölderlin's word, according to Blanchot, is instead "anterior to the day, and always anterior to itself, it is a before-day" (PF: 127/121). In Blanchot's reading, this absence is a nonrelation that cannot be erased in favor of its presence as a relation, because the poet's experience is *of* the rupture of the immediate and any mediation of this is derivative.

By emphasizing the impossibility of saying, Blanchot is not denying what Heidegger has said by casting his thought as "impossible," but is indicating that saying is always conducted in the face of an extreme alterity. For Blanchot, saying is always accompanied by an irrecuperable loss, which although never absent from Heidegger's thought is not thought through here to such a degree, and it is precisely the reasons and consequences of this that comprise the essential difference between poetry and thought. For Hölderlin the experience of this rupture is central to his understanding of tragedy, and in particular, to his decision to liken the poet to a "false priest" in his intrusion upon the gods; for it is precisely in these terms that he describes Oedipus four years later in his "Remarks on *Oedipus.*" Here, Oedipus is shown to adopt the priestly office when he "interprets the oracle too *infinitely*" and presumes to pronounce upon his own fate (SW5: 197/102). As was the case with Semele, this transgression brings about the actualization of the tragic for Hölderlin, as the awesome union of man and god in which this hubris, or as he calls it, *nefas* (the blasphemous *word*), leads to the expulsion of Oedipus and the turning away of the god. But where this move would in the Aristotelian model of tragedy lead to a catharsis and resolution for the audience, Hölderlin refuses this by finding this turning-away to be an endlessly repeated moment in the poet's existence in which the infidelity of man and god is their only possible loyalty. Neither Oedipus nor the poet can confront that which continually turns away, but in turning away a relation is still obtained if we understand that this turning-away becomes a *nonrelation* of deferral in repetition.

Thus this transgression and expulsion come from the very *written* nature of the work itself, which directs us to the heart of Hölderlin's existence as a poet: his practice, and, as we will see in chapter 4, it is in this that we find the key distinction that separates Hölderlin from Heidegger, although it is partly as a result of his failure to read Hölderlin in this essay that Heidegger comes to learn the "cultivation of the letter" that he later understands as the only way of approaching the essence of language (W: 194/276). It is precisely this tragedy of writing that seems to be at issue in the last lines of stanza 8, which are drawn from Hölderlin's prose notes for the hymn: "But oh my shame! (when of a self-inflicted wound my heart is bleeding, and deeply lost is peace and freely-modest contentment, and unrest and lack drive me to the abundance of the gods' tables, when round about me)." Prior to this Hölderlin states that poetry will only succeed for those poets who "are pure in heart, / Like children," for only as such could they withstand the lightning of the gods that otherwise would "sear" their hearts. It is this situation that is violated by the poet's "self-inflicted wound," which is his compulsion to approach the gods immediately that then breaks the contract of their mediation. But in doing so, the union with the gods is laid out in the same movement that wounds the poet, thereby bringing together both attraction and separation, and lack and abundance. Thus it is from this violation that the poet achieves his goal, as his approach and rejection by the gods entails a movement that repeatedly converges upon them; not as a subject, but as the movement of writing, which turns and returns from compulsion to expulsion.

While this might seem to be returning to a Heideggerian thought of the perpetual striving of earth and world that is the work of art, the work of the poet has very different stakes, for his word is the (non)relation *of his existence*, and hence his saying is a work of great personal risk. However, the textual basis of this interruption means that its self-inflicted wound does not come from the poet but *is* the work itself, as it is the rupture *of* the word, the very word that is the work, which breaks up the poem's development and appears as its fragmentation and collapse. Thus it is possible to say that the rupture of this tragic wounding finds itself in its loss, not as a saying or thought, but as a failure that cannot be taken up since it can only be spoken of elliptically. As such, Hölderlin would not simply be presenting a depiction of tragedy but enacting it, "there," in the final epode in the final word, we would find it, deferring its own end and thereby suspending itself in its own disintegration, which is closest to the dissembling of what is.

While Heidegger was by no means unaware of the nature of tragedy, as his own treatments of Sophocles illustrate, his omission of the last epode of Hölderlin's hymn means that he fails to pick up on this aspect of the poet's work. Moreover, as Heidegger's reading of the hymn stops before its disintegration he not only misses the tragic dimension of the poet's experience, but also and more importantly, he misses the enactment of this experience in the poem itself through its encounter with its own finitude. Heidegger's thought thus misses out on a chance to move from a depiction of the limits of language to an experience of them and as a result, we have to ask if this is a weakness in Heidegger or in philosophy: Does the nature of this encounter with the limits of language mean that it is only to be found in poetry, which is essentially concerned with its language, or is it possible for the language of thinking to also turn in on itself, to find its own limits and to thereby experience its finitude?

As we will learn in chapter 4, Hölderlin speaks of this tragic encounter as a chiasmic movement of union and separation resulting in emptiness, its sign "= 0," since within its extended ellipsis of turning away it resembles or represents nothing (SW4: 274/89). If Heidegger achieves this tragic emptying of the word anywhere it is in his private manuscripts of the 1930s and 1940s, in particular, *Contributions to Philosophy (from Ereignis)*, and the late lectures on language, especially "The Essence of Language," which will be discussed in chapter 5. However, even within these texts we have to be aware of the way in which the limits of his writing become configured by the relation of thought and language. This configuring is the same "setting-into-work" that was developed in "The Origin of the Work of Art" and, as was pointed out there, this setting up obscures that which gives thought and language and that it is given to thought to think. Nature, we need to remind ourselves, *loves* to hide; it is always turning its face away from us, concealing itself in endless disfiguring. We cannot con-front or en-counter that which turns away; thus the only approach to this divergence is to allow its concealment to presence *as* concealment and thereby remain loyal to its dissembling and cryptophilia as what is most essential to it, and in doing so we enable it to dissemble itself by way of us.

. . . The Position of the Word . . .

Thus, we can say that Heidegger's differences from Hölderlin arise from his understanding of the nature of the *word* in which, as Blanchot has noted, "it seems that the commentator was more sensitive to tradition than to Hölderlin's experience" (PF: 126/120). In other words, the failings of Heidegger in this essay are not just due to those inherent in language, but also arise as a result of the philosophical tradition of which Heidegger, but not Hölderlin, was a part. Although Heidegger was fond of calling for a "poetic thinking" or "thinking poetics," this was always done as a philosopher and not as a poet. Even his designation and celebration of Hölderlin as the pre-eminent "thinking poet" depends on a philosophical configuration of his poetry, overlaying whatever thought Hölderlin himself may have sought to develop.

This last point is especially problematic as the justification for this overlaying derives from the "self-positing" that already occurs in Hölderlin's poetry. According to Heidegger, Hölderlin's status as "*the poet of poets*" comes from the fact that his poetry is about poetry, in such a way that he only becomes a poet through his poetry (EHD: 34/52). He is the necessary result of poetry: called forth by language as it is opened through its self-reflection in the poem, he is in the impossible position of only becoming a poet after responding to the call of language in his poems. The originary nature of this self-positing authenticates Hölderlin's position as *the* essential poet and fixes him in place as such by making his actions not only *essentially* self-positing, but also those by which an historical epoch and nation is also founded (EHD: 76–77/97–98). In doing so, Heidegger has diverged from Hölderlin's own position on the opening up of the word by configuring this moment as constitutive of being, insofar as language through its opening sends being into its particular historical configurations, while Hölderlin's thought is instead centered on the tragedy of this opening in which a divergence from nature appears that can never be turned back.

The ex-centric nature of this opening seems focused for Hölderlin by the incompleteness of "As when on a holiday . . ." as it is incomplete at the very point in which its culmination was designed. But for Heidegger this incompleteness "is only the result of the profusion which flows from the innermost beginning of the poem" (EHD: 75/97). This is the excess granted in the "word," "which sustains everything else: 'But now day breaks! I waited and saw it come, / And what I saw, may the holy be my word'" (EHD: 72/94). To make *this* the culmination of the poem, in which the poet's word announces his advent as a poet, brings together Heidegger's and Hölderlin's differences quite profoundly as it leads to placing the greatest configurational pressure on the most delicate point of figurality. This is not unjustified for the opening of the word is "the event of the holy" from which the poem and the poet come forth, but there is also the greatest risk of the radical instability of this self-positing being ignored at this point in favor of phrasing it in terms of a self-establishing leap into the open (EHD: 76–77/98). This is the same kind of maneuver by which the work of art set itself forth as a work and was thereby fixed in place as such, and in doing so Heidegger seems to have transferred the *work* of poetry from the poem to the poet.

This setting up of the figure of the poet *is* his essential identity: it is the essence of his identity to be so configured against nature. Like the work of art, Heidegger seems to construe the poet as a figure (*Gestalt*), which means that the identity of the poet is con-figured in contradistinction to nature and appears as an event of sudden im-position or presencing. *If* we are to follow this line from the work to the poet, then this seems to neglect not only the complexity of disfiguring that was part of the work of art, but also the double emergence of nature and word that occurs in the poetic saying. By moving from the work to the poet, Heidegger appears to have replaced this subtle combination of presentation and representation with something much simpler. In the poem the poet, like nature, was called forth in a way that was both presentation and representation; his appearance was both that *of* a poet and *as* a poet. This duplicity led to the mutual effacement of both presentation and representation such that neither was possible on its own; instead the poet became nothing more than a presentation of his own representation, which is to say, a repetition of nothing. To stage this as a self-positing leap in which the poet establishes a transhistorical founding of truth would appear to do a great deal of violence to this complexity, but this is a possibility that is never absent from the opening of the word and is part of the essential divergence and dissembling that make it tragic.[13] Hence, the responsibility and care that comes with saying and the concomitant need for reticence, which Heidegger later responds to by withdrawing from figuring the poet in this way.

What has been lost in this reading is the possibility of rethinking the *mimēsis* inherent in the duplicity of the poetic word. For Heidegger, *mimēsis* is wholly determined by its relation to the Platonic *eidos*, and thus is embedded within an understanding of truth as adequation. Because he rejects the latter he also rejects the Platonic idea of art as *mimēsis*, that is, as a merely derivative form of appearance (copying) that is separated from truth (EM: 193/197).[14] Instead, he sees the work of art as an event *of* truth, that is, as a self-positing leap whose *Ur-Sprung* is the ground of its own presencing. But this self-positing is at risk of ignoring the duplicity of its presencing that would limit the possibility of such setting-up, and this in turn can lead, as Heidegger discovered, to a dangerous treatment of the political as a self-positing and transhistorical entity. For Philippe Lacoue-Labarthe, this rejection of *mimēsis* derives from thinking it solely from within the Platonic scheme as a form of *technē*, as merely impoverished production. Instead, he urges us to think of *mimēsis* as an "originary secondarity," that is, as the "deputising function (*la suppléance*) demanded by the essential 'cryptophilia' of *phusis*."[15] This (non)original *mimēsis* is necessary both in order to counter the separation of presentation and representation that is at the heart of the metaphysical idea of presence, and because of the way in which Heidegger's own thoughts on the duplicity of origins (*Ereignis*) are often overshadowed, as his reading of Hölderlin shows, by his interest in the self-positing of the work as a *Gestalt*. Although Heidegger's thinking of *Ereignis* seems at times to be a tacit rethinking of *mimēsis* as the event of repetition, its experience needs to be supplemented by an awareness of the finitude that it brings, that it is not only an event of appropriation but also of dissembling or expropriation (*Enteignis*).

The significance of this point centers on the naming of nature, for in the act of naming Heidegger wishes to preserve that which is named, while in Hölderlin's work we find that what is named "is" only through its names. The distinction is profound as it means that for Heidegger the dissembling of names in Hölderlin's work needs to be brought into the univocity of that which it attempts to say, while this saying is only possible for Hölderlin by way of dissembling, for the immediate can only be approached through its mediations and any attempt to transgress this law only leads to expulsion and thus to further dissembling. As Blanchot puts it, "nature is not Nature until after the naming it receives from the poet"; there is no sense of the poet naming that which already is and thereby discovering its original name; instead the poet's act of naming brings it forth in an entirely singular manner, which is thus susceptible to an inescapable recession (PF: 126/119). Although for Heidegger, "Hölderlin never knew the force of the primordial word *phusis*," he was still able to "put into his poem something else that, to be sure, stands in a concealed relation to that which was once called *phusis*" (EHD: 57/79–80). This "something else" is Hölderlin's word, "the holy" (*das Heilige*), which for Heidegger is that which heals (*heilen*) the rift between poet and nature through its saying; it is the whole (*heil*) saying that "stands in a concealed relation" to *phusis*, which enables Hölderlin's hymn to be one in which the name "nature" is "already overcome." As Heidegger goes on to say, this "overcoming is the consequence and sign of a saying that starts from a more primordial point" (EHD: 58/80). In other words, in "the holy," Hölderlin has found a way of saying *phusis* without knowing it, but this is *phusis* as Heidegger understands it, as the whole that is the hidden name of being.

Despite its common ground, "the holy" for Hölderlin cannot be subsumed into this understanding of *phusis*, for it is that which indicates that the rift between poet and nature *cannot* be healed and made whole; there can be no saying of nature in itself. Language in general is evidence of this utter separation, and "the holy" in particular is evidence of the endless and futile yearning to bridge this separation. Although Hölderlin was aware of the linguistic kinship of holiness, healing, and making whole, this could not erase the fact for him that the saying of these words would always undermine their meaning. Naming seems to have a completely different meaning for Heidegger and Hölderlin, as for one it is possible while for the other it is not, but this is only to be expected, since Heidegger, as a thinker thinking from within his own historical decision, cannot but translate Hölderlin into what is most proper to his own.

While there can be no question of this being a mistranslation, what has to be recalled is that Hölderlin's word is, by virtue of his persistent rewriting, already in translation. If Heidegger erases this in favor of presenting his own thought he is not engaging in anything illegitimate, but runs the risk in doing so of casting Hölderlin's work into a form that it not only does not possess, but also actively resists. This is the case with Hölderlin's "overcoming" of "nature," for which Heidegger refers to an early draft of another hymn written shortly after "As when on a holiday . . ." Here Hölderlin wrote some lines in which he named "nature," but, Heidegger notes, "in a pencil revision, the poet subsequently crossed out these lines," and this he takes as a sign of Hölderlin's "overcoming" of "nature" by the substitution of a more "primordial" word (EHD: 58/80). This is in philological terms highly suspect, and directly contradicts Heidegger's use of early drafts at other points, such as when he prefers the earlier use of *entwacht* (awakens) in line 39 of "As when on a holiday . . ." rather than the later *entwächst* (grows) (EHD: 66/88). But more importantly, it demonstrates quite strikingly what Blanchot described when he stated that "the commentator was more sensitive to tradition than to Hölderlin's experience." For here the *practice* of Hölderlin's rigorous, obvious, and necessary rewriting, which makes meaningless the idea of "overcoming," is passed over in favor of a move that directly recruits him to a Heideggerian philosophical strategy, that is, to a history of being, which is quite alien to his work. Blanchot's comment on this is damning in its simplicity, for the lines of this draft, "although subsequently crossed out, were nevertheless still formulated" (PF: 126/119).

Trying to read poetry into a philosophical project is inevitably going to lead to a reduction of its practice, in which light Heidegger's curious slip at the beginning of his essay becomes more telling. Hölderlin's text of "As when on a holiday . . ." Heidegger tells us, "rests upon the following attempt at an interpretation," that is, Heidegger's interpretation (EHD: 51/74). This paradox was pointed out to Heidegger in a letter from a student in 1953, and writing back he promptly concurred that the sentence was "impossible," and that in any new edition of the *Elucidations* this line should be deleted (EHD: 207/237). However, in a strange revisiting of Hölderlinean practice this intention was never carried out and the line persists to this day, intruding its own material refraction into the text against the flow of his projected thought. What we are to make of this is difficult to say, but the fact that Heidegger's own texts are not immune to this kind of disfiguring suggests that we should not be so certain about his or our abilities to hold meaning in our reading or writing. When it comes to poetry this impossibility of speaking certainly renders any attempts at naming equally impossible; this is the paradox at the heart of poetic practice and without recognizing it all of Heidegger's engagements with poetry are undermined.

Perhaps the tragic experience that Blanchot and Hölderlin speak of, and that seems to distinguish their relationship to poetry from Heidegger's, is at work here. Perhaps it is precisely the *experience* of the word as a textual caesura that separates poetry from thought, because this rupture *is* an *ex-periri*, a "trial" or "test," found by passing through (*perao*) or beyond (*pera*) a limit (*peras*). (Equally, in German, *Erfahrung*, "experience," from *fahren* "to transport," contains a concealed relation to *Gefahr*, "danger.")[16] These limits are the limits of thought, which as we saw in the addendum to "The Origin of the Work of Art" are the outlines within which the work is "fixed in place." Thus this experience would be excluded from a thinking that was not an experience of the word and, although thinking could never succumb to the excession of the word without also succumbing to its disruption and evasion and thereby perhaps becoming something other than thinking, there could still remain a role for a thinking into being. What this role might be, and whether we could ascribe it to Heidegger's thinking, cannot be answered here, as it will be necessary for us to negotiate the relation between thought and the caesura before any attempt to do so.

Part Two

The Repetition of Language

4

Suspending
The Translation of Tragedy in Hölderlin's Essays

> The conception of the idea of poetry as that of prose determines the whole Romantic philosophy of art. . . . Above all, however, this fundamental philosophical conception founds a peculiar relation within a wider Romantic circle, whose common element, like that of the narrower school, remains undiscoverable so long as it is sought only in poetry and not in philosophy as well. From this point of view, one spirit moves into the wider circle, not to say into its center—a spirit who cannot be comprehended merely in his quality as a "poet" in the modern sense of the word (however high this must be reckoned), and whose relationship to the Romantic school, within the history of ideas, remains unclear if his particular philosophical identity with this school is not considered. This spirit is Hölderlin, and the thesis that establishes his philosophical relation to the Romantics is the principle of the sobriety of art.
>
> —Walter Benjamin, "The Concept of Art Criticism in German Romanticism," 1919

Heidegger's encounter with Hölderlin's poetry has exposed the particular nature of the poetic word as one that both offers a relation to what is, but also undermines that relation in doing so. This, for Hölderlin, would seem to constitute the tragic nature of poetry, in that its writing reveals its word to be endlessly evasive and resistant to that which it is attempting to reach. His response to this problem is to pursue this textual finitude as the basis for a renewed understanding of translation. This does not mean that Hölderlin simply turns this impossibility into a possibility, but instead comes to an understanding of what the finitude of language implies about the nature of its relation. In turning to Hölderlin now I hope to be able to show not only the depth of his thinking on this issue of the relation of language, but also to indicate how the complexity of his writings grants to his thinking a liminal position that means, as Walter Benjamin pointed out in the epigraph, that his work is both within and without the sphere of poetry. It is this singularity that motivates Heidegger's readings and that enables him to read Hölderlin as both a figure of the tradition and as the most futural figure of our modernity who exposes us to the necessity and possibility of a writing to come. This proves to be a most important point, as it reveals a significant aspect of the relation of language to temporality: the nature of the moment of the word.

To begin this inquiry we cannot continue to think of Hölderlin simply as a poet; instead we must treat with all seriousness the fact that he was essentially a writer. The oeuvre to which the name "Hölderlin" is attached consists of many different types of text: poems, plays, letters, translations, essays, a novel, and other assorted fragments and notes. Moreover when we look closer and find that his poems consist of a wide range of odes, hymns, and elegies, and that his novel is epistolary in form, it becomes apparent that writing was for Hölderlin primarily an address; like an ode or a letter it was written toward someone, something, or somewhere. Whether directed toward the past or the future, nature or the gods, friends, colleagues, or lovers, the style that seems to hold over all of Hölderlin's writing is that of the *apostrophe*; the projected address or call whose conditions are that of radical instability and indeterminacy. For inherent in the apostrophe is the possibility of failure, as the call is issued under conditions of extreme loss: that it will either go unheard or unanswered, and Hölderlin's work persists in the inescapable nature of this uncertainty. All but two of the letters that make up the novel *Hyperion* are written by Hyperion himself, and the poems, plays, essays, and letters also seem to be written both "toward" and "against" (*gegen*) this absent and perhaps unreachable other.

This raises the next important aspect of Hölderlin's writing, as its apostrophic nature is partly responsible for its fragmented quality. In the years before his collapse Hölderlin seemed to be only infrequently capable of bringing his projects to conclusion as he seldom had the response from his peers or his works that would enable him to bring his thoughts to completion. Instead, his writing seems to develop under these very conditions of abandonment, by nature; by the gods; by friends, lovers, and colleagues; and eventually by himself. Rarely did he attain the response he desired and yet if we look closer at these scattered fragments that make up his letters, essays, and poems, with their notes, variants, and marginalia, it is possible to see that in this plethora of incompleteness he may perhaps have found the response that he was calling for, since the mode of apostrophe, while initially futile in its address, is itself the very response that it is calling for, such that it is sustained *by* its lack of completion. The apostrophe is not calling for any fixed response that would bring it to resolution; rather, its projection is its own response, in that it holds open the dynamic of writing, which perpetuates the relation to the other as other that is the very condition of the call. Thus, writing for Hölderlin is such that longing, absence, and separation are the conditions of its relation to the other and any alteration of these would necessarily erase that relation. While his writing is thereby preserved from utter futility, it can never escape the tragic conditions by and in which it persists.

Although this means that Hölderlin's writing is grounded in loss, this loss can itself be attended to in *translation*, in the passing encounter that takes places in its transport. Translation and poetry are both tragic in Hölderlin's thought as their passage can only be suspended temporarily, that is, translation is both in and of time; it is born out of it, out of its turning in the self-estranging encounter of the caesura, which is the interruption of the "pure word." Thus there can be no resolution or fulfillment to this reflexive turning because these moments are transient and only realized in retrospect as having occurred. The rupture that takes place in the caesura cannot be held; it is that which brings about the burgeoning of a new time, but as such can only be apprehended in its absence, after the fact, *nachträglich*, we could say.[1] Hölderlin sees in this transition the interaction of the personal, the poetic, and the social, all of which are linked into an account of change in which nature and art are translated into themselves through each other. This relation Hölderlin wishes to explore in terms of the destiny of modernity in its relation to ancient Greece and in particular, in his own relation to Pindar and Sophocles. There is in this relation the tension of coming after, which arises out of the problem of succeeding; how can one combine following with autonomy, tradition with innovation?

Hölderlin's response, as I will show, is to undermine each position by translating it into its other, by making of succession a caesura and autonomy a remembering. In this way, what is past is no longer simply past, and what follows is not simply subsequent; an overlaying of positions has taken place in which *before* and *after* become mobile terms, interpenetrating and never absent. As in a palimpsest it is not impossible to discern before and after, but each infects the other, destroying its authority and limits such that past becomes future and vice versa. This effect is worked out by Hölderlin in his translations, that is, in practice rather than in theory, such that his understanding of the role of translation changed from first seeing it as a tool to achieve better poetry, to later seeing it as the very goal and purpose of poetry. While he began by making standard translations from Greek into German, he then moved into a mode of strict lexical transfer, and then into a more substantial reading through the Greek into its hidden "oriental" aspect, thereby translating both Greek and German into something richer and more "lively." It is also significant that after working on Pindar and Sophocles in this way he would then turn to translating his own poems, rewriting them in such a manner as to bring out their own absence while still holding them to the earlier texts so as to expose the hidden transport of their words.

Crudely, one might say that Hölderlin moves from translating the meaning of words in the standard sense, to a translation of the words themselves in a literal, etymological sense, to a translation of the gaps between the words, which is not to say the spirit of their meaning, but a more textual translation of that first translation that enabled those words to be so inscribed. This is not to find in the spaces between the words the place from which language itself speaks, but to allow the mark of language itself to appear *as* its disappearance into words. This disappearance is not a relation but a rupture that Hölderlin seeks to approximate by rewriting his own poems into a suspended position that lies between words and that which precedes them. This rewriting holds open the transition into words at the moment that they pass between appearance and disappearance, but this practice is excessive; it can only persist by its own endless repetition. These words then speak as memories of forgetting that indicate an intangible absence and that make present that absence as such, as the gap between words, the ellipsis that has always already occurred.

Thus, to seek an exposition of Hölderlin's poetry by examining his essays is not simply difficult, but probably misguided. These brief, fragmentary, and unfinished pieces were mostly written for Hölderlin's personal guidance rather than for any public edification. Consequently, we are faced in reading them with a range of private, unexplicated, and inconsistent themes that are often strung together with little regard for punctuation. In addition, it is often difficult to assess in what order they were composed, so there is little internal help to be gleaned from comparing the various texts. However, trying to piece together a clear and systematic presentation of Hölderlin's thoughts on poetry and tragedy is perhaps not the goal we should be seeking. Instead, what these prose works seem to suggest is more that of a primer for thought, or notes set down as he worked on other projects, like the translations of Pindar and Sophocles or the writing of his play *The Death of Empedocles.* They are, as he points out in an essay from 1800, "thought-experiments" (*Denkversuchen*), in the most literal sense of being attempts or essays into thinking. These experiments "cancel themselves" by "striving" into extremes, thereby making thought possible by creating "the difference necessary for knowledge (*Erkentniß*)" (SW4: 256/75). Thus they are a first foray on the way to other works, their dense and elliptical quality marking the "text" from which his other works are translated. It is due to this density that these texts resist exposition and instead actively propagate the turning of thought into other modes, into its differentiation as the words of poetry and drama.

It is with this in mind that we should read these texts: with an eye to translating them ourselves by finding those places where the turning of thought takes place, where it begins to reach outward into an other text. In allowing ourselves to become estranged in this way we find in Hölderlin's words what is most proper to our own, which is also what lies closest to his: its differentiation of itself. This way of reading arises from a remark made by Lacoue-Labarthe in 1978, in an essay appended to his translation of Hölderlin's version of *Antigone*, a remark that to my mind has still not been fully pursued:

> The Hölderlin who seems to me urgently to require examination (and decipherment) today is the theoretician and dramatist (as regards the essential, the one is inseparable from the other). It is the Hölderlin of a certain precise and sure trajectory in the theory and practice of the theater, in the theory of tragedy and the experience or the testing—and this entails translating the Greeks (Sophocles)—of a new kind of dramatic writing. Perhaps simply of a new kind of writing: one which is, as he himself and his epoch said, "modern."[2]

What follows is an attempt to examine and follow through on the implications of this claim, for although Lacoue-Labarthe has himself worked on the aspects of the theatrical in Hölderlin's work, by unwrapping the relation between catharsis and the caesura, and speculation and representation, there has not been an equal level of attention paid to the "new kind of writing" that arises within Hölderlin's work on tragedy.

It is important to recognize the subtlety of Hölderlin's position before we can proceed, especially because of the way in which Heidegger's reading insists on the "abysses" that separate Hölderlin from his contemporaries, as much as from any literary or aesthetic concerns, which may explain his scant regard for Hölderlin's essays and other poetological writings (BPE: 463–64/326).[3] This may be necessary in order to configure Hölderlin as an epochal poet, but cannot but hinder our attempts to understand his writings.[4] Instead, we have to understand, as Lacoue-Labarthe has illustrated, how Hölderlin's thought develops out of an early influence of idealism and dialectics into something, which although never completely detached from it, critically disturbs the possibility of such thought. I say "critically," as it is evident that of all his peers it is Hölderlin who sticks closest to a certain Kantian rupture of thinking, for which we must see evidence in his use of the caesura, although he will go further than Kant or even Schiller by attempting to pursue the possibility of an "intellectual intuition" through aesthetics. While his early theoretical writings are largely influenced by Fichte or Schiller, there is a change that occurs around 1799–1800, the same period in which "As when on a holiday . . ." is composed, where his thought becomes more complex and distinctive. This change coincides with the failure of his attempt to write a "modern tragedy" around the character of Empedocles, and thus the question of the role of the tragic in his thought assumes a dominant role, and so too, but more implicitly, does the concomitant question of "writing."

. . . The Chiasmic Ground of *Empedocles* . . .

That Hölderlin should see the tragic word appearing at this intersection of poetry and nature is made clear by his work on Empedocles, who as a philosopher, poet, politician, physician, and priest was a paradigmatic worker of the intersections of matter and spirit. This accumulation of disparate but convergent forces all focus on the power of the word to bring about change, which is emphasized by the revolutionary nature of Empedocles' religious and political behavior. Although sketchy, the histories of

Empedocles all agree on the various key events of his life: He was a priest in the Sicilian town of Acragas in the fifth-century BCE who betrayed the priesthood by revealing forbidden knowledge; he was a gifted physician whose miraculous healing powers saw him rewarded with the crown, which he abdicated by calling for a republic; he was a philosopher whose poem *On Nature* detailed the cosmic revolution of *philia* (love) and *neikos* (strife), which unify and separate all things; and finally, he declared himself a god and threw himself into the volcanic crater of Mount Etna. All of these elements stress the transgressive nature of Empedocles' character, as he crossed the boundaries of life and death, and men and gods, and ably demonstrate the attraction Hölderlin must have felt for his story.

Hölderlin tried three times to write a tragic drama called *The Death of Empedocles* and each time failed; it is not possible to say exactly why this happened but the sheer overdetermination of Empedocles' character may well have been a problem. Any one of these stories would have provided the basis for a tragic drama, but their excessive proliferation makes this impossible, as any sense of their being a drama at work would require some room for the protagonist to negotiate their fate. Empedocles seems to actively deny this possibility by giving too many reasons for him to die, only to refuse even this dramatic device by proclaiming his suicide an entirely free and self-willed action. Thus the very source of Hölderlin's fascination is also the source of his inability to dramatize the story, for the tragic word fails in the face of this excess; although there is tragedy here there is no drama; it cannot be encompassed.[5] As such, Empedocles appears in the first two versions of this drama more as the figure of an idea, than as a genuinely dramatic character, and as a result the plays lack any real antagonist, which is central for any tragedy. In the third version the character of Manes is introduced to balance Empedocles' impatience with patience, but by then Hölderlin's ideas about the general direction of his work had already changed.

In trying to compose his drama Hölderlin wrote a brief but unfinished essay in 1799, just before working on "As when on a holiday . . ." called "The Ground of *Empedocles*," which sought to make sense of the relation of art, and specifically poetry, to nature. The key insight of this paper is to realize that the continual movement between unity and separation, which is actualized in the suffering of time, can only be restaged in tragedy by its recapitulation. The justification for this comes from the work of Schiller who believed that art was the means by which nature was able to complete itself, and thus the means by which the artist in his turn could approach nature. This is the basis for Hölderlin's belief that aesthetics could make possible an intellectual intuition, that is, a direct apprehension of being. But this direct intuition is only possible through the mediation of art, which is in the ambivalent position of being both the opposite and the culmination of nature. This is what leads Hölderlin's thought into a dialectics, in which nature is both canceled and completed through art, thus introducing temporality as the passion of nature. Tragedy, as the form of art that most closely follows this passion, is thus most capable of fulfilling nature, but it can only do so through its own dialectical passage.

That is, the drama must itself actualize this suffering by setting up a movement of *translation* between the opposing dynamics of the natural, or "aorgic," and the artistic, or "organic."[6] The practice of translation in this model is such that the organic can only reveal itself in the aorgic, and vice versa, that the aorgic only becomes itself in the organic: "nothing at all can become understood and enlivened if we cannot transport our own soul (*Gemüth*) and our own experience into a foreign analogous material." The material referred to here is the language of the drama, its words, which must be estranged to an extreme, for the "more foreign they are, and the less the visible material of the poem that forms the ground resembles the soul and the world of the poet, the less may the spirit, the divine, as the poet has received it in his world, be denied in the artificial foreign material." It is this translation that takes place in the language of the drama, which although it makes possible the depiction of the tragedy, also affects the poet as he composes it. Through his actions "the tragic poet, because he expresses the deepest intimacy (*Innigkeit*, also: "intensity"), wholly denies his character, his subjectivity, and also the object present to him, he carries them into a foreign personality, a foreign objectivity." As a result of this translation the drama can unfold, for then the divine itself can appear as "a third, more different, more foreign material than the poet's own soul and his own world" (SW4: 150–51/51–52).

The goal is not simply the representation of a tragic drama, but the presentation of the tragic in the work of the poet through a transformation of his language, which thus brings about the translation of parts and whole, art and nature, and man and gods. But there is a problem here, as the figuring of the character of Empedocles has failed to achieve sufficient distance from the poet and thus has failed to be a truly tragic character. Just as with Heidegger's early work on Hölderlin, the early part of Hölderlin's work on Empedocles contains much evidence of an identification of the poet with his character, and as a result the drama becomes a representation of a tragic character, instead of being tragic itself. By figuring himself as the tragic protagonist he has impatiently sought to embrace nature directly, and this has the effect of undermining the necessary indirection of the writing that must act to mediate the movement of nature and art. The free figuration of the tragic through writing has been prevented by this identification and this has stopped it from emerging, for its necessary separation is already configured by the dimensions of the writer. Hölderlin's response will eventually be to move away from the figuring of characters into a figuring of the writing itself, so as to *dis-figure* his relation to nature through writing and thereby enter into the separation of the tragic. This writing would no longer be on tragedy since it would be tragic itself, but what kind of writing is this?

Hölderlin's awareness of this problem is only slight in this essay but we can detect points of tension that will become significant later on. At this point, he describes the movement of separation through a complicated chiasmus of the organic and the aorgic, in which nature becomes art only insofar as art becomes nature. Despite its dialectical basis, no final, unified state is reached, for this crossover brings about a unity that cannot last. Equally, this is distinct from the *polemos* of earth and world that Heidegger configures into the separating and gathering outline of the drawing that is the work of art. What occurs in Hölderlin's version of this moment is an extraordinary double crossover in which the organic finds itself anew in the aorgic that has become organic, and vice versa, that the aorgic achieves its fullest expression only through realizing itself in the organic that has become aorgic.

This union and discovery can only take place because the two movements happen together, but because the two occur at the same time this moment of greatest *Innigkeit* is also the moment in which they must split apart, for the organic in finding itself in the aorgic become organic is thereby thrust away from it. This discovery of identity, as both the mark of unity and its death, is when the word appears as the presence of the divine, which thereby shatters the just achieved unity and sends each back into its separation again. For Hölderlin all this is united in the character of Empedocles, but this complicated gathering of opposites that leads to apotheosis and death indicates that the figuration of the poet is also destined for dissolution.

This is a significant realization for Hölderlin, as it makes of Empedocles' story a tragedy "demanded" by "the fate of his time." Empedocles' age "demanded a sacrifice, where the whole man really and visibly becomes that wherein the fate of his time seems to dissolve, where the extremes really and visibly seem to unite in one, but precisely for that reason are too intimately united, and in an ideal act the individual must decline and pass away" (SW4: 156/56). Before it reaches this extreme the transformation of Empedocles' character demonstrates the complexities of this movement. For "what is regarded in his world as more subjective," namely the powers of thought to organize and differentiate in art, "is in himself more objective," and conversely, "what is regarded by others in his world as more objective," namely the disorganized, undifferentiated world of nature, "is with him and for him more subjective" (SW4: 154–55/55). In this way, what is subjective (art) becomes objective (nature), and vice versa, such that what was speechless (nature) now gains speech and what was only spoken (art) now becomes real. Only by losing himself can Empedocles speak in the voice of that which was speechless and so these words only arise out of the dissolution of his voice.

To support this we can turn to a brief fragment on the "significance" (*Bedeutung*) of tragedy, written while he worked on his Sophocles translations in 1802–3, in which Hölderlin sketches out this chiasmic model very concisely: "Now in the tragic the sign in itself is insignificant, ineffective (*wirkungslos*), but the original is straight out (*gerade heraus*)." This distinction refers to the tragic figure as the sign of nature (the original), indicating that tragedy is the means by which nature completes itself, for if "the sign in itself is posited as insignificant = 0, the original, the hidden ground of every nature, can also present itself." Thus the meaning of tragedy is to be "understood through paradox" (SW4: 274/89). In doing so, Hölderlin has opened an approach to tragedy that repeats the intrinsically religious meaning it had for the Greeks, in which tragedy was the means of a very real presencing of the gods or of nature, rather than a representation. For on the one hand he is saying that nature can only present itself through the sign, in other words, appearance is always mediation, translation, but on the other hand by way of the possibility of tragedy to resemble nothing by means of its dissolution, this appearance of nature is straight out, that is, it is appearance in the sheerness of its appearing. Thus, nature presents itself in tragedy through the medium of its opposite, through a metaphor, only insofar as this sign of nature is ineffective, *workless*, indicating that the appearance of presencing as such can only occur by way of a dissembling of this appearance into nothing.

We have seen how this prepares the stakes of the poetic word for Empedocles, which arises out of the way that "time individualizes itself in Empedocles" (SW4: 158/57). But this naturally raises the issue of what is at stake for Hölderlin; if dissolution is the fate of the character then is it also the case for the poet? If so, how is it possible to write a modern tragedy, or is it the case that this dissolution opens a new relation of language, of writing? This question is central to Hölderlin's existence not just as a poet, but as a person, for as the essay on Empedocles sought to demonstrate, the nature of poetic language is intertwined with our relation to the world and to time, which is constitutive of our self-understanding and identity. Understanding how this problem may be addressed in this age requires an understanding of how this age developed, and it is with this in mind that Hölderlin turned to translate Sophocles. At this point a second remark from Lacoue-Labarthe's essay will indicate the significance of the transition from Empedocles to Sophocles, while keeping us aware of the contextual stakes of Hölderlin's position:

> The theory put forward in Hölderlin—and this would apply to more than just those texts which are usually classified as such—*is*, through and through, speculative. At least it can always be interpreted in this way, read in this way, and written in this way. For it is probably in just this fashion—above all, when it wished to extricate itself from this constraint—that the theory itself was first read and written. But this is not to say that it *reread* itself and *rewrote* itself in this manner—especially when it did not want to extricate itself from this constraint, in which it also saw its resource, its protection, and, perhaps, its "remedy."[7]

It is precisely in terms of translation that Hölderlin will find a way of turning writing into rewriting, thus suspending its theoretical configurations, dis-figuring it, and thereby rendering it "ineffective." Translation is then able to accomplish what Hölderlin originally stated to be the aim of tragedy, namely, to be "the metaphor of an intellectual intuition" (SW4: 266/83).[8] But the effect that this worklessness will have on the historical horizons of translation will have a radical impact on our understanding of what is at stake in modernity as a result of writing, and what is thus realized as "modern writing."

. . . The Caesura of *Oedipus* . . .

Although it appears that he intended to translate all of Sophocles' works, Hölderlin only completed versions of *Oedipus Tyrannus* and *Antigone*, which were published with commentaries in 1804. The reception of these works is well-known, and although part of the derision they received is due to the abysmal manner in which they were edited for publication and the poor quality of the original texts Hölderlin was using, which led to something in the region of a thousand errors, the main source of bemusement lay in the radical nature of their translation.[9] While the originality of his translations is no longer in doubt, this does not make them any easier to elucidate, a fact exemplified by the commentaries, which seem to be opaque to the point of being hermetic. What we can ascertain is that they arose from a period of involvement with Sophocles' work that stretched back to 1799 and that included four separate and distinct attempts at translation. With each new start the mode of translation changed as a result of the previous attempt, so that we can surmise that on each occasion Hölderlin became dissatisfied with his results and started again in a different manner. The overall effect of these changes was to lead Hölderlin to a position of such familiarity with the meter and the syntax, as well as with the words and their meaning, that his understanding of the role of translation had itself become translated. Now he felt himself capable of translating "Sophocles" himself into what he could have been, had he not been confined to the poetic modes of his time.

The necessity of doing so was outlined in an oft-quoted letter written in December 1801 to his friend Böhlendorff, where he applied his understanding of the chiasmic relation of art and nature to an analysis of the poetic mode of ancient Greece: Because the natural mode of the Greeks was "sacred pathos" it was necessary for them to pass into its opposite, "sobriety," in order to develop their art. For his own age Hölderlin makes the opposite diagnosis: as the natural mode of the Germans is "clarity of presentation (*Darstellung*)" they must learn the "passion," which was natural to the ancient Greeks, if their art is to develop. If tragedy is concerned with an attempt to return to what is most one's own, then, Hölderlin writes, "this is the tragic for us, that packed up in any container we very quietly move away from the realm of the living, not that, consumed in flames, we atone for the flames we are not able to control." The tragic for Hölderlin means a return to the natural element of quietness, order, and compartmentalization. This "sobriety"—which is not the "Junonian" sobriety that was acquired by the Greeks, but one that is truly our own, as "we may not even have anything the *same* with them"—is also that which is most elusive, for "that which is proper (*Eigene*) must be learned just as well as that which is foreign (*Fremde*)," and we "learn nothing more difficult than the free use of the Nationelle" (SW6: 425–26/149–50).

(As an aside, it is significant that Hölderlin should use the neologism "Nationelle," a liberal slogan of the French Revolution, as it indicates the social, cultural, and political dimensions that he sees as inherent to his practice of poetry and particularly, translation. But, as a later paraphrase of this line indicates, "the free use of what is one's own (*Eigenen*)," we should not look to the modern political meaning of "national," but to the chiasmic translation of our nature. It is thus highly revealing what Heidegger writes on this word as it indicates the difference between his and Hölderlin's understandings of the "proper": "the 'Nationelle' means the land of birth (*nasci, natura*), because as the beginning it determines what abides." However, because of its difficulty and ambiguity Heidegger refuses to comment on this idea any further, adding only that our approach should be tempered by the fact that "Hölderlin finally left behind him that part of his way, which he thought through under the title 'patriotic reversal,' by overcoming (*verwunden*) it" (EHD: 159/206). But as the word itself lacks nationality, in not being either French or German, this would suggest a radical impropriety, for it is a word without source, a neologism, which might explain why it is that which, in being what is most one's own, is also what is most difficult to learn.[10])

Explaining how his translation is to be done takes up much of Hölderlin's commentaries, but what is intriguing is the way in which they take up the relation of time and language to explore how the tragic brings about this chiasmic reversal. In developing this, Hölderlin moves substantially on from the position he held as he worked on the Empedocles tragedy, and it seems that the very structure of the chiasmus has changed with the change in approach. The crucial change that has taken place, and that signals Hölderlin's own response to the problems of classicism, is that the relation between the ancients and the moderns has been doubled by being internally divided. The "modern" no longer has to discover how to relate to itself by uncovering its relation to the "ancient," for these terms are already in a process of relating to themselves through their internal struggle between what is "foreign" and what is "proper" to them.[11] As such, there is neither an "ancient" nor a "modern" position from which or to which translation must operate, and moreover, these terms have never had any substantial existence.

Translation for Hölderlin exposes time as not being made up of positions, but of tendencies in which each term is always in excess of itself, differentiating and unstable to the point of becoming lost to itself, and thereby unreachable. This would in the most precise manner dis-figure history, by removing the possibility of using such figures as historical markers, thereby leaving it unconfigured, volatile, strange, not founding, but rather losing itself, becoming errant. This "poetic view of history" as Hölderlin calls it in a letter to Leo von Seckendorff, radically undermines the classical view of history as an evolving series of different ages, by insisting that any particular age is divided to the point of fracturing by virtue of its struggle with its own otherness, its own past and future, which means that history doesn't progress from age to age but exists in layers of internal division and estrangement (SW6: 437). This renders any period ex-centric, differentiating it also from Heidegger's destinal model of the sending of epochs out of the withdrawal of being, by replacing it with an understanding of time drawn from writing, that is, as operating under a *palimpsest* of internal differentiation that knows no progress or decay. In this view division does not arise out of the change from one tendency to another (e.g., clarity to passion), but by the eruption within the word of its own alterity; thus the movement from the foreign to the proper does not occur by a faithful clarifying of translation but by its interruption and suspension.

It is important to qualify this though, as the more immediate concern of these commentaries is the issue of translating Sophocles, which arises from the problem of writing a modern tragedy. Consequently, Hölderlin seeks to draw out the nature of the "lawful calculation" (*gesezliche Kalkul*) that he feels is required by any modern tragedy. This law is the key to understanding how poetic craft can be "taught, and when it has been learned, can always be repeated reliably in practice." While his concern for a social and cultural renewal through poetry is significant, and indicates an important political dimension to his writings—in continuity with the much earlier radical pronouncements of "The Oldest System-Program of German Idealism" coauthored with Hegel and Schelling—it is only the result of the main property of this law, which is that it enables mankind "to see with every thing, that it is something, i.e. that it is recognizable in the medium (*moyen*) of its appearance" (SW5:

195/101). Thus it is only by directing our attention to the singularity of things as they relate to their appearance that the poetic craft can be repeated. While this hints at the phenomenological relation between singularity and repetition, the purpose of this law is to enable the poem to achieve a differential singularity, that is, to find itself within the palimpsest of its temporal and linguistic appearance.

To achieve this suspension Hölderlin introduces the *caesura*, a development described by Benjamin in 1922 as being of "fundamental significance for the theory of art in general, beyond serving as the basis for a theory of tragedy," and, as I will indicate below but unfortunately cannot pursue here, Benjamin's explication of this "significance" in terms of its effects on translation and writing offer suggestive alternatives to Heidegger's own approach to Hölderlin's writings.[12] The caesura disrupts the structure of a work, which would ordinarily develop in such way that different sequences "are produced one after the other," by allowing these representations to appear "more as balance, than as pure succession"; this then enables each part to be seen in itself and in its relations. Within tragedy the effect is heightened, as we have seen, by virtue of its sign's dissembling into nothing, such that "the tragic *transport* is properly empty, and the most unbounded."

> Thereby in the rhythmic succession of representations, in which the *transport* presents itself, it becomes necessary to have *what in prosody is called caesura*, the pure word, the counter-rhythmic interruption, in order to meet the rushing alternation of representations at its peak, in such a way that it is then no longer the alternation of representations that appears, but representation (*Vorstellung*) itself. (SW5: 196/101–2)

Tragedy hereby presents itself as a differential harmony in which each part is present as itself and as part of its medium; thus there is no diachronic representation of content, or story, but only the presencing of representation. However, the pure word of the caesura has not only suspended the parts of the tragedy, but also time and subjectivity, since by withholding their development each thing is beheld in its singularity and we are thereby confronted with its finitude. Within the tragedy this occurs when Oedipus comes up against Tiresias' word and is suddenly removed "from his own life-sphere, the midpoint of his inner life into another world." This "pure word" is not Tiresias' own, but is the law of fate, of finitude, which for Oedipus, just as for everybody, "tears (*reißt*) him into the eccentric sphere of the dead" (SW5: 197/102).

Oedipus' fate comes from his "almost shameless striving to be master of himself," his "insane questioning after a consciousness," which implies the same speculative desire, the same transgression of the divine, that Empedocles portrayed (SW5: 199–200/104–5). This is not just the fate of the tragic character or of idealism, but of the essence of tragedy itself; for by introducing the caesura Hölderlin has made the writing of tragedy itself tragic, as it ruptures the same presentation of the divine that it is attempting to deliver: Oedipus' fate has become Hölderlin's, and by implication, Sophocles' writing of *Oedipus Tyrannus* has revealed the fate of all poetic attempts at writing tragedy. The significance of this play for Hölderlin lies in its self-presentation of tragedy, which reveals the fate of all modern writing. What Oedipus' strivings reveal is not the self-presence of consciousness, but its finitude, just as the poet's desire to present the divine in writing similarly fails by only being able to present its own finitude. The caesura that enables things to be seen as themselves can only do so by suspending them, thereby revealing them only insofar as they are finite; the union with the divine that the poet seeks is thus only possible in separation, through its distance and rupture. This has immense significance, for it implies that the tragic operation, while necessary in that it grants the primary division by which things can be beheld as such, is also that by which the union with these things is marked as impossible. This duplicity is brought together in the caesura, which, although it is found in Sophocles, only now, by virtue of Hölderlin's translations, assumes its fate as the mark of modern writing, and the consequences of this are great, for the translation of tragedy brings about its own effects on Hölderlin's age.

In Empedocles' age the chiasmic reversal of the organic and the aorgic was made possible through sacrifice, but now "in an idle time" there is no longer the possibility for this kind of exchange, as god and man "participate in one another in the all-forgetting form of infidelity." Because the gods have departed the agency of sacrifice has become impossible; instead it is only through the recurrence of this departure, through infidelity, "that the course of the world shall have no gap in it and the memory of the heavenly ones does not end." Time and the gods can only persist without interruption by our turning away from them, a turning that is made possible in writing itself, which alone can repeat the separation or caesura that brought about this infidelity. The modernity of tragedy is not only realized in writing, but *as writing*, for in its turning away, man "forgets himself and the god," and at this "extreme limit of suffering there stands nothing more than the conditions of time and of space." The mutual infidelity of man and god then reveals itself in a moment in which time "turns categorically, and beginning and end cannot be brought to rhyme with each other at all" (SW5: 202/108). There is still a chiasmus of sorts here between man and the divine, but its transport is empty: the translation of the caesura into writing has suspended its rupture at the point of its opening, its turning away, such that it can only open and never re-turn.

This tragic and endless separation Hölderlin marks with the name of *physeos grammateus*, "nature's scribe," which signs the appearance of tragedy with its dissembling: "The presentation (*Darstellung*) of the tragic rests primarily on this, that the inordinate, how god and man couple, and the boundless becoming one in anger of the power of nature and man's innermost, thereby comprehends itself, that the boundless becoming-one purifies itself through boundless separation. *Tes physeos grammateus en ton kalamon apobrechon eunoun*" (SW5: 201/107). The Greek phrase is a semi-citation from an entry on Aristotle in a tenth-century Byzantine encyclopedia and translates as "nature's scribe dipping his well-meaning pen." Hölderlin has changed the phrase by the removal of Aristotle's name, to which the accolade of "nature's scribe" was attached, and altering *eis noun* to *eunoun*, changing the action of the scribe from the original "dipping his pen into meaning." Given the proximity to Aristotle's thoughts in which Hölderlin's ideas on tragedy seem to have developed, it is perhaps not unusual to come across this citation, and considering the number of errors in his translations it is possible that the change from *eis noun* to *eunoun* is simply a slip. But neither of these points shed any light on the juxtaposition Hölderlin has made by placing this excessive definition of tragedy next to a description of the action of nature's scribe, unless we are to read the latter as somehow being a gloss on the former, in which case the omission of Aristotle's name may indicate how Hölderlin has translated the definition of tragedy, by obliquely referring us to what has also been omitted from this definition: the resolution of its action through catharsis. Instead Hölderlin favors an "inordinate" (*ungeheuer*), which is to say, immeasurable, that is, impossible, union purified "through boundless separation." If this is to be understood by way of the gloss as also being the action of nature's scribe, then it suggests a relation between writing and nature that can never be re-solved.

But if the implication is that the presentation of the tragic is somehow echoed in the action of nature's scribe, then this would suggest not just that writing re-presents nature as tragedy, but that this is the writing of *nature's* scribe, thus indicating a movement in which nature repeats itself as writing in a movement of becoming-one that brings about a self-comprehension leading to endless scission. This chiasmic moment is found in the pure word, which brings nature to form for the first time through its rupture, and is thereby the *inscription* of *phusis* in itself. This self-inscription is a repetition that is both within and without nature, as it is the self-effacing trace of its figuring. Thus this rupture *of* time and space, by which nature comes to be, not only precedes nature but also only occurs from out of it, such that if it is originary it is only by way of its repetition. However, insofar as this is also the presentation of the tragic this repetition implies that there can be no resolution here as there was for Aristotle, for the rupture of this inscription commits us to a turning without return, a turning that is the writing *of* nature (*physeos grammateus*). We have to be clear on this point, for it is the *caesura* that ex-poses presence and for Hölderlin this is a term of poetry or more precisely, writing, which *transcribes* and *de-scribes* presence, both marking and re-marking it, figuring and dis-figuring.[13] By recalling the draw-ing of the work of art we can perceive how Hölderlin's approach has attenuated its outline to an extreme by emphasizing the abyssal and repetitive experience of this writing.

As a result, Hölderlin's alignment of *phusis* and writing has exposed a *mimetic* movement in which the writing of the tragic is a (non)originary *mimēsis*, the very dissembling presencing that was the event of the work of art and the inappropriable limit of language. Beyond its textual and personal implications, this possibility also has a crucial impact on Hölderlin's attempts to write a modern tragedy, for, as Lacoue-Labarthe notes, it entails that the "modern" is "something like the *après coup*, in the strict sense, of Greek art: that is to say, the repetition of what occurred there without ever taking place, and the echo of that unuttered word that nevertheless reverberated in its poetry." This repetition avoids the problem of imitation that so concerned classicism in Hölderlin's time by neither imitating nor completing the Greeks, but turning to that which was present there only as an absence. As Lacoue-Labarthe goes on to say, this explains the significance of translation and rewriting, for "it was a matter of making Greek art say what it had not said—not in the manner of a kind of hermeneutics attempting to find the implicit in its discourse, but in quite a different manner. . . . It was a matter of making it say by this means, quite simply, that which was said (but) *as that which was not said*: the same thing, then, in its difference."[14] While this echoes Heidegger's similar attempts at a "retrieval" (*Wiederholung*), "recovery" (*Verwindung*), or "remembrance" (*Andenken*) of philosophy, Hölderlin's notion of modernity is, as we shall see, more prosaic, which thus has an impact on the framing within which such a repetition is conducted.

As for Hölderlin, this mimetic movement is not an imitation, but the repetition *of* differentiation, "the *en diapheron eauto* (the one differentiated (*unterschiedne*) in itself)," as his rewriting of Heraclitus puts it.[15] The radical nature of such endless repetition arises from its relation to writing, and not saying, for only in writing is there found the dissembling of presence as the repetition and rupture of nature. A note of caution must be struck here, for it is not the case that Hölderlin had a theory of *mimēsis* or *phusis*, and so our understanding of *physeos grammateus* must be limited by our awareness that this is a singular textual point. *Mimēsis* is not being described by Hölderlin; rather the writing of the pure word or caesura is itself a demonstration of it through its repetition and finitude. But this raises the important point that the tracing of inscription cannot be grasped; it can only be felt through the singular absence that empties the word in writing. This is a difficult point to accept in terms of our understanding of a poem, for it requires a poem to be both the representation of nothing and the presentation of itself, which it does by presenting nothing but the representation of itself, which is the caesura. It must keep silent to prevent its words from being taken for what they say, rather than what they are, since what they are is nothing but the rupture of their (non)originary repetition.

While Heidegger's awareness of this need for silence can be found in his detailed attention to words it is often the case, as his encounter with Hölderlin showed, that his need for a decisive reading overrides his reticence. This is unsurprising, for the required reticence is not a capacity of speaking but of writing, as the absencing of de-scription eludes the articulation of speech, even the most reserved. Here lies the tragedy of words in that we are bound to failure, and while our failing is itself indicative of the dissembling of nature and thus extends a certain proximity to us, this proximity is also lost to us through dissembling. Moreover, this failing is necessarily the case, for nature only appears as a caesura, as a rupture that refuses speech, except for that writing that arises from its repetition.

. . . THE ECCENTRICITY OF *ANTIGONE* . . .

The effect of this caesura on the chiasmic structure of tragedy is taken up in the "Remarks on *Antigone*," which directly addresses the issue of its contemporary meaning. By moving from *Oedipus Tyrannus* to *Antigone* Hölderlin inverts the traditional sequence of Sophocles' plays and brings about in its place a relation that confronts the issue of our relation to Sophocles. This move from the Greek to the Hesperian (Western, Occidental) was at the center of his letter to Böhlendorff and is constitutive of the move that Hölderlin has to make in order to translate Sophocles and to understand what is required for modern tragedy.

Oedipus Tyrannus, with its emphasis on the tragic fate of its protagonist whose fault is to seek too urgently after his own consciousness, is often considered the quintessential modern tragedy, and Hölderlin seems to agree with this position insofar as its development by Sophocles rests on the most complete acquisition of a *sobriety* in its execution. But, as we have seen from the chiasmus discussed in the letter to Böhlendorff, this sobriety is modern only insofar as it is not natural to the ancient Greeks; it is what Sophocles has to acquire. *Antigone*, by contrast, is considered the most Greek of Sophocles' dramas in that its execution relies on the irresistible *passion* of its protagonist. This passion is what Hölderlin believes is necessary for the Hesperians to acquire to counter their own natural clarity. For this reason, the transition in his translations from *Oedipus Tyrannus* to *Antigone* moves Hölderlin into a more direct confrontation with what is necessary to the nature of a genuinely modern tragedy, one that does not simply reflect what we naively are, but what we are not, and thus what we must pass through in order to become what we most properly are.

This does not mean a return to, or even of, the passion that made *Antigone* the most Greek of ancient dramas, for this quality was concealed in Sophocles, as it was what was natural to him. Instead, as he explained in a letter to his editor Friedrich Wilmans in September 1803, Hölderlin proposes "to present Greek art to the public more vivaciously (*lebendiger*) than usual, it is foreign to us due to the national convenience and bias it has always relied on, by bringing out further the orientalism it has denied and correcting its artistic bias, wherever it comes forward" (SW6: 434). That is, Sophocles needs to be translated into what he most essentially is but never actually was and, as Hölderlin remarked in another letter six months later, this estrangement must be attempted "even if I should expose more boldly, up to (*gegen*) eccentric inspiration (*Begeisterung*), what is forbidden to the poet" (SW6: 439). Beißner notes that *gegen* here should be read as "towards" rather than "against," which thus implies a movement away from what is natural (for the Germans: clarity) into what is strange (passion), in order to recover what is natural (sobriety). Only by making the foreignness of Sophocles more foreign can an encounter with it enable modern tragedy to become modern. This unwraps the strange movement of *eccentricity*, which follows the rupture of the caesura by endlessly diverging from itself, leading to an ex-centric movement without return.

Before we proceed any further it will be wise to pause for a moment to take account of what has so far been said. Hölderlin's understanding of the tragic has arisen from his attempt to negotiate the problem of how the poet approaches nature and concomitantly, how man approaches the gods. As the structure of the tragic implies the impossibility of maintaining any such union Hölderlin moves, in the "Remarks on *Oedipus*," to make use of the caesura as a means of suspending the moment of this union, such that it can be re-presented in the *writing* of the tragedy. However, this maneuver does not go far enough, for the problems Hölderlin faces not only center on the writing of tragedy, but also on the writing of a modern tragedy.

Thus the problem of relating art and nature, and men and gods, must be layered with the further problems of relating modern and ancient, and German and Greek. Thus the problem of writing tragedy enters into the problem of translation, and if we anticipate briefly, this would suggest that the suspending action of the caesura, which enables the writing of the tragic to proceed, must somehow be developed to take account of the impossible relation of translation. In doing so the transport that normally occurs in translation, where Greek *becomes* German, or vice versa, is suspended by its rupture in writing, not to reveal one language or another, but rather the transport itself. It is by this suspension that the writing of a modern tragedy occurs, not so as to present the modern itself, but rather the endless passage toward it.

Within this passage is found the possibility of the modern as a repetition of what was never present in Sophocles, and such a repetition is only to be found by rupturing the normal practice of translation and following the "eccentric" path of what it has always concealed. This is signaled from the very beginning of Hölderlin's version of *Antigone* by a particular moment that has since been seen as symptomatic of the supposedly misguided nature of his translations in general. Ismene's second line in the play contains the phrase: "*delois gar ti kalchainous ethos,*" which in the standard English translation becomes "you sound so dark, so grim." Hölderlin's translation instead opts for "*du scheinst ein rothes Wort zu färben,*" which can be rendered as "you seem to dye your word red" (SW5: 206). The key word in the Greek, *kalchainous*, comes from *kalchaino*, meaning "to brood" or "to have dark thoughts," but it literally means "to make red."[16] As such it would seem that Hölderlin is simply holding to a very pedantic and word-for-word translation that takes each word at its most literal meaning. This was the response of contemporary scholars and even erstwhile friends like Schelling and Schiller, who ridiculed Hölderlin's translations for what they saw as crude, nonsensical, and possibly irrational readings that ultimately had no justification or fidelity to either Greek or German. But removing the metaphoric figuration from *kalchainous* was not an arbitrary or meaningless endeavor for Hölderlin, as it follows from the more general and rigorous model of translation that he was following. Unlike his contemporaries who felt that the goal of translation was either to modernize Classical texts or to antiquate modern language, by bringing the German to the Greek or vice versa, Hölderlin's aims were more complex and challenging.[17]

By understanding metaphor etymologically as a *meta pherein* or "carrying over," translation (*Übersetzung*) for Hölderlin becomes transport (*Übertragung*) or transition (*Übergang*), which is to say that the aim of translation is not so much the carrying over of meaning from one language to another, as the opening up of an awareness that such transport is the nature of language itself. As such, Hölderlin's readings of Sophocles draw on this constitutive nature of transport by treating both Greek and German as languages that are already engaged in translations of themselves. By turning eighteenth-century German back toward fifth-century BCE Greek, Hölderlin is not juxtaposing two static systems that require relation, but engaging the inner movements of each language out of themselves, their own transports, into a moment of encounter that does not reveal the transition of any particular meaning, as much as transition itself. By suspending the translation of *kalchainous* between its ordinary Greek or German versions he presents us with a moment of sheer transport; by refusing to accept its figuration, by dis-figuring it, Hölderlin empties the word of meaning and it emerges instead as a rupture. This is not a movement from Greek to German or vice versa, nor is it a movement from antiquity to modernity; rather its interruption opens up the movement of language as language; outside of meaning or history, it suspends the ordinary use of transport as relation in favor of the unconfigured, pure transport of the tragic itself.

The peculiar potency of Hölderlin's "red word" is that it presents this estrangement while remaining singular, for removing the figuration of *kalchainous* leaves its metaphoric transport empty; it no longer means "to brood"; it no longer means at all, in the sense of conveying understanding. Instead it is a simple mark, a word that does not signify, less a word than the disappearance of meaning as the deferral of transport. But in becoming insignificant, ineffective, the word does not disappear entirely for in doing so it indicates the general possibility of meaning, of transport as such, suspended in its conveyance so that it does not represent anything but simply presents itself. This is precisely what was at issue in the brief fragment on the significance of tragedy mentioned above, where nature could only appear through the transport of a sign that had become = 0. In rewriting Sophocles' word in this way nature has appeared as the emptiness of pure transport: Antigone's word is not red, but by interrupting the ordinary translation Hölderlin has released a language in which the word has become an image, as Blanchot (and Benjamin) would say, of its own appearance insofar as it presents nothing but the representation of itself, its own empty translation. As such an image, the word is poised between presence and absence, at the brink of disappearance, refusing configuration by the singularity of its rupture, and in doing so becoming the non-relation of a certain relation between Greek and German: the density of an impossibly singular word.[18]

This suspense of relation is doubled in the action of the play by the conflict between Creon and Antigone. Instead of Oedipus' confrontation with himself in the guise of fate, we have with Creon and Antigone a more balanced and thereby irresolvable conflict in which their opposition is constituted by each "weighing equally one against the other and different only in time" (SW5: 269/113). This intransigence is evidence of the caesura of modern tragedy in which the chiasmic relations of nature and art, men and gods, have been internally stretched, giving rise to an endless suspense rather than discovery.[19] This moment only comes about when both currents are brought to a point of simultaneous transgression and estrangement, and in this moment there is a move "from the Greek to the Hesperian" (SW5: 267/111).

This also indicates the significance of Hölderlin's placing of *Antigone* after *Oedipus Tyrannus*, for the role of the gods has changed in this transition. Zeus, in becoming "Father of Time," has become "a more proper Zeus" and this has converted "the striving out of this world into the other," which characterized the modernity of Oedipus, into the "striving out of another world into this," which characterizes the modernity of Antigone and thus also Hesperia (SW5: 268–69/112–13). This is the aim of Hölderlin's chiasmic encounter with Sophocles: for by confronting Sophocles' work with its own aorgic side, Hölderlin is able to realize his own organic side, which is not just the execution of his art, but the actualization of the fate of Hesperia. As the name indicates, Hesperia is the land of evening and so modernity must pass into darkness, like the silent passing of the dead that was mentioned in the letter to Böhlendorff, to become itself.

This point is easy to misread, for Hölderlin is not so much concerned with the historical reality of Sophocles and ancient Greece, as the confrontation of opposites, such as passion and sobriety, or nature and art, and the rigorous suspension of their resolution. That this is most fully realized in Hölderlin's translations is not so much a result of what they are translating, but of the extremity of foreignness that is engaged. Consequently, it would be wrong to read the transition from Greece to Hesperia too literally; there is no chronological progress being marked here, for the Greece and Hesperia that concern Hölderlin are simultaneously present as the matrix of our time. But it would also be wrong to read this as simply metaphorical, for the presence of these terms relies on the distinction of their temporal dimensions; the Greece that concerns Hölderlin is a very real historical presence. That is, ancient Greece is present now as the past, just as Hesperia is present as that into which we are heading. The importance of Hölderlin's translation lies in exactly this: that his holding together of Greece and Hesperia holds open the present moment in its transport. It is only by virtue of the way in which poetic language can suspend transition at the moment of its occurrence that we are able to be present in it.

In this moment Hölderlin's poetic and historical concerns converge in the literal reading he gives to metaphor as transition. The poetic word as metaphor makes this transition possible because in it is found both the dissolution of the old and the simultaneous emergence of the new. This process is detailed in an unfinished essay written after "The Ground of *Empedocles*" that has become known as "Becoming in Passing Away" ("Das Werden im Vergehen"). Here Hölderlin seeks to examine the nature of historical change by looking at the moment of transition from old to new that underlies the relation of nature and art, and man and the divine, for "in the very moment and degree in which existence dissolves, the newly-arriving, the youthful, the possible, also feels itself" (SW4: 282/96). The chiasmic translation developed in "The Ground of *Empedocles*" is here the very nature of temporality, for the actual point of crossing over, the metaphor of the present moment, requires the co-presence and exchange of both tendencies for it to appear.

What might appear as a dialectic between these opposing tendencies is undermined by the fact that their existence is not overcome through the emergence of the new moment. Instead, their presence is rigorously maintained in terms of balance and opposition by the "lawful calculation," which suspends the moment of becoming by ceaselessly interrupting it, turning it back onto itself and refiguring its chiasmic matrix so that it can persist. In this moment the writing of the poetic word is critical, for only it can reconfigure the dissolution of the old "as that which it properly is, as a reproductive act" (SW4: 284/97). It does so by reintroducing the moment to itself as a repetition, by prefiguring it as that which has already occurred and thus as that which has already been translated into something new, which is what Hölderlin's translations and rewritings of Sophocles set out to accomplish. This means that the new moment is engendered by being antedated, by its transition being marked as that which has already occurred, which is the only means by which it can occur. But in doing so the poetic word makes possible a moment that it can never encounter; the actual transition has always already occurred and the word can only mark this, even though doing so makes possible a further transition. This may cast some light on a remark in Hölderlin's "Remarks on *Antigone*," which says that the "Greek tragic word is deadly factive (*tödtlichfactisch*)," while that which holds now is only "perishingly factive (*tödtendfactisches*) . . . not properly ending with murder or death" (SW5: 269–70/113–14).[20] This would seem to imply a relation between words and their effectuation, which in *Oedipus Tyrannus* was somehow direct in a way that is no longer the case. It is this delay that marks the Hesperian word, which is always isolated from its effects, mediated.

. . . The Rhythm of *Dysmoron* . . .

The idea of the poetic word as an endless, differentiating repetition certainly has a consonance with Heidegger's approach, but as we have seen, for Hölderlin the experience of this repetition is unavoidable and tragic, as it exposes him to a "categorical turning" by which the historical and linguistic dimensions of his existence are radically destabilized. It is precisely this effect of Hölderlin's practice that Heidegger seems to have overlooked in his determination to gauge the being-historical destiny of Hölderlin's work as a whole. For this reason we must pay especial attention to the particularities of Hölderlin's practice in order to uncover the manner in which he experienced the rupture of the poetic word. This will enable us in chapter 5 to assess more clearly the differences that persist in their approaches when Heidegger comes to encounter this rupture in his later works on language. Although brief, the essays and notes that Hölderlin has left, alongside his translations and rewritings, provide an insight into the manner in which he approached the eccentric aporia of the word, and over the remaining pages of this chapter I will outline some of the main points of his writing practice.

Although we cannot know exactly why Hölderlin eventually gave up on his attempt to write a modern tragedy, his notes for the third version of the Empedocles drama indicate how far he had moved from a dialectical model, but also how his attempts become undermined by the difficulty of achieving the chiasmic balance necessary for the presentation of the tragic. It is perhaps because of this that the third version of the play is also abandoned despite its drastic revisions, and why Hölderlin turns to Sophocles instead, to write a modern tragedy by way of translation. The notes on Sophocles seem to indicate a return to Kant concomitant with this, in that the criticality of representation is the vehicle of realization, which is thus always an eccentric, and therefore deferred realization. But, such a criticality cannot be the basis for subjectivity, as it is marked by an endless internal scission such that the transport of this intellectual intuition carries the poet into an errancy without return. This leads to a union through separation, and completion through fragmentation; the ambition of Empedocles is still present but it is now stripped of any possibility of fulfillment.

It must be pointed out that Hölderlin is not seeking to define union as separation, nor is his writing designed as incomplete; rather its practice prevents it from being anything else. Writing itself is the source of Hölderlin's failure, which becomes implicitly thematized in his translations and rewritings, something he seems partially aware of, enough to recognize that what emerges through this failure is something in itself. This is the writing of nature as the movement of "the one differentiated in itself," the immeasurability or inordinacy of its coupling revealed through its divisions. This impossible definition of tragedy from the notes on *Oedipus Tyrannus* is revised in the translation to the Hesperian, inherent in the move to *Antigone*, where the corresponding remarks state that "The tragic presentation rests on this, that the immediate god, wholly one with man . . . that *infinite* inspiration, separating itself sacredly, grasps itself *infinitely*, that is to say in opposites, in consciousness that cancels consciousness" (SW5: 269/113). In separating, consciousness is able to grasp itself only infinitely, so that in attempting to reach itself it comes up against the impossibility of union and cancels itself out, which indicates the moment of the caesura as pure transport; the suspension of the foreign and the national.

The transition in Hölderlin's writings from Empedocles to Sophocles characterizes this change insofar as the failure of the Empedocles tragedy arises from the attempt to make a drama around the figure of an idea, that is, not a dramatic encounter, but the representation of an infinite ambition. There is no drama in the Empedocles tale for he has no antagonist; he is simply a figure of desire. In transferring to Sophocles this problem is remarked quite explicitly, as Hölderlin has turned from a tragic figure to a tragic writer. His concern can now become properly tragic, as he is no longer engaged with the idea of an infinite ambition, but the vicissitudes of translation and writing. In this he finds a tragic engagement with the material, which is dramatized *as* the writing of the tragedy. His notes on Sophocles demonstrate this by their attention to the structure and mechanics of a tragic representation, and their focus on the ramifications this has for the social practice of poetry and the political effects of the tragic. As he points out, the tragic is both empty in itself and that by which the tragedy is brought into dramatic equilibrium, that is, the antagonism is held in the moment of its opposition in order to present it as such, rather than trying to resolve it. Thus a fidelity to the tragic requires this excessive ambition: to present the unpresentable, which realizes itself not as the tragedy, but in its writing. The catharsis by which this hubris is emptied does not occur in the specular scene of tragedy, but by way of the endless rupture of its pure word.

As Benjamin has indicated, perhaps the most remarkable development in these essays is that of the "lawful calculation," whose implementation works precisely against that of the writer's poetic inspiration or passion.[21] The actualization of this law depends on bringing the "sobriety" that is most our own into the operation of the poet's language, and the form that Hölderlin gives to this is that of the caesura. The operation of the law brings about two simultaneous movements that echo those ascribed to the changes in Empedocles' character, for on the one hand it works to diminish the involvement of the poet's subjectivity, while on the other hand and in direct proportion to the other movement, it works to bring the object of the poet's work into writing. While this might initially refer to nature or the divine, what the caesura actually brings about are the conditions for the autonomy of writing, as the reduction in subjectivity implies the concomitant loss of the object toward which it was oriented and in its place writing emerges as a saying from itself or autology. For Hölderlin, the significance of this critical rupture has been obscured because "the main tendency in the modes of representation of our time is to hit upon something, to have a fate (*Geschik*), since fatelessness (*Schiksaallose*), *dysmoron*, is our weakness" (SW5: 270/113–14).

If *dysmoron*, "lack of measure (*moira*)," is our weakness it is because the theological and historical markers of our world have been removed. While it may be our nature to avoid this measurelessness by finding a fate, this will not bring us closer to ourselves, as the fate of sober wandering is what is most proper to us in the modern age, but as a result it is also what is most concealed from us. Poetry is able to bring us into measure with that which has no measure, the hidden or departed, through its caesura, which places the transport in equilibrium, even if that balance is always unstable and deferred. So, through "lawful calculation" Hölderlin hopes to be able to bring about the conditions not only of poetry, but also of modernity, for the combined action of this law works toward engaging the finitude that is writing's possibility. Hölderlin's key insight in this was to realize the importance of writing to any understanding of the nature of poetic language, but this point can only be grasped fully if we consider the singularity of Hölderlin's essays as writings *of* the caesura, for it is both by and for this rupturing that these writings develop.

But there is a fault in this turning, as the caesura brings the piece into a presentation of itself by placing its parts into equal weighting. But this cannot be done, for writing is always fragmentary and incomplete; thus any balance will be unbalanced by its dissymmetry and eccentricity. As a result the turning of writing, by which it attempts to find this balance by folding its prior and successive moments into itself, leaves it in fragments that are both finite and endless: a writing that is never the same as it is always differentiating, repeating, and deferring. At the beginning of the "Remarks on *Antigone*" Hölderlin compares the manner of poetry's operation to that of philosophy in exactly these terms, for "philosophy always treats only one faculty of the soul, so that the presentation of this one faculty makes a whole, and the mere hanging together of the parts of this one faculty is called logic." Instead of making the one into the whole by presenting it as logically combined, poetry works in the other direction by treating "different faculties of man, so that the presentation of these different faculties makes a whole, and the hanging together of the more autonomous parts of the different faculties can be called the rhythm, in a higher sense, or the calculable law" (SW5: 265/109). In maintaining the law of the caesura poetry finds a *rhythm* that preserves the difference of the parts in relation to the whole by treating them as autonomous fragments.

Thus, as Hölderlin indicates in this note from 1799, the poet's duty in following this rhythm is to interrupt the normal ordering of parts into wholes to achieve a greater balance of periods:

> One has inversions of words in the period. But greater and more effective then must be the inversion of the periods themselves. The logical position of periods, where the ground (the grounding period) is followed by becoming, becoming by the goal, the goal by the purpose, and where the subclauses are always only attached at the end of the main clauses to which they refer—is certainly only very seldom of use to the poet. (SW4: 233/45)

This inversion leads to the fragmentation of poetry, to an ellipsis of repeating, differentiating periods.[22] But how do we read such words? The answer might well be that we do not, that this radically finite writing cannot be read in the normal sense, as it is not involved in representation. Reading it does not tell us anything. Instead we have to suspect that the word simply presents itself, and that as a result, it is we who are read, in the sense that we are drawn into its endless finitude. This suggests that the language of the poetic word is translation, for by way of it we are translated, and what does it mean to be so translated but to be inscribed with finitude? It is as such that we become who we are, as this transcription exposes us to a finitude that is as elusive and unspeakable as it is ineradicable. For Hölderlin, this translation occurs *in* writing, when the caesura interrupts a poem with a "counter-rhythmic" movement that exposes it as a poem, and thereby exposes us by way of its finitude to a measureless and endless divergence. But the caesura itself does not appear, because as a rupture it only appears by way of the mark of its disappearance; it is not a figure as much as a disfiguring, which disfigures the appearance of the work by exposing it to an absencing. Thus the caesura cannot be marked, but can only be recalled as that which has occurred without appearing, thereby leaving a trace of absence, a re-(mark), which neither is nor is not, for it renders such a distinction impossible; rather it is indistinct, inapparent.

A poem is not involved in representation or imitation, but repetition as difference, and inasmuch as it ruptures presencing through its temporal and material punctuation it is the limitation that interrupts being. For Heidegger the poetic word is the turning in which presencing takes place, the site where the event of being occurs. This was once done through the power of the gods' names, which configured what is through their measuring power, or meter, but this capacity has now passed into the poetic word as the only place in which the trace of the gods remains. The poetic word would then be that which gives measure to our presence as it brings our presencing about. Although the caesura of a poem brings about its appearance it has no measure to give, for it is a rupture of ex-centric, measureless finitude and thus does not expose us *to* our presencing, but exposes us *from* any presencing into an endless prosaic absencing. Such words are the mark of an interruption that cannot be housed, or provide housing, for they evade any such maneuver, any work to which they might be put. These words bring change, but cannot be made to do so, for by them the poetic practice undoes itself, becoming workless, ineffective. As the term implies, the eccentric path of Hölderlin's writing is a writing without fixed course, without guiding lights, it is a disastrous writing. Hölderlin worked for years to write a modern tragedy; it is necessary that we continue to do so.

5

A Void

Writing and the Essence of Language

> But because the word is not grounded in the sounding of words, but rather as the wording, which rings as what it is only from the initially soundless word, then the words and arrangements of words in writing and in books can break up, while the word remains.
>
> —Heidegger, *Heraklit,* 1943

As this remark indicates, Heidegger's relation to the word is not straightforward; while it would seem on the surface to be directed away from the kind of close textual exploration that we have seen Hölderlin engaged in, a second reading suggests that for Heidegger the textual concerns of poetic writing must become refined such that their explorations are not just directed toward the details of the wording, but to what occurs in the text when the wording breaks down. Within this approach we find the entire basis of Heidegger's understanding of the word: the wording (*Wortlaut*) as we ordinarily see it is the result of the word's prior sounding (*Lauten*), such that the wording is the *sounded* word (*Wortlaut*); that which remains after its sounding.[1] But the initially soundless sounding from which the word itself rings is that which gives writing in the first place, and it is to this that Heidegger's attention is directed. In Hölderlin's work writing was a response to the demand of the tragic, the only response that could suspend its movement, and so the poet's relation to the word was the most serious but most difficult task to approach. In this chapter I will indicate how Heidegger's relation to the word develops through his understanding of the pain and finitude inherent to the essence of language, which will in many ways counter the weaknesses in his earlier reading of poetry but in doing so will also bring him up against the impossible demands that constituted Hölderlin's relation to the word. First, we need to return to "The Origin of the Work of Art," to a remark that indicates how closely Heidegger's own thoughts on tragedy set the stage for his inquiry into language, by outlining the problematic status of any language that attempts to speak its own essence.

Although tragedy never occupies a position of such significance for Heidegger as it does for Hölderlin, his remarks on it have attracted a considerable literature that has demonstrated the key role it plays in his inquiries into the essence of politics.[2] As my own inquiry is into Heidegger's changing understanding of the nature of language I will not pursue these major remarks, but turn to one more pertinent: "In tragedy nothing is staged or performed, rather the battle of the new gods against the old is being fought." At first this would seem to be a predictable aside, given Heidegger's concern with a polemical reading of art in this essay, but we need to read on: "In that the linguistic work arises from the speech of the people, it does not talk about this battle, rather it transforms the speech of the people, so that now every essential word fights this battle." The linguistic work is the tragedy itself, which is not *about* the battle between the old and new gods, but instead brings that battle to language by engaging every word in it. In light of what goes on throughout the rest of the essay it is worth lingering on this distinction between a language that stages and one that transforms, for Heidegger's own language in this essay is very much one that stages his thought; bringing it forth in images that demonstrate his ideas. But here in this aside we uncover the possibility and significance of a language that does something else, one that is able, by staging nothing, to change the nature of saying from performance into essence, from representation to presencing.

It is of considerable note that this point should follow a similar reversal in our understanding of religious sculpture. Here, a statue of the god "is not a portrait, so that it is easier for one to know how the god looks, but is a work that lets the god himself presence and thus *is* the god himself" (H: 29/22). If Heidegger is keen on turning our understanding of the language of tragedy away from a perspective that views it as representational, it is because he wants to turn us back to an understanding of language as presencing. This is to make the language of tragedy itself tragic, which is to move away from the common understanding of theater as display into an understanding in which it directly enacts that of which it speaks. This is to return tragedy to its ancient religious origins as something deeply disturbing, not theater as *mimēsis*, understood as simple imitation, but as the staging of nothing but itself: its presencing *as* language.

While the possibility of such a language necessarily follows from the direction of Heidegger's thinking it is another question entirely what status such a language might have. This is what makes Heidegger's later works so difficult to assess, for he is not so much thinking *about* being and language and the relation between them, as he is attempting to bring this relation to language itself. But this means that he is no longer engaged in philosophical reflection and so it would be a mistake to reinsert this work back into the discipline by asking *what* he is saying in these lectures. There is no content here that we can learn or ideas we can discuss; the role of these lectures is not to teach but to prompt; Heidegger's position as a thinker has changed such that his works now seek to pursue an experience, rather than an understanding. This exposes the singularity of the work, as there is no method or *technē* contained within these lectures that can be generalized into an understanding; instead they are concerned with bringing the relation of language to language such that it can speak from itself as itself. There is something of the religious or theatrical endeavor here, in that Heidegger is attempting to bring *us* into an experience with language.

If such is the project of Heidegger's later works we can see how far he has come from his early thoughts on logic and phenomenology. The compelling aspect of this development is how much Heidegger's later thoughts on language remain within a concern with the key problems of intuition and expression; how do we gain access to the world without reducing it and how we do bring it to language without objectifying it? The *logos* of phenomenology took Heidegger a long way toward answering these problems by allowing him to see how this *logos* was itself part of the movement of presencing as its self-explicating hermeneutics. By the 1930s Heidegger had begun to find these terms, *phenomenology* and *hermeneutics*, more of an obstacle than a guide, hence his move in "The Origin of the Work of Art" to a language of more common terms like *earth*, *world*, *rift*, and *event*. That Hölderlin was a constitutive part of this change in approach was confirmed at Heidegger's seminar in Le Thor in 1969, when Beaufret recalled that Gadamer had once said of Heidegger that it was Hölderlin who "had first loosened his tongue," to which Heidegger assented by saying that through Hölderlin he had learned "how useless it was to coin new words" and that the necessity for thinking lay instead "in turning back to the essential simplicity of language" (S: 351/51). For it is in simple words, which by themselves do not seem to speak but instead hold themselves back, that we find the relation of language itself coming to speech. It is out of this demand not to impose a form on language that Heidegger turns to the silent wording of language and to a concomitant approach of reticence and namelessness, of holding oneself back so that language can find its own way to speech; this "active silence (*Erschweigung*) is the 'logic' of philosophy" (BPE: 78/54).

In adopting this approach in which language is released into its own language, Heidegger is entering the area of the "enthused" that Socrates interrogated in Plato's *Ion*.[3] Enthusiasm refers to the experience of being inspired or possessed by the god, *en-theos*, and thus is the province of mystics and poets. For Ion such an experience is entirely singular, as it only arises when he hears or recites the poetry of Homer. What engages Socrates is the fact that although Ion recites and interprets the work of Homer, this process is rendered dubious by Ion's lack of knowledge. Because Ion is unable to explain the source or nature of his excitement, and lacks the knowledge of which he speaks, Socrates concludes that he has no knowledge and is simply "inspired." Enthusiasm becomes the mark of this inexplicable speech and thus the mark that differentiates such language from philosophy, which by its possession of a method or *technē* can be analyzed and learned and thus practiced as a general understanding. Poetry, as inspiration, lacks this *technē* and thus is irretrievably singular.[4] It is this distinction that has given us the history of philosophy but it holds a conflation. Firstly, there is the argument that poetry cannot designate its sources and is thus ignorant of its content, implying that its knowledge comes from divine inspiration, if not simple charlatanry. The second point is that this inability derives from a lack of method, the implication being that *technē* is the sign of true knowledge. This contains a circularity for it suggests both that *technē* is the indicator of truth, and that truth is only to be found through *technē*: truth is thus what is demonstrable. Poetry in lacking both *technē* and truth is thus doubly displaced by philosophy.

However, Ion does have a method of learning and reciting that he is fully aware of, but as this cannot be fully explained it is deemed unreliable. The enthused nature of his language does not exclude it from having a method, nor from being knowledge, but it does distinguish it from those types of knowledge that can be demonstrated through an analysis of their methods. This is because the knowledge of poetry is not contained *within* its language, such that one could say that poetry is about some state of affairs. Instead the knowledge *is* the language itself, which means that it can be learned or repeated but it cannot be generalized into the object of analysis. This recalls Heidegger's earlier understanding of *logos*, for the enthused nature of poetry means that it is not just a form of *praxis*, since part of its enthusiasm is the loss of any agentive capacity on the part of the poet; when he is reciting Ion is *ekphron*, outside of *phronēsis*. Thus the poet does not "do" (*praxein*) poetry, anymore than he "makes" (*poiēin*) it; poetry happens *to* the poet *as* language, which would suggest that if it is anything then poetry is an "affectedness" (*pathos*, or *Befindlichkeit*, "disposition").[5] But as a result, there is a need for a sobriety, as Hölderlin called it, in our response to this *pathos*; inspiration needs to be balanced by care: it is no accident that Ion is described as *ekphron*, as it is precisely "out of" his capacity of *phronēsis* that poetry draws him, and by which he must thereby respond.

Despite his interests in poetry and mysticism Heidegger was neither a poet nor a mystic; however this did not prevent him from entering into the singular experience of language by way of his thinking. When he was asked by a student to explain where his thinking got its "directive," Heidegger conceded that he could "provide no credentials" for what he had said "that would permit a convenient check in each case whether what I say agrees with 'reality.'" But despite this, his thinking does have a way, as he goes on to point out, for it follows "the path of a responding that examines as it listens." While he admits that this path could lead astray, following it thus "takes practice" and practice "needs craft" (VA2: 58–59/186). That there is a precise development to this craft is apparent from the fact that it supports a "thinking experience that is reconstructable (*nachvollziehbarer*)" (US: 200/104). But the presence of repetition does not necessarily imply objectivity, which was Socrates' concern, for despite Ion's evident facility the effects of his poetry could not be isolated and determined. So although there is a craft to Heidegger's thinking, it cannot, like Ion's recitations, be brought to account against any supposedly external criteria. As he often remarked, there is no "Heideggerian philosophy," instead his later works indicate a way of thinking that can be repeated but not represented.[6] This is not to say that he is enthused in the manner of the poet or mystic, for it is not the divine that speaks in Heidegger, but rather an attempt to allow language itself to speak.

However, the issue at stake is not the accountability of speech, for it is not the case that Socrates' words have any greater evidence behind them; the issue is rather: how are we to respond to a language that speaks with the voice of the muses, or in Heidegger's case, with the speech of language itself? The argument that Socrates raises against Ion can be seen to be a way of avoiding this difficulty by only concerning itself with Ion's lack of knowledge, but as Heidegger insists, that of which he speaks is that which addresses "the innermost nexus of our existence," and thus cannot be so easily avoided for it calls to us to respond in our being (US: 149/57). Thus how Heidegger responds will be of concern, for language draws us into a tragic experience, since to have a language that speaks without becoming present, in that it does not manifest any apparent meaning, is to have a language that speaks nothing. This is why it is so disturbing and why its sources are adduced as being divine or mysterious, for it brings us up against a limit of meaning: that which speaks and yet says nothing is both inescapably concrete and incomprehensible. Language as such, if that is what this speech is, is the end of our being, our inability. If this is what also forms the innermost nexus of our being, then we are faced in language with the existence of our own emptiness and finitude, a material and temporal limit that indicates our mortality. The *fact* of language is tragic and this is what Heidegger is attempting to negotiate in his lectures on language, for in this fact we find being, in the turning of language at its limits.

. . . BEARING OUT . . .

It is with this fact in mind that we should approach Heidegger's reading of poeticizing (*Dichten*) as renunciation (*Verzicht*) in his writings on Stefan George. Meditating at length on the final stanza of George's poem "The Word," which reads, "So I renounced and sadly see: / Where word breaks off no thing may be," his concern is not only with the use of renunciation or with the results its interruption brings about, but also with the physical, textual basis of this rupture: that of the colon that separates and joins, *cleaves,* the two lines. In doing so, Heidegger comes close to saying that this colon is itself the mark of the draw-ing (*Riß*) of language, of the language *of* language, which only arises where words break off (US: 189/94, 210/142). What occurs here "is" not, for language is not a thing that *is,* as Heidegger noted in 1945, the relation of words and being "can be thought of neither as ontic nor as ontological."[7]

That this renunciation is not a negativity, but the utmost affirmation of language, arises from the fact that it occurs when we give ourselves to the withdrawal that takes place within the appearance of words. And in doing so, we are not only entering into the very movement of language but also into that which enables us to be, such that there arises in this withdrawal the "essential relation between death and language" (US: 203/107). For within this withdrawal we come up against "the sound of language rising like the earth," its physical, textual resistance to appearance, the rupture that is found when language turns back on itself (US: 196/101). The colon indicates this withdrawal with a mark of closure and opening that interrupts language, creating a pause or caesura (which Hölderlin called "the pure word," that is, a word that is only word and is thus intrinsically unstable, acting less as a word than as a mark of wording), but in doing so it also projects beyond this limit into what lies beyond, without indicating *what* lies beyond. We see nothing with it and cannot put it into words; its pause is a bodily, textual halting.

It is worth pausing here to explore the implications of this point, that the rupture of language is physical, for Heidegger is often accused of neglecting the material dimension of language, although his later works consistently refer to the "pain" that is intrinsic to language. This should not, he insists, be imagined "anthropologically as a sensation that makes us feel afflicted," but instead refers to both the material resistance of language, which was earlier called the "earth," and its differentiations by which separation occurs, which has been discussed as the "draw-ing" (US: 24–25/205). The peculiar property of the draw-ing, which both separates and unites, leads Heidegger to term it the "dif-ference" (*Unter-Schied*) in his 1950 lecture "Language," given significantly in memory of Max Kommerell (US: 22/202). Albert Hofstadter's translation of this term as "difference" is adequate insofar as it registers the breaking of the term *Unterschied*, meaning "difference," but fails to indicate what has been exposed by this breakage.

As Heidegger makes clear, the specificity of *Unter* and *Schied* are at issue here, *Unter* meaning "between" or "below" and *Schied* referring to a "cut." That these two terms combine in "difference" is what Heidegger is drawing out and as his concern is to defamiliarize this word by indicating its hidden workings it is possible to suggest a parallel translation as "intercision." Doing so brings out the ambiguous nature of this difference as that which is both a cut into and a cut between, hence the oscillation between "incision" and "intersection." This point is particularly focused in a key passage from "The Essence of Language" where the neighborhood of poeticizing and thinking arises out of just such a paradoxical cut. Equally, the inter-cision as differentiation carries this word into the proximity of the "between" (*Zwischen*) and the "decision" (*Entscheidung*) of being, as well as the lineage of complexity found in the "draw-ing."

In its separation, the dif-ference leads into differentiation, that is, it draws each being into its own, but as that which leads beings into their being it is outside both, as Heidegger remarks in a footnote added to "The Anaximander Fragment": "The dif-ference is infinitely different from all being, which remains being *of* beings. It is therefore inappropriate any longer to designate the difference with 'being'—whether it is with an 'i' or with a 'y'" (H: 364/275). Thus dif-ference seems to resist naming or discussion (in the sense of *Erörterung*), as Heidegger's variety of names for it makes apparent and furthermore, it seems to undermine or escape the unity of being that lies outside its names, for the dif-ference "is" *only as* its instability and dissembling, it has no underlying ground. This suffering of language disturbs the confidence of Heidegger's earlier position regarding the naming power of words and leads to an awareness that if language persists through this dif-ference then it does so by way of its suffering, that is, *through its pain.*

This persistence only occurs insofar as pain can "settle" or "bear" (*Austrag*) the between of the dif-ference, its threshold, thereby enabling it to persist as it is. This does not mean that pain fixes or hardens the dif-ference into stasis; rather the dif-ference persists because "pain essences enduringly in the threshold as pain." As I will discuss in the next section, the references that Heidegger makes to "pain" in the 1950s seem to suggest a rethinking of *pathos*, but for the moment I want to focus on the dense etymological play that Heidegger is making here, for the verb *austragen* literally means "to carry or bear out," which brings it into relation to the Latin verbs *portare* (to carry) and *ferre* (to bear). These terms are to be found in such significant words as transport, support, rapport, deport, defer, transfer, differ, offer, and suffer, as well as fertile, which also leads to the Greek root *pherein* (to bear) that we find in *meta-pherein* or metaphor. The bearing or carrying out that pain accomplishes provides language with a supporting transport that both transfers and differs; it carries out and carries apart, and bears up and bears out. This etymological paronomasia is being deliberately used to open up the way in which we listen to language, such that we can hear beyond its terms into its own inner transport, its differing *as* language. Thus while *Austrag* comes to mean something very close to difference and metaphor, and transference and diaphora, this does not mean that we should focus on any one of these words, but on their transport as the dissembling of language, its passion or *pathos*, its endless patient suffering in which pain does not simply join the draw-ing, but "is the dif-ference itself" (US: 24/204).

To understand what this means we need to realize that if the dif-ference settles or "stills" each thing into itself, in such a way that it "is always more in motion than all motion and always more restlessly active than any agitation," and if the speech of language is the "peal" (*Geläut*) of this "stillness," of the dif-ference itself, then this peal "is not anything human" (US: 26–27/206–7). Consequently, we have to be aware of the fact that in our response to language, any "uttering (*Verlauten*), whether in speech or writing, breaks the stillness," but this breakage *is* our response for as breakage it is an echo of the dif-ference; pain calls to pain as the only thing that can respond to it, as the only means of its persistence (US: 28/208). This chain of repetition recalls Socrates' model of enthusiasm as a sequence of magnetic affects that hold together muse, poet, rhapsode, and audience (and himself, and Plato, and us, etc.) in a mutually supporting and inspiring suspension. The secret of this echoing lies in its silence, which allows the repetition of affect to be made while keeping it in reserve, enabling language to presence within words *as* reserved, *as* this silent echoing. Thus the breaking of stillness brought about by human utterance is prefigured in this echoing that is the splitting and joining of language itself.[8]

This mode of presentation is given an exemplary demonstration in the opening pages of this essay, where the manner in which Heidegger repeatedly disrupts the phrase "language speaks" (*die Sprache spricht*) brings us to a point of hearing something new and concealed. Nothing occurs in the repetition of this phrase or its companion, "language is language," but there is nevertheless a dislocation of presence; an absence that makes itself present as absent. In doing so, Heidegger does not reveal language, but suspends us over the abyss of its withdrawal and thereby brings us up against its limits (US: 10–11/190–91). If human being takes place out of the speaking of language, it is insofar as humans are called into what is most their own, their mortality, by language (US: 27–28/208). The speech of language, in its pain and rupturing, exposes humans to their mortality. In this speaking, pain is that which remains, that which persists in reserve as that which cannot be spoken, that which repeats and withdraws, that which denies itself to the poet as the limit of language, whose impossibility is thereby present as an endless dying, a "wandering toward death" (US: 20/200). Our own speech rests in this relation to the speech of language, but this relation requires reserve so that our responses can be attuned to its resonance, as well as to anticipate its repetitions.

Such speaking is found in poeticizing when it takes its measure *from* language, such that man is "bespoken" (*Versprechen*) by it, but language itself as the dif-ference is without measure or relation, which means that poeticizing can only have a "strange" measure, one without a metric (US: 12/192; VA2: 72/223). To write poetry is thus to take a measure from the unknown *as* the unknown, to stay with the strangeness of the measure by finding that which persists and remains as unknown. If we recall Hölderlin's own thoughts on meter and the dual role of the caesura as both rupture and equilibrium, then the combination of incompatible tendencies into a chiasmic transport will only attain balance through rupture and thus will only persist in eccentricity. Hence, as a strange measure it is from the unknown but never of the unknown, which *as* unknown is always in withdrawal, distending and distorting the possibility of measure.

As a result, poeticizing as measuring opens up the relation between gods and mortals, and earth and world, but in doing so it takes a measure from that which is without measure. That is, poeticizing opens itself onto, and steps aside in favor of, the absence of the gods and the impossibility of death, the darkness of the earth and the dissembling of the world.[9] As we will shortly see, this poeticizing no longer nominates beings into the clearing as figures of truth, but empties itself into language; it is not work, not *poiēsis,* but "releasement" (*Gelassenheit*), the *pathos* of listening in "apartness" (*Abgeschiedenheit*), to which the work in its own way must try and respond for it "is" only as a saying-after, "*Dichten heißt: nach-sagen*" (US: 66–67/188).[10] The word of such poeticizing is essentially ambiguous, in that it speaks both to that which it opens onto, and to that which it leaves behind, and so the word is a departure both in the sense of a leaving and a journeying, caesura and metaphora, ex-perience (US: 70/191–92).

. . . THE PAIN OF LANGUAGE . . .

The word that Heidegger gives to the relation that being has to the human is *Brauch*—meaning both "need" and "use," indicating that being both needs and uses the human to be—and the mode within which this usage occurs is language. This is to say that it is by way of language that being needs and uses the human and thus by way of language that being comes to be. In this one word we find the most demanding and ambivalent aspect of Heidegger's thinking of language, for if being needs and uses, *enjoins*, humans in order to be, and if it is by way of language that this relation is conducted, then there is a deep dissymmetry in this relation that exerts an extreme pressure on the very possibility of gathering it together in any kind of relation. For as we have seen, the human relation of language is borne by finitude such that any attempt to respond to it will only encounter the extremes of rupture. In this section I will examine the development of *Brauch* with a view to highlighting the implications of this aporetic pressure, for it brings out a long-running difficulty in Heidegger's thinking of how we are to approach the ground, origin, or essence when it withdraws and occludes itself and occurs only as such. This will lead to the question of how this aporia resounds within the essence of language, and thus how we are to think and write of it when it seems to occur as a *traumatic* recurrence, a trace of darkness that cannot be recalled, but that also cannot be forgotten as it is that which constitutes the duplicity of the need and use of language.

By examining how this darkness occurs it is possible to suggest that the *Brauch* of language is the manner in which finitude *gives itself*, for in its ambivalence *Brauch* indicates how the darkness in the essence of language is the source of both its appropriation *of* the human and its expropriation *from* the human. It is this ambivalence that is at work in the conjunction of *Brauch* with *Ereignis*, *Geschick*, *Austrag*, and *Geviert*, which structures Heidegger's later understanding of the relation of language and the human, but while this opens up the manner in which the human bears out the measuring and sending of being in the opening of language, what has not been recognized is the manner in which language expropriates itself, which leads to a caesura of memory and thinking in our attempts to respond to this *Brauch*. Thus any attempt to approach the essence of language must proceed from this point, and in doing so we not only come to see what Heidegger's thought on this point entails, but also how the reading of this darkness exposes a *writing* in which the human relation of language exists, since language writes in finitude.

Thus the difficulties inherent in Heidegger's later thinking of language lie not only with the performative dimension of his work by which he seeks to bring the essence of language to language, but also with the very relation of thinking to language that seeks to accomplish this presencing, for the task is one of attempting to counter the oblivion of thinking that is in some way constitutive of our time. Thus this is a question of history as well as language, and more significantly a question of the response to oblivion, and whether such a thing is even possible given

Heidegger's position on the oblivion of oblivion. What I want to raise here are the demands that the finitude of language places on thinking and the responses Heidegger makes to this, for I feel that there is a pause between language and thinking that can neither be recovered nor removed, but that recurs and punctures our attempts to respond.

The essay entitled "Der Spruch des Anaximander" is taken from a longer work composed during Heidegger's postwar isolation following his enforced retirement from teaching at Freiburg University, and it develops an extremely close and detailed reading of a fragment (*Spruch*) from the very dawn of Western thinking. Anaximander's saying (*Spruch*) was the subject of Heidegger's thinking five years earlier but at that point the issue of *Brauch* had not achieved its later significance; thus when its discussion emerges in the last pages of the Anaximander paper it signals a major new development in his thinking. His aim in reading this fragment is not to demonstrate that it conceals some archaic originality but rather to expose the manner in which the development of Western thinking arises out of its changing relation to its languages. Thus to think through the human relation of language is primarily to think *through* translation, and as such find a way to respond to the immense demands that the history of our language tacitly places on us. Language needs and uses our thinking and so it is only by way of our thinking that this *Brauch* can itself be brought to language, and in doing so it brings about a particular historico-linguistic reading; a translation of thought into the time *of* language, a time that as we shall see carries its own endlessly unanswerable demand. Consequently, Heidegger spends much of the early part of the paper discussing the being-historical provenance of the saying as a fragment from the very beginning of Western thinking, and the resulting philosophical and philological difficulties faced by its translation, and concludes by following the now current tradition of treating only the last two clauses cited by Theophrastus as being Anaximander's actual words, of which he then proceeds to examine the last first.

> . . . *kata to chreon; didonai gar auta diken kai tisin allelois tes adikias.*
> (. . . according to necessity; for they pay one another punishment and penalty for their injustice.)

After deliberating on the essence and relation of *dikē* ("order," *Fug*) and *adikia* ("dis-order," *Un-Fug*) as what he calls the "jointure" (*Fuge*) of the transition of being, its passage between the finitudes of beginning and ending in which beings "while" or "linger" (*weilen*), Heidegger states that this clause thereby "names what presences in the manner of its presencing." In doing so he can then return to the fragmentary first clause, which therefore "must name presencing itself" if it is to precede the second clause, insofar as the second clause, in detailing what presences and the manner of its presencing, must refer back to presencing itself. But this first clause is more difficult to explicate as it consists of only three words: *kata to chreon*, which, as Heidegger notes, is ordinarily translated as "according to necessity" (H: 362/273). The first word presents no problems, for *kata* simply designates a movement of falling in which what follows is as a result of a descent or a decline. This fulfills Heidegger's contention that what the second clause explicates comes as a consequence of what is designated in the first; thus the remaining words must indicate the nature of presencing itself: "*to chreon* is the oldest name in which thinking brings the being of beings to language."

This is quite a claim, but Heidegger unravels it somewhat by explaining that *chreon* must be understood in relation to what is described in the second clause by *dikē* and *adikia*, such that *chreon* "disposes" (*verfügt*) matters in such a way that order and dis-order *can* belong together as the whiling of the jointure of being (H: 363/274). But this does not elucidate *to chreon* in itself, and furthermore, this understanding is made more difficult and more significant by the manner in which Heidegger has read the saying, since by claiming that the first clause designates the nature of presencing while the second names what presences he has indirectly exposed the ontological difference in the pause between the clauses. So the difficulty of understanding *to chreon* is doubled in that it is also marked with the oblivion that covers our forgetting of being and the ontological difference. Thus, the *kata* that opens the saying itself marks the fall that has been the destiny of being since Anaximander; this fragment *announces* the history of being with its *kata*, and it is thus that it stands at the dawn of Western thinking for Heidegger, as this fall is "the event (*Ereignis*) of metaphysics." What is forgotten cannot be recalled as it is of the essence of presencing to fall into concealment, but the oblivion in which this forgetting has itself been lost can be lifted once we understand how it has "imprinted" (*geprägt*) a trace of itself, "which remains preserved in the language to which being comes," which is the very language in which we find the oldest name for the being of beings.[11]

Heidegger is not hereby implying that ancient Greek is the only language in which this trace of being remains, but is rather calling our attention to the nature and status of the thinking transition that is constitutive of translation for him. In this transition we do not simply step back into the language of the ancients, but into the coming to language of being, which is thus also the coming to be of language; the very stepping forth of the presencing of language that in doing so indicates the nature of presencing itself. This is the nature of the mark imprinted on language, the trace indicated in the transition between the two clauses, the pause that is the *differing* of the presencing of language into presencing and what is present, "in such a way, indeed, that presencing comes to word *as this relation.*" This is what is named by *to chreon*, which Heidegger calls the "early word of being," and now that we have situated this word ontologically we can ask after its meaning (H: 365/275). Heidegger begins by placing *chreon* next to *cheir*, "the hand," and *chrao*, "to deliver," suggesting that in such a delivery what is transferred is kept in hand, along with the transfer itself. In this, *to chreon* would indicate that which delivers and preserves presencing by its manner of handing it over and keeping it held in this handing over, and in order to maintain the unique nature of being's word Heidegger offers a translation that is equally strange: *Brauch* (H: 366/276).

In explaining this choice Heidegger directs us to the root of *Brauch* in *bruchen* ("to brook," in the sense of "to enjoy the use of"), which is related to *fruchten* (to bear fruit), thereby suggesting an understanding of use grounded in joy, in which our taking joy in something lets it come to presence as such (H: 367/277). As a result, *Brauch* ("usage," but perhaps more helpfully, "enjoinment," if we emphasize the silent "joy" in "joining" that also "enjoins," that is, claims and directs us) refers to "the way in which being itself essences as the relationship to what is present"; it is that which hands over what is present to its presencing, in the whiling of its jointure. That is, enjoinment is what disposes the passage between the finitudes of our existence and is thus itself "that which is without limits" (*to apeiron*). Enjoinment is not something that is present but destines what is *as* present, which means that it links its whiling to its decline, in which its jointure is surmounted by oblivion (H: 368/277–78). So, although the translation of *to chreon* by enjoinment has arisen from a prior translation of thinking into the destining of being, this unique transition carries with it the inescapable decline in which such traces of thinking are themselves lost, thereby laying the burden on us to persist in our attempts to deliver language into its presencing once more.

It is this demand and difficulty that underlies Heidegger's understanding of enjoinment as the relation *of* language, for if it is the case that being needs and uses, enjoins and enjoys, the human to be, then it is by way of this enjoinment that the human itself comes to be, and if it is the relation *of* language that delivers and bears this enjoinment, then the double genitive itself indicates this reciprocal determination, for in the relation of language to the human the relation that belongs to language itself takes place, and it is by way of this coming to be of language that being occurs. Language then becomes the privileged site in which the being of the human is possible, and by virtue of this the possibility of being as well, but this possibility carries with it its own decline, which is thus the exigency that language bears to us as the condition of human being.

It is from this point that Heidegger can then articulate the responsibility of thinking in the face of the demand of language, and he does so in his letter to Beaufret that followed the Anaximander essay: "Thinking accomplishes (*vollbringt*) the relation of being to the essence of the human being. It does not make or cause this relation. Thinking brings this relation to being solely as something handed over to thought itself from being. Such offering consists in the fact that in thinking being comes to language" (W: 145/239). This bold claim is the basis for the essential step from poetry to thinking that figures Heidegger's later works, since in such thinking language is itself released into its essence from out of the grip of "logic" and "grammar," and thinking is thereby appropriated to being, such that thinking comes to belong to its essence insofar as it comes to hear being in *its* coming to language; thus language itself becomes "the clearing-concealing advent of being" (W: 146/240, 158/249). If being is as this relation to our own existence in which it enters into its essence and also conceals itself, then it is coextensive with our existence while remaining hidden, it is this "nearness" that then comes to be as language (W: 164/253).

As a result, it becomes apparent that the human is essential to the truth of being, which thereby raises the question of ethics, of how we are to be if we are to bring this truth to language (W: 176/263, 183/268). In that ethics inquires into the abode (*ethos*) of the human and that language has been indicated as this abode, the proper direction for an ethics is to examine the limits of language inasmuch as it is here that the relation of language itself comes to presence, thereby articulating the ethical demand of the human more clearly (W: 187/271). In this way, Heidegger moves outside ontology or ethics as such and isolates the task of thinking as the thinking of language, which is for him neither a theory nor a practice but a *recollection* (*Andenken*) of being in which it has no result or effect, but instead simply occurs as "saying" (*Sagen*) (W: 188/272). It is only by understanding the nature of this saying that we can come to understand our dwelling in the world, our *ethos*, for such saying, by thinking out of the limits of language, provides the *measure* of existence, in that it recalls us to our provenance in finitude. Thus, this recollective thinking "in its saying merely brings the unspoken word of being to language" (W: 192/274).

The exact nature of this unspoken word and the difficulties of finding its measure are given extensive thought in the following years and develops into what Heidegger calls the *Geviert*. The four points of this dwelling are the limits indicated by the earth and the gods, and the sky and the mortals. However, the measuring out of our dwelling is achieved only insofar as a space is drawn out between the finitudes of our existence, and thus if our existence spans this draw-ing then it is, as Hölderlin remarked in discussing the temporality of modernity, "measured (*gezählt*, that is, counted, reckoned) in suffering" (SW5: 268/112). Because we can only find our dwelling by taking a measure from a finitude that is without measure (*to apeiron*) we are condemned to dwell in a relation of suffering, and it is this that starts to put Heidegger's thinking of language under pressure. In recognition of this dilemma he turns to an examination of pain, as I have mentioned, as something approaching a *pathos* of thinking.

In "The Turning," delivered in the "Insight" lectures of 1949, Heidegger discussed the difference between "overcoming" (*überwunden*) and "recovering" (*verwunden*) by saying that the latter "is similar to what happens when in the human realm one recovers from a pain," for in doing so what is thus "recovered" is passed over "in a way that restores it into its yet concealed truth," whereas when something is "overcome" it is simply lost, destroyed, or left behind.[12] For Heidegger this distinction is a necessary part of the turning needed in our historical relation to technology, as it enables us to come to terms with the essence of technology as that which is part of our own essence. But to compare this process with that by which "one recovers from a pain" suggests an other possibility, in the guise of what remains impossible to recover because of its *traumatic* nature, but that instead provokes a repeated marking of its absence, an inability to turn away from its endless limitation. This is the underside of translation that subtends its particular readings and instead takes place as an endless pressure on our thinking of language in the face of its unanswerable demand.

However, this understanding is outside Heidegger's reading, for as he states in his study of Trakl's poetry, where pain is precisely that which appears as "infinite torment": "This does not mean unending agony. The infinite is devoid of all finite restriction and stuntedness. The 'infinite torment' is consummate, perfect pain, pain that comes to the fullness of its essence" (US: 68/189). This emphasis on consummation repeats the earlier analysis in the 1950 lecture that pain is that which endures by virtue of its persistent presencing, but the significant point in 1952 is pain's "converse essence" by which it achieves its consummation. This converse essence of pain is its draw-ing, which "as the backward-tearing (*zurückreißender*) draw-ing first properly tears onwards (*fortreißt*)," for it "is that backdraft (*Rückriß*) in pain by which it reaches its mildness and its disclosing-conveying power," and that thereby reveals its "essential simplicity" (US: 60/183, 58/181). Obscure as this may be, Heidegger seems to be suggesting that pain is a figure for the double-sided movement of presencing *in* its simplicity (much as he had in the 1950 lecture by saying that pain is the draw-ing *and* the dif-ference), that is, as a onefold, rather than a duplicity, it is the *ge-* of the *Sprachgebrauch*, that which holds together the human relation of language in its need and use.

This will then enable him to say later, in much more brief remarks, that pain is "that which gathers most intimately," as it is the "gravity" (*Schwergewicht*) of the soul that enables mortals to "rest in their essence" (W: 232/306; US: 222/153). As Heidegger points out, pain marks the between of the dif-ference, the interval that is the center of the relation measured out in the *Geviert*, the infinite hollowing out of our finitude (US: 22/202). But in this reading the possibility of an unrecoverable pain, which would arise out of the very endlessness of the *Brauch* of language, has been skirted around, and furthermore, by its insistent marking of this abyssal demand pain betrays itself as *writing*. Thus the thinking of language comes up against an aporia in the alterity and finitude of pain, the recurrent silence of trauma, which it is thinking's task to recover and poetry's to measure, but that can only be accomplished by way of our own expropriation into the limitlessness of an immense measure. If this is what is indicated in the turning of thinking to language, then where are we bound, unless this is a leap away from saying into its renunciation?

The tone within which these themes are worked out needs to be emphasized for in "The Anaximander Fragment" the relation of language is discussed out of a meditation on eschatology and the never-ending passage into the evening that characterizes Western thinking. While this recalls Heidegger's long studies of Nietzsche and nihilism, it has to be placed alongside the reading of Hölderlin that prefaces the other major work of 1946: Heidegger's inquiry into whether Rilke is a poet for and of our needy (*dürftiger*) times. It is Hölderlin's elegy "Bread and Wine" that asks the question of what poets are for in such time and it is no accident that it is the same work that Trakl cites in his "A Winter Evening," which is the focus of Heidegger's discussion of language in 1950. It is during this time that Heidegger is engaged in developing an understanding of dwelling to counteract the nihilistic influence of technology, and it is to Hölderlin that he turns again in his 1951 paper ". . . poetically man dwells . . ." to understand how the quartering of existence by finitude is measured out in the poetic word. This in turn comes before his reading of Trakl on the "undergoing" (*untergehen*) of the human *Geschlecht.*

What I wish to suggest by bringing out these conjunctions is that there appears to be a tacit rereading of Hölderlin's notes on tragedy here, in that it is a question of drawing out the sober measure of our age, of finding the word from which the poets, who would be for and of our time, would speak, and coming to a free usage of this word. But why is it that philosophy turns to literature when it reaches the limits of its language? Or, more pointedly, what is it about the limits of language that seems to activate a *literary* response? And how does this relate to trauma, insofar as it is precisely the traumatic that does not permit language, and yet, there is literature, at the edge of language . . . what is this presence of literature?

. . . INTO THE SPACE OF RENUNCIATION . . .

Heidegger's turn to the language of poetry in the 1930s arose from a need to find a means of approaching that which phenomenology obscured. "The Origin of the Work of Art" announced this development by introducing poetry as a movement of naming and saying that repeated the movement of being in a manner that was originary, that is, it repeated it for the first time and so let it be. At that point Heidegger was only engaged in sketching out the possibility of such a language, which was exemplified for him in the poetry of Hölderlin and in the fragments of the Presocratics. However, the relation of this poetic language to thinking entailed that it could not remain as just an outline; language itself had to be thought, which meant bringing thought into the fabric of its movements. This step was needed otherwise thought would find itself in the same relation to language as it had to poetry: describing it rather than following it into its own movements. For thought to enter into a relation to language meant that thought should take on those dimensions of language that had become apparent in Heidegger's work thus far. These dimensions are still largely phenomenological, as has been outlined, for they are based in the finitude of appearance, in that the language of poetry has indicated a movement in which language brings itself to language by way of its own staging and pain. While these dimensions indicate the tragic nature of language, we will need to see how far Heidegger is able to pursue its *written* basis.

Beginning exactly twenty-one years after the lectures on "The Origin of the Work of Art" finished, Heidegger's mature views on language are presented in "The Essence (*Wesen*) of Language," the first two parts of which were delivered in December 1957 and the third some seven weeks later in February 1958.[13] Coming during a period of intense revision of his earlier work, in which extensive notes were added to "The Origin of the Work of Art" and, following his work on Paul Klee, a second part to that essay was being considered, these lectures on language seem both structurally and thematically to be a restaging of the earlier lectures, and are thus a possible candidate for their missing final part. The displacement that has occurred in Heidegger's work over the years is announced by the changes in the title, in which the matter of his thought has moved from the work of art to language. This directly takes up what had remained unfinished at the end of the earlier lectures, and that Heidegger had revisited in the addendum that was added to them in 1956. Writing about his reservations, Heidegger had concluded that the "questionableness (*Fragwürdigkeit*) that prevails here gathers itself at the proper place of the discussion, where the essence of language and poetry is touched upon" (H: 74/56).

The problem of language had raised itself because although it was the basis of what was addressed in the work of art, it could not be understood from within a thematics of "work," so in making this transition from art to language the other terms of the title are also placed in doubt. Consequently, we find the most substantive shift in the move away from a discussion of origins into one of essence, for language *as* the origin of the work of art proved to be an impossible origin, since its repetition undermined any possibility of origination outside its iteration. This prompts the more basic discussion of essence, as well as signaling the problematic relation that language as iteration has to origins. Moreover, since his work of the 1930s, essence has been understood by Heidegger as a verb, such that an essence is that which *essences*, much as the work of art became an understanding of the way in which art *works*, so the essence of language concerns the manner of its essencing.

These transformations in Heidegger's titles are not simply an interesting aside, for they indicate what he is attempting to expose within the lectures themselves. Throughout the three lectures on language Heidegger uses his title as a "guideword" by returning to it at key points to reconfigure its terms, its limits, and thereby expose something of the essence of language itself. To be exposed to language as such is Heidegger's aim in these lectures, which follows from the physical and dramatic staging that has developed within his thought as its necessary mode. The title reveals these theatrical and bodily elements by making us the witnesses and accomplices to a manifestation, to an experience of language. What Heidegger is attempting here is not a display of thinking in the representational sense of theater, but an exposure to that to which we are engaged, in the ancient sense of theater as an audience in which we are involved with the mystery. While this is possibly transformative it is more immediately painful and disturbing; its presentation is a rupture from which we are tempted to turn away unless we realize that this rupture *is* what we are being presented with, for it is the appearance of language itself, which is nothing but its own appearance. In attempting to think the essence of language it is necessary to enter into a relation with this void, not to fill it or cover it over, but to hold it open by restaging it, for in this relation is language.

Responding to such a language is not easy, but is essential to our understanding of it as we cannot approach such a language without also responding to it, and finding a way of responding is what Heidegger is attempting in these lectures. If we are to take seriously our position as the audience needed and used, enjoined, by language in its self-presentation, we have to allow ourselves to become involved in this presentation. Doing so means that we have to put aside our attempts to describe what is at work in Heidegger's essay, and instead find a means of allowing its language to repeat itself through our own work. It is through its repetition that language becomes different and thus reveals itself by way of, rather than within, our work. By making our reading a restaging we are entering into the area of translation that Hölderlin labored at under the name of the tragic, for the measure of our success in achieving this restaging is precisely the extent to which we become displaced or ex-posed, *by* language, so that language itself appears only where our own speech is lost.

As the medium of our work language is embedded in what we say and write, and being immersed in it we cannot bring it out of ourselves in order to examine it objectively; instead it has to be found in passing. As a result, Heidegger's work on George in this essay, and its continuation, "The Word," plays out the encounter of poeticizing (*Dichten*) and thinking (*Denken*) in a manner that indirectly approaches its language. In doing so, these lectures do not describe the relation of poeticizing and thinking so much as enable it, but insofar as this occurs the relation itself cannot be encountered as it takes place *through* the movement of the lectures. Heidegger's attempt to bring this relation about through language, to stage its occurrence through the transformations of the lectures, means that his own position changes as he moves along; passing from poeticizing to thinking through language and thereby letting language itself appear. There is a double indirection at work here, as Heidegger stages the encounter of poeticizing and thinking to expose the essence of language, which in turn exposes the relation of poeticizing and thinking. This strategy underlies the deceptively simple approach that Heidegger adopts here and considering that these were public lectures it is difficult to imagine how those who attended could have followed their very discreet and deliberate staging.

This is a significant point, for it indicates something of what Heidegger is attempting, something of the deferral that is needed when seeking to approach the matter at hand, which as he states at the very beginning of the first lecture is, "to bring us face to face with a possibility of undergoing an experience (*Erfahrung zu machen*) with language" (US: 149/57). Immediately we are confronted with something unusual, which signals the nature of the path we are about to take: we are not to hear a lecture *about* language, but to attempt to *undergo an experience with language.* This is not a descriptive or analytic program but one more direct and personal; it is closer to a dramatic or religious endeavor, or perhaps more accurately, a *critical* encounter, in that Heidegger is setting out to bring us face-to-face with an *experience* with that which most concerns us. Moreover, this is not an experience *of* language, but an experience *with* language; it will be our companion more than our subject, our guide to that region that is itself. This is congruent with Heidegger's earlier aim to examine language through itself rather than through something else, for if we are to come close to language it must be done through language, if we are to experience *its* language. Of course, this makes the attempt much more intangible as we are already engaging in it every time we engage in language, so the necessity is for us to become aware of it as such.

As Heidegger points out, to "undergo an experience with something, be it a thing, a person, or a god, means that this something befalls us, strikes us, comes over us, overwhelms and transforms us." As such, "the experience is not of our own making," so if we are to experience language we must endure it, suffer it, submit to it, and through this, language comes about. By doing so, we enter the possibility of finding out something about "the innermost nexus of our existence," which is to say, we make possible the discovery of *our relation to language* by allowing ourselves to become "concerned by the claim (*Anspruch*) of language" (US: 149/57). Such a "claim," as we will find out, has a resolutely textual form; language in effect puts its mark on us, and in doing so we are concerned by it; we are its concern. As Heidegger will put it later in speaking of the conjugation of poeticizing and thinking, this mark is "the inscription in which our destined (*geschicklich*es) existence has ever been inscribed" (US: 224/155). For our existence to be "destined" by this inscribing means that its experience changes us; we are turned by it in such a way that nothing is left unchanged, and if we recall that the speech of language "is not anything human," then it is apparent that we become human through our relation to that which is not human. Language is simply language, nothing else; but by entering into an experience with its strangeness we become ourselves. This is not possible simply by speaking, for while we are engaging in language by speaking, our relation to language is itself hidden.

The task is thus to find a way of speaking that allows language to speak rather than ourselves, but this can only take place when we cease to speak through language, "when we cannot find the right word for something," when the right word is not apparent or does not exist (US: 151/59). It is on the strength of this point that Heidegger turns to poeticizing as that mode of speaking that attempts "to put into language something that has never yet been spoken," and that thus may serve as a guide for our own attempts to say what cannot be spoken. George's poem "The Word" allegorizes this experience by passing from the joy of the youthful poet who revels in his facility with language, to his later realization that it is only when this facility disappears that the relation of language to things emerges. Much like Heidegger's configuration of the poet in his own earlier work, the poet in George's poem has the power to bring things into being by naming them; naming calls them forth into what they are. This echoing of the thinker in the poet is made explicit by Heidegger in a footnote that directs us to his own experience of linguistic failing: when he was led to withdraw the third division of the first part of *Being and Time* and to defer its presentation until its language could be found. This turning from poeticizing to thought, which thereby places thought within the context of poeticizing, follows from what Heidegger will say about the neighborhood of poeticizing and thinking; that each can only find itself not in, but by way of, the other. In doing so the word plays a pivotal role for, as the poet in George's poem finally finds out, it does not do the work of thinking or being but stands outside both, limiting their possibilities.

In light of this awareness of the resistance of the word there is more attention here than previously in Heidegger's work on the material presentation of the word and its significance. This is found not only in his attention to the position of the colon in the last stanza of George's poem, but also, as has been indicated by his use of deferral, by the fact that this emphasis will only become apparent through the material presentation of his *own* work. It is unlikely that Heidegger's development of these points would have been fully accessible to the members of his audience at these lectures; thus it is only through their publication and dissemination that the subtlety of these maneuvers has become apparent, which is to say that their meaning has been delayed by Heidegger, held in reserve *by* their inscription. Just as the poet had to renounce his former relation to the word in order to enter that realm where the word itself speaks, so too has Heidegger realized, as he indicates by recalling the deferral of his earlier work on time, that the indirection required by the word must be fully embedded within the manner of his thinking and therein must await its own language. But, as we will see, this deferral also has an effect on the possibility of Heidegger's own attempts to stage an experience with language; there being no possibility of appearance where there is only deferral.

The poet's experience is initially that of the ability of names to bring things into being; this is his craft, but then he discovers that there is one thing he cannot name and in that moment it disappears: "straight it vanished from my hand." We are not told what this "prize so rich and frail" might have been, but in its departure the poet learns a more searching lesson than that of his ability to name things to their being, something that turns him away from his earlier craft:

So I renounced and sadly see:
Where word breaks off no thing may be.

(*So lernt ich traurig den verzicht:*
Kein ding sei wo das wort gebricht.)

This realization, that the nature of language is exposed in the breaking of the relation between word and thing, is itself, according to Heidegger, what is enacted in the last line of this poem, for this line "brings the word of language itself to language" (US: 153/60). To understand how this could be possible close attention needs to be given to the *wording* of these lines. In its ordinary sense of phrasing or syntactic arrangement, "wording" is translated by the German *Wortlaut,* which has the literal meaning of "sounded word," meaning that which persists and subtends outside the sounding or speaking of the word; the wording. To refer to this as a "sounded" word would suggest that it follows the sounding of the word, but as the epigraph in this chapter indicates, Heidegger's view is the opposite. The sounding of the word is instead grounded in the fact that it is *already* a sounded word, in that it rings from out of the initially soundless word of language; thus sounding (speaking) can only be achieved insofar as the word is already sounded. Thus speech depends on what might be called, following the "worlding" of the world, the "wording" of the word: how words become themselves through their essencing as words. This "wording" of the word has nothing to do with its syntactic arrangement, for it persists even where words break up.

To uncover this essential wording from out of the ordinary sense of the term, Heidegger looks to those places in these lines where the words break up and lead into soundlessness. While the last line indicates that the relation between word and thing is only apparent when the word breaks off, the condition of this appearance is drawn out of the phrase "may be" (*sei*) and out of the movement of the stanza as a whole. The colon at the end of its first line momentarily suspends the movement of the stanza and indicates that the last line is *where* the renunciation of the poet's former power leads ("*den verzicht:*"): "What follows the colon does not name that which is being renounced; rather, it names the realm into which the renunciation must enter" (US: 157/64–65). Furthermore, because "renouncing is a manner of saying, it can be introduced in writing by a colon" (US: 210/142). That is, it is by way of a textual intervention that the poet can pass through the renunciation of saying. This renunciation is thus a suspension of the rhythm, a "counter-rhythmic interruption," which operates exactly according to Hölderlin's requirements that it should "meet the rushing alternation of representations at its peak, in such a way that it is then no longer the alternation of representations that appears, but representation itself."

As Hölderlin discovered, this leaves an opening into which the poet passes, although the words he uses are more drastic, the movement being an *Entrückung*, a "rapture" or "removal," and a *reißen*, a "tearing," into the other side of finitude: "the eccentric sphere of the dead" (SW5: 196–97/102). In doing so the poet encounters the ambiguity of words, in which the "may be" in the last line is both a renunciation of the power to name things to their being ("no thing may *be*"), and an avowal (*Zuspruch*, a word that relates to *Spruch*, meaning "motto," "maxim," "saying," or "aphorism," that is, those textual fragments that provoke or suggest by referring us elsewhere) of that to which this denial of power leads ("no thing *may* be"). It is worth recalling here the parallel development in "As when on a holiday . . ." where Hölderlin declared:

> But now day breaks! I waited and saw it come,
> And what I saw, may the holy be my word.
>
> (*Jetzt aber tagts! Ich haart and sah es kommen,*
> *Und was ich sah, das Heilige sei mein Wort.*)

For George, the double meaning of "may be" is such that it can mean both that nothing *is* where words break off, and that there "is" nothing where words break off. This possibility is only found in the absence of words, and it is this absence that Hölderlin also speaks of: "may the holy be my word" is not speaking of a word that is, but that which is where one can only say "*may* be." Significantly, both poets find this possibility through rupture; the loss of the word for Hölderlin is brought about by the sudden arrival of the dawn, as this breakage exposes the absence of the word and thus the relation that is possible in this absence. For George, it is his inability to name the *word* that is the rupture that sends him into its absence, which is both marked *and* brought about by the colon. In both cases it is only a possibility that is found, a possibility intimately connecting the word and what is, which is only exposed through its rupture. Without this possibility, that is, when its rupture occurs, which is to say, within impossibility, there "is" no thing. Both poets have indicated to

Heidegger that there exists a relation in rupture, a relation of supposition or avowal, where there is an empty (im)possibility: the "may be" "is the relation itself" (US: 177/83).[14] This (non)relation is itself marked by the pause and opening found in the colon, that is, not in the words themselves, but in what occurs between them, in their wording.

This departure from normal syntactic wording is often pursued by Heidegger through a paratactic suspension of relation between words, which are then intercut by colons to indicate the unknown and open nature of their relation. In doing so, the *use* of language is renounced such that language itself can appear, for language only "*speaks* where there are no words, in the interval between them, which the colons indicate" (WHD: 114/186). What has been opened out by this loss of relation, of this relation without relation, is a language outside configuration, a language that does not construe "as." This apophantic "as" that guarantees presence by setting up the relation of being and beings, is precisely what has been erased by the colon. Instead, this rupture introduces an other relation between them, in which there is simply repetition, echoing, and displacement: *die Sprache spricht.* When Heidegger speaks at the beginning of "The Way to Language" of the need "to bring language as language to language," the important point is the third iteration in which the configured relation is itself suspended by being brought to language. This is to speak language *from* language, and in doing so the guideword "loses its formal character, and unexpectedly becomes a soundless echo which lets us hear something of the proper character of language" (US: 232/113).

To return to George's poem, the word that is translated as "renunciation," *Verzicht,* could also be rendered as "abdication" or "resignation" (*Entsagen*). Heidegger offers these alternatives by referring to the Latin, *dicere,* "to say," and the Greek, *deiknumi,* "to show," which were earlier used in his explication of the meaning of *Dichten* and also reflect the German verbs, *ziehen,* "to pull or draw," *zeigen,* "to point or show," and *zeichnen,* "to draw or mark" (US: 158/65). The refusal of signification or indication means that the sign can only refer to itself, which opens the renunciation of the poet into the complex singularity of the draw-ing, which suggests that it is also a "withdrawal" (*Entziehung, Absagen*); a mark that in re-marking itself places itself in erasure, which is to say, in palimpsest. In a sense drawn out more fully in Heidegger's lecture "The Word," which follows "The Essence of Language," this rupturing or renunciation of the power of the word is not so much a self-*denial* as a denial of *self,* and is thus an affirmation of what is outside this power, rather than a negation, such that it "is in truth a nondenial of self (*Sich-nicht-versagen*): to the mystery of words" (US: 220/151). In avowing *himself* in this way, the poet is drawn into the space that the colon opens: the space where the word breaks off and the withdrawal of language occurs.

However, the poet cannot experience this withdrawal itself but instead receives what Heidegger calls an *Ur-Kunde*, a note that provides "original" documentary evidence, *archē*-tidings (*Urkunde*: a "writ," "scrip," or "certificate," from *Kunde*: "tidings"). Thus it is a promise of knowledge, of an origin, rather than the origin itself, a note that betokens and carries an injunction but does not produce what is to come, an inscription that calls for language in its absence (US: 159/66). There is a sense of the tragic exigency here that Heidegger seems to confirm by his reference to the mourning (*Trauer*) felt by the poet in his renunciation, but this is a mourning that "is in relation with what is most joyful" (US: 222/153). This would appear to be referring to the fact that the knowledge received cannot be spoken or read, but is by virtue of this closer to the essence of language. But that Heidegger should use a term of writing to denote this promise or grant (*Zusage*: "saying-to") of language is of key importance, as it suggests that the manner in which language conceals itself in the drawing of the earth perhaps has more relation to the repeatedly self-concealing marks of a palimpsest than has so far been recognized. As much as he discusses language in terms of speaking and listening, there is, as we will shortly find out, a stronger if more discreet presence of the textual, material underside of language.

In receiving this *Ur-Kunde* the poet undergoes an experience with language such that, through the renunciation and avowal of the word, he enters into the relation between word and thing. This relation does not simply connect two parts together that in themselves precede that relation; instead the "word itself is the relation"; it is both that which connects and that which withdraws into itself (US: 159/66). This means that the poet's experience with the word, much as was the case with the work of art, is an experience of nothing, but relation: that which gives being, but that itself is not. However, in giving an account of this abyssal poetic experience, Heidegger has not been poeticizing himself, but thinking, for the encounter of poeticizing and thinking means that each are engaged in a countering relation to each other. This countering (*entgegnende*) word reveals the country or region (*Gegend*) in which the relation of the two takes place. We have then entered into the neighborhood of poeticizing and thinking, into that which lies between them, that which appears when words disappear. As such, Heidegger has come full circle with both poeticizing and thinking and it is here that the first lecture ends.

Before doing so Heidegger returns to the beginning of the lectures, as his reading of poetry has enabled him to situate himself within its neighborhood such that the opening statement can now be rephrased as an attempt "to bring us face to face with a possibility of undergoing a *thinking* experience with language" (US: 163–64/70, emphasis added). The addition of "thinking" indicates a greater understanding of the position from which he starts, but also makes the region of the discussion more questionable, thus a rephrasing of the title is required, rendering it: "The Essence?—of Language?" This places the presumption of each word, and their relation, into question, thus reconfiguring the guideword by placing its supposition within the promise of language, which is always to come. But if the promise is to come then our questioning can only occur within the avowal of this promise, within the space of our waiting, for every "posing of every question already stands within the grant and promise (*Zusage*) of what is put into question" (US: 165/71). This means that our questioning is itself in question, as it can only arise out of a prior listening to this promise, out of which its questioning occurs as its avowal. What is promised by language but withheld is its essence, for it is out of its essence that language avows itself, but as a result, when language itself speaks what is withheld is brought forth, such that "the essence of language becomes the grant and promise of its essence, i.e. the language of essence" (US: 166/72). The essence of language occurs *as* this avowal, which is thus *the language of essence* in that it speaks from out of its promise.

Heidegger's guideword, like George's poem, has begun to fall apart just where its words are lacking, but in breaking it up Heidegger has fulfilled his own promise of enabling us to undergo an experience with language. For with its reversal the title has become "the echo of a thinking experience," whose transformation indicates the transformation inherent to our experience with language (US: 166/72). As such, the repetition and inversion of the guideword has not only opened up a chiasm, but also plunged us into this movement, for by its transformation the title has itself released the withheld promise of language, as Heidegger proceeds to indicate:

> If we are to think through the essence of language, language must first promise itself to us, or must already have done so. Language must, in its own way, avow to us itself—its essence. Language essences as this avowal (*Zuspruch*). We hear it constantly, of

> course, but do not give it thought. If we did not hear it everywhere, we could not use one single word of language. Language essences as this avowal. The essence of language makes itself known (*bekundet*) to us as the saying (*Spruch*), as the language of its essence. But we cannot quite hear this *Ur-Kunde*, let alone "read" it. It runs (*lautet*): The essence of language: The language of essence. (US: 170/76)

Twice we are told that "language essences as this avowal," somehow priming us for what is to come, making us pause by way of the repetition, until the moment of its realization is possible. Again we are told that the essence of language makes itself known to us as the language of its essence, and as before this declaration is given the name of a text, which we cannot grasp. But then Heidegger gives us this *Ur-Kunde* itself; for the transformed title reappears after the pause of the first colon *as the essence of language itself.* Just as with George's poem the use of the colon indicates the realm into which we are called, but the extraordinary nature of this claim is due to its status as an inscription: as the *Ur-Kunde.* That it is textual is confirmed by Heidegger's dismissal of our possibility of "reading" it, and his use of *bekundet, Spruch,* and *lautet,* all of which suggest a written manifestation. But even if we cannot approach it as we might an ordinary text, then perhaps it shares the same relation to writing as saying does to ordinary speech, as the claim nevertheless remains that language comes to language, as Christopher Fynsk puts it, "in something like a writing."[15]

It is impossible to assess what kind of status such an inscription might have as we are told that we cannot read it. Instead it simply presences as a line, a few words, whose existence *as* the essence of language seems demonstrated *by* its evasiveness. In this we find part of what Heidegger is taking up in drawing this essence out as textual, for writing has the compelling and frustrating presence of being both near and far, unavoidable yet ungraspable; it is *essentially* fragmentary. Moreover, the *Ur-Kunde* transcribes the essence of language by way of a few words, that is, as marks that implicate their own absence, their soundlessness. In doing so a key distinction is marked between writing and saying, as Heidegger makes clear later on when he states that there "is no word for this mystery, that is, no saying which could bring the essence of language to language" (US: 223/154). As George's poet found, there is no word for the word, so it can only be presented by way of its own soundless wording. Thus the wording of the words opens up its inscription to an iteration without end, without terms, a relation of endless repetition and reversal. Perhaps sensing the abyssal character of the *Ur-Kunde*, Heidegger remarks that in order to "read" these "words" the words after the colon will have to be changed, as what is meant by "language" and "essence" have become emptied by their chiasmic reversal. While this change will occur over the following two lectures, the matter of Heidegger's thought has already taken place: the key words: *Ur-Kunde*, *Zusage*, and *Zuspruch*; what occurs when words fail; and the concomitant relation between poeticizing and thinking.

As a result, Heidegger does not progress over the remaining pages as much as return repeatedly to what has already been said. This repetition is required to draw us away from the habits of calculative thinking into a listening to language, a following of its ways. In doing so, one of the more basic understandings of "experience" is developed as it was stated at the beginning of the lectures: in coming from outside our experience with language is not something we can control, but must submit to, and through this we become transformed. Moreover, in coming to us it comes because it pertains to us, and in transforming us we become transformed *into* it in a movement that follows the chiasmic transformation of the guideword, in which the essence becomes language only insofar as language becomes its essence (US: 167/73–74). Equally, Heidegger's key words also change in their relation to the region that they enter: as they are read into that region they become the words that arise from it; they become both the way and the region (*entgegnende* turns into *Gegend*; *Zusage* turns into *Sage*), both the saying of its site and the place of its speech, its *topo-logy*.[16]

. . . IN PALIMPSEST . . .

Following from the injunction carried by the *Ur-Kunde*, Heidegger calls the transformed guideword a "demand" or "imposition" (*Zumutung*), and like the *Ur-Kunde* its appearance is a mark of rupture (US: 170/76). What emerges in it is a mystery, a darkness, something unknown, not a thing at all, for it is nothing that "is." Neither poeticizing nor thinking can lessen this mystery, neither separately nor together, for their neighborhood is itself a "supposition" (*Vermutung*) that only echoes the imposition of the guideword (US: 174/80).[17] These slippages from term to term, and from relation to relation, follow the "current" (*Strömung*) of language itself, which does not work to illuminate its darkness but simply layers it so that it becomes a "manifold" or palimpsest that reveals itself through its concealments (US: 153/61, 178/84). If the essence of language is this reserved promise, then when it speaks the language of essence must be the promise of its reserve: what is concealed in its relation, in the "and" of "poetry and thought," or "word and thing," or in the very relation that is lacking and thus exposed in the guideword, "the essence of language: the language of essence" (US: 176/81).[18] For the neighborhood of these terms can only arise out of the emptiness of their relation, which is revealed by their chiasmus without revealing *what* this relation is, such that it is only through this renunciation that the relation can emerge in its essence as a promise. The nature of relation is what is most mysterious here since if we are unable to think it in itself, outside of its terms, then only rupture can make it apparent and then it can only do so by exposing its lack, but this lack of appearance is what is most essential to it, in that it appears by way of its withdrawal (US: 177/83).

There is an indirect comment on "The Origin of the Work of Art" here, as the implication of this discussion of relation is that language, as relation, does not speak in figures or images as much as it images itself as words (US: 176/82). That is, there is no "setting-up" or "installing" of truth in language, but rather the evasion of such configuring by way of a movement that is no longer concerned with the truth of being but its topology, the saying of its place or region, as which language occurs. In doing so language itself does not "appear," since it refuses appearance, even that of an indirect staging; rather it displaces the movement of presencing away from the clearing into an "entangled" (*verstrickt*) movement, in which its essence is not a site but a way, "a going that is like a going away" (US: 169/75, 171/77). Furthermore, if the word is that which enables things to be, but is not a thing in itself, then it does not lead to being by adding something onto things; instead it enables things to be by repeating them, that is, by adding nothing to them and thereby re-presenting them as nothing, but themselves (US: 180/86).

If language does not speak in figures or images in the ordinary sense that is because its speech is of the word. This speaking is of the relation that Heidegger has just indicated as being outside our ability to grasp, but despite this he proposes to call it "saying" (*Sage*), before retreating again by refusing to indicate what "saying" might mean. It has nothing to do with speaking or language as we commonly understand them, but is instead that region in which poeticizing and thinking find their neighboring. The common meaning of *Sage* as "legend" or "fable" is not registered by Heidegger, but the nature of this kind of saying as both anonymous and repeated would seem relevant for our understanding of the origins of poeticizing and thinking as always already hidden by repetition. Although it is different for each, both reside within this region without having any knowledge of what it is in itself, as it is what gives them to be through its "promise" or *Zusage* and so is always in withdrawal. In 1945 Heidegger developed his most elaborate account of this region, and in doing so remarked that "it is the region of the word, which is answerable to itself alone."[19] Thus it is the region of the pure or solitary word, because the "word for the word can never be found" as "the word, the saying, has no being (*Sein*)" (US: 181/86–87, 223/154). As he points out, in saying this, we "are struck by the sight of something other," for if words have no being, then they are not things that are; they *are* not at all (US: 182/87). Words are nothing, which means they have no relation to truth, history, or presence, for they do not appear in any way. This is what the poetic experience with language has led to, but in the sight of something so other, what are we to say?

If we cannot say of the word that it is, then we must say that "it, the word, gives" (*es, das Wort, gibt*), but what does it give? The "word gives: being" (*gibt das Wort: das Sein*), by being nothing more than this giving, this promise and avowal "to be," this is its relation, its sup-position, a projected but endlessly deferred presencing (US: 182–83/88). The key addition of the colon to George's poem has been repeated by Heidegger here, temporarily suspending the movement of this phrase, turning it from "the word gives being," to "the word gives: being." Nothing has been added but the simple mark of a pause or break, a caesura, but in doing so the relation of the word to being has been suspended and thus its *wording* has appeared. The word that gives is only ever implied, never present, and thus is an origin only as a supposition, as the *Ur-Kunde*, and its wording is thus the mark *of* deferral. It inscribes the space of being but withdraws from it, because it is nothing more than its spacing, its mark of lack and rupture by which it becomes a space, a neighborhood in which relations can take place. Heidegger calls this "the mysterious nearness of the far-tarrying power of the word," which draws near only by holding apart.[20] As the approach of the word only takes place out of this reserve, the encountering of poeticizing and thinking can only occur in their separation and distance: "divergence (*Auseinander*) is their real face-to-face encounter (*Gegen-einander-über*)" (US: 184/89–90). Thus in their neighboring poeticizing and thinking are

> held apart by a delicate, yet luminous difference, each held in its own darkness: two parallels, in Greek *para allelo*, by one another, against one another, surpassing (*übertreffend*) one another each in its own way. Poeticizing and thinking are not separated if separation is to mean cut off (*abgeschieden*) into a relational void (*Bezugslose*). The parallels intersect themselves (*schneiden sich*) in the in-finite (*Un-endlichen*). There they intersect themselves with a cut (*Schnitt*) that they themselves do not make. By this they are first cut (*geschnitten*), i.e. engraved (*eingezeichnet*) into the design (*Aufriß*) of their neighborly essence. This drawing (*Zeichnung*) is the draw-ing (*Riß*). It tears (*reißt*) poeticizing and thinking into their nearness to one another. The neighborhood of poeticizing and thinking is not the result of a process by which poeticizing and thinking—no one knows from where—first pull (*ziehen*) one another into nearness, which thereby first comes about. The nearness, which nears, is itself the event, by which poeticizing and thinking are directed into what is proper to their essence. (US: 185/90)

The complexity and intangibility of the draw-ing is indicated here through the combination of terms for cutting, drawing, pulling, tearing, and intersecting. This is in turn complicated by the positions of poeticizing and thinking themselves, which intersect not by crossing each other, but by somehow being cut into themselves from their between, which in doing so tears them into an openness that is their neighboring. It is compelling that the neighborhood of the draw-ing should again arise out of an inscription, as evinced by the use of the word *eingezeichnet*, but this is developed no further. Instead the draw-ing withdraws into its own impossible figurality, for if it is akin to writing this can only be as its abyssal condition, its dif-ference, which writing could only approach through its resistance or rupturing.

This neighboring restages the separating and gathering movement of the draw-ing in "The Origin of the Work of Art," but not in a manner that draws it into the thematics of configuration. Here the play of finitude in the cut of the draw-ing is one that interrupts two parallels, and thus occurs in the in-finite, that is, outside its terms, in a relation without end that is decided from within its ex-centricity and is thus endlessly differentiating in a palimpsest of relations (US: 68/189, 207/139). This cannot be the founding movement of history or nation, as its movement is one of divergence rather than setting-up, unless, like Hölderlin, we entirely reconsider what is meant by "history" or "nation" from the perspective of its palimpsest, in which case its saying would be underwritten by the draw-ing as its *topo-graphy.*

What is indicated by the draw-ing is not only the neighborhood in which poeticizing and thinking find their countering, but also their repetition. For in marking out this nearness Heidegger notes that nearness and saying are the "same," by which we should recall the elaboration of the same as tautology. This "saying of the same" changes the guideword, as was promised, by replacing language with "saying" and essence with "nearness," such that the essence of language "is" the nearness of saying, which is the event of regioning (US: 190/95). Thus if the essence of language: the language of essence, then the event of regioning takes place *as* its regioning, which is the saying of its nearness. In reading the guideword as a tautology what takes place is not the interrelation of separate parts, but a repetition that is both its separation and its nearing. This is how Heidegger proposes the guideword to be read and so, contrary to first impressions, its transformation has not made it less abyssal; instead, changing words that are identical for ones that are the "same" has inscribed its repetition more profoundly. For the guideword cannot refer back to itself, as it is decentered by its lack of ground, so if there is a sense of the same returning then it can only do so if it never comes back to where it is, but is removed in an endless detour. Thus, as we will see in chapter 6, there is no saying of nearness outside of its interminable repetition, in which the event of nearing would only occur by way of its deferral, for any sense in which the promise of language was fulfilled could only do so by betraying its essence.

But in speaking in such a way the guideword has brought us back to where we are, the regioning of our nearness, more powerfully than would have been possible without it. But, this speaking cannot be heard or read in any ordinary way; instead it "is much more important to consider . . . the physical element of language, its vocal and written character" (US: 193/98). For, as Heidegger explains, by this approach we can come to understand how "body and mouth are part of the earth's flow and growth," such that in attending to its speech "we hear the sound of language rising like the earth" (US: 194/98, 196/101). Language comes to speak then as the voice of our own finitude, the singular *logos* of *phusis* that only refers to itself, but in doing so it becomes different: repeating itself with layers of dissembling and thereby becoming dark and hidden. If phenomenology revealed the existence of this concealment then it is through tautology that we can come to understand its manner and necessity, for tautology is the language of hiding. But in bringing this hiddenness to language we are brought face-to-face with that which withdraws from nearness and resists opening, and as a result, the essence of language only comes to language as a singularity that cannot be broached but persists as an extreme rupture.

This encounter with the limit of language is thus an encounter with our own limits; here the "essential relation between death and language flashes up, but is still unthought. It can however give a hint of the manner in which the essence of language draws us into its concern and so relates to itself" (US: 203/107). Language relates to itself through us, by way of our speaking, but in doing so we experience its coming to language as our limits; thus this finitude is the condition of relation, for by its rupturing "the sounding word turns back to soundlessness, back to whence it was granted: Into the ringing of stillness, which as saying moves the regions of the world's fourfold into their nearness. This breaking up of words is the proper step back on the way of thinking" (US: 204/108). Thinking finds itself in an extreme exigency by way of this experience with language, for it thereby encounters not only its own limits, but also our own mortality; this is the singularity that the essence of language brings to language and confronted by it how are we to respond?

It would seem that this is a question that Heidegger has left open, for if his starting point was to try and find a language that could articulate the meaning of being, then he has found that the language within which this *logos* can be brought to expression is one that is irreducibly singular. Thus for thinking to come into proximity with such an experience is not only to find a topological saying that "moves the regions of the world's fourfold into their nearness," but also one that exposes thought to an endless topographical iteration. This repetition is, as Ion discovered, a limit experience for thinking, as it entails a

> perpetual repetition from episode to episode, development on the spot, interminable amplification of the same—that makes each rhapsode not a faithful reproducer, an immobile rehearser, but the one who carries forward the repetition and, through it,

> fills in the gaps or expands them through the medium of new turns (*péripéties*), opens, closes the fissures and, finally, by dint of filling the poem out, distends it to the point of volatilization. (EI: 572/390)

For Socrates this rhapsodic mode is disturbing as it has no discernible origin, but this is how it persists, giving rise not only to the poet's enthusiasm but also to his ejection therefrom, which leads to the unavoidably tragic nature of such language. For once ejected Ion cannot return to the poem except by way of its repetition, which is precisely the means by which he is ejected. It is to this experience that Hölderlin was particularly sensitive, for in translation and rewriting he found a mode of repetition that persisted by way of interruption, but in whose caesuras he was himself also tragically bound. For Heidegger, this rupturing of relation is an aporia, in response to which his thinking can only step back before its unanswerable demand, perhaps, as he had remarked earlier, "the rhapsodes are those who bear the tidings (*Kunde*) of the poets' word" (US: 115/29). But in so bearing the pain of language where and how are we taken, and what "new kind of writing" does this rupturing of relation lead to?

6

Fragmenting
L'iter-rature of Relation

> In this relation that we are isolating in a manner that is not necessarily abstract, the one is never comprehended by the other, does not form with it an ensemble, a duality, or a possible unity; the one is foreign to the other, without this strangeness privileging either one of them. We call this relation neutral, indicating already in this manner that it cannot be recaptured, either when one affirms or when one negates, demanding of language in this way not an indecision between these two modes, but rather a possibility of saying that would say without saying being and without denying it either. And herein we characterize, perhaps, one of the essential traits of the "literary" act: the very fact of writing.
>
> —Blanchot, *The Infinite Conversation,* 1969

This inquiry began by trying to find the place of poetry within Heidegger's thinking and what it has uncovered is that the nature of poetic language indicates something very significant about the language of philosophy. For Heidegger the task of the language of philosophy was to articulate the meaning of being, but his encounter with poetic language has shown that this meaning can only be brought to language as a rupture, with which we can have no relation insofar as it severs all relation. The logic of this finitude, by which the rupturing of language persists, is grounded in its endless repetition, but as Hölderlin's translations indicate, any attempt to respond to the caesura by rewriting it only restages its tragic scission. Heidegger has also found this rupturing excessive, as is found by his attempts to respond to the dissembling of the earth, the textuality of poetry, or the essence of language. While he came to understand this excession as tautology, as the saying of the same of being in its differentiations, this leaves the possibility of this saying in question, for it is a repetition that only persists by way of the finitude of writing. By uncovering this finitude in the essencing of language Heidegger came to see how any thinking *of* language is an experience in which we are exposed to the tragic; but how can this become the language of philosophy?

The answer, of course, is that by this point in the development of his thinking Heidegger is not interested in pursuing any "philosophy" of existence or being, but is instead pursuing something much more akin to his earliest concerns with a care or *phronēsis* of the *logos,* one that cannot be separated from its *pathos.* Thus the experience of the limits of language, which Heidegger has pursued through his readings of poetry, is an experience of the limits of our own existence, of absence and loss, so coming to terms with this experience has the utmost seriousness and urgency. But this is an experience of rupture, one that we can have no relation with, so what form can its *phronēsis* take and what kind of language does this lead to? In these last few pages I will briefly sketch out two responses to this concern, the first from Blanchot and the second from Derrida, both of whom are intent on trying to find what kind of writing can come after Heidegger. Both have followed many different strategies, but the two that I will explore will be Blanchot's fragmentary and Derrida's poematic, which both arise out of the issue that has permeated throughout this inquiry: *repetition.* As such, they are in no way "solutions" to the "problems" of Heidegger's work, but rather arise out of the ellipses of his thought; those points where it could not return to itself but instead exposed its outside.[1] It is these points that we must repeat if we are to find a means of coming after Heidegger, not to rectify or conceal their omissions but to pursue this absence as its greatest demand.

The nature of this particular exigency is perhaps most noticeable if we consider a topic I have not explored so far: Heidegger's politics. It has become customary to treat Heidegger's readings of poetry, particularly Hölderlin's, as harboring a covert political agenda that not only places his language at considerable risk of entering the same arena of aestheticized politics that formed such a major part of National Socialist doctrine, but also of thereby appropriating poetry to a language that has no regard for its singularity, for what poetry is in itself. There is a corollary to this that reads Heidegger's later works as a retreat from his failed political engagements of the 1930s into a quietism or mysticism that is essentially conservative, if not reactionary, thereby tacitly confirming the political agenda of *Heimat* and *Boden* that he had sought to propagate more explicitly in his earlier years. From this reading it would appear that Heidegger is damned on all counts and my own attempt to draw out the language of his "poetic thinking" from the politics in which it is so indissolubly merged would thus seem to be naive, misguided, or willfully perverse.[2]

This is clearly a serious problem, but what concerns me about this political damnation is the ease and certainty with which Heidegger's language as a whole becomes tarnished by such accusations. In registering the manner in which his work of the 1930s conceals maneuvers and tropes of a "totalizing" political agenda that is concerned with the inner truth of historical decisions and epochs, we are providing an invaluable and essential insight, but this should not convince us that Heidegger's language itself has any hidden unity or aim, as it is no unitary thing that could have such properties. My concern with this approach is that despite its importance it fails according to its own criteria by not pursuing the singularity of Heidegger's own language. Heidegger's errors arose precisely where he failed to consider the reality of what was at work in language, and thus if we are to respond to his work we cannot allow ourselves to fall prey to the same failing by not considering the reality of what is at work in his language.

Only by doing justice to the singular fact of language can we do justice to Heidegger's thinking, in all its aspects. In doing so, the criticisms of his work are in no way lessened, but we can raise the possibility that he began to address these errors himself in the most discreet yet rigorous manner in his work after the war. We may never be able to understand or accept his silence on the Shoah, but this does not give us the right to fill that silence for him.[3] Instead we should turn to his own words, for while his language had been irreparably implicated by his actions of 1933, actions that were never fully rejected, his turn to a thinking of language in the 1950s could be said to be following, albeit indirectly, the utmost political exigency, as it concerns the impossibility of saying and the difficulty of holding to this necessary impossibility. It is not my concern to say that this is what Heidegger's postwar work is about, and to thereby replace one political image with another, but to attend to the more subtle demand that arises *out of his work*. It is this demand that still addresses us today, one that we have barely begun to recognize; that of the necessity of responding to the fact of language: that it "is" only by way of absence, which directly pertains to our own existence.

It is to this fact that we find the work of Heidegger and Hölderlin being drawn, which draws us away from "philosophy" and "poetry" into thinking and poeticizing, toward what gives rise to and also undermines them, what draws them through its erasure. As we have seen, the demands of responding to this extraordinary *Not* (lack and necessity) have pushed Hölderlin and Heidegger into an extreme contortion of writing, whose repetition both answers to this exigency and provokes a further one. Writing itself becomes a cipher for this exigency by way of which absence is *secreted*, that is both hidden and produced, that is, dissembled, such that its absence persists in its absence. This would be a relation of *mimēsis* rather than *poiēsis*: the relation without relation that occurs in cryptophilia where the relation of hiding is also a hiding of relation.[4] Here the relation is itself dissembled such that there is no gathering together, for writing does not draw poetry and philosophy into being, but mimes the repetition of absence by which poeticizing and thinking recur. For both of them, this repetition answered to the lack out of which their work arose: for Hölderlin this was figured as the departure of the gods; for Heidegger it was the forgetting of being, but for each the practice of writing strove against the possibility of their being able to answer to this lack. In writing, their work was drawn into a further demand, a greater exigency, which for Hölderlin was the tragic and for Heidegger was the nothing, that which writing always comes to, which always disfigures it. The repetition in writing empties it, displacing it into an other relation to which we cannot enter, with which we have no relation, for it is perhaps repetition as such, the palimpsest of its *an-archē*-writing, the opening of an endless finitude by and to whose erasure we are drawn.

As such, the caesura of writing seems to focus the point at which poetry and philosophy differ, by indicating how its nonrelation becomes a relation according to the different exigencies it brings out in each area. This suggests that a relation of nonrelation transpires between poetry and thinking insofar as each interrupts the other as they intersect themselves along their own parallels: limiting by evading each other. It is from this point that Heidegger's thought gathers itself and in doing so exposes the uncrossable proximity that separates it from poetry. As soon as it is espoused this relation dissolves; its singularity only persists in secret, and if a poem in responding to this secret finds a way of secreting itself, then perhaps thinking must also develop this if it is to reach this relation. Doing so might well be the limit of thinking, beyond which it ceases to be, and if this is so then thinking must come to terms with this loss, and in this recognize its own singularity. But in recognizing this loss, the recognition itself must become *un*-marked if thinking is to approach poetry, for otherwise thinking would only remain aware of itself in its loss and unaware of its proximity to its other, since it is the self-destruction of a poem that thinking retreats from. In remaining itself thinking resists singularity, for it is only in dissolution that the singular mark can be found *as* the mark of its singular loss.

Responding to this other relation provided the demand of Blanchot's later writings, in which he sought to turn aside from "poetry" and "philosophy" to seek that from which they are drawn. To do so meant resisting the figuring of this course as either poeticizing or thinking, by trying to find the path of writing's own (dis)figuring. This gave rise to a writing of the *fragment*, which did not seek to go beyond Heidegger and Hölderlin as much as to secrete itself within their borders. Writing at the limits of poeticizing and thinking entailed a writing that persistently interrupted itself, giving itself to its own fragmentation and thereby writing. Moreover, the fragmentary for Blanchot is always to be associated with the *neutre* (both "neuter" and "neutral"), which emerged as a response to the problem of how we can have a relation with the other that neither objectifies nor subjectifies it. The neutral relation would be that which persists between self and other while remaining outside their relation, for it is that which occurs out of the effacement of the self, and remains after the interruption of the other. Neutral speech would thus be the speech of effacement and rupture, what Blanchot calls "the speech of writing." In this speaking, the other persists without being revealed, as it does not appear through the neutral relation but exists outside it, the neuter being that which neither reveals nor conceals but fragments.

. . . "WITHOUT RETURN" . . .

In 1959 Blanchot was invited to contribute to a Festschrift for Heidegger's seventieth birthday; the piece that he submitted, entitled "Waiting," would later be greatly expanded and published in 1962 as *Waiting Forgetting* (*L'attente L'oubli*). This latter work marks a transition in Blanchot's writing, away from the narratives of his earlier years into a fragmentary writing combining both fictional and nonfictional elements. This deliberate disruption of language unsettles the traditional relation between narrative and reflection and leads to a writing of extraordinary depth and subtlety. As a result, there is no possibility of doing justice to such a text within the contexts of the current project, but the earlier piece, "Waiting," offers a glimpse of what is underway, as well as providing us with an insight into Blanchot's relation to Heidegger.

The difficulties of responding to the demands of a Festschrift are immense and obvious, but are only made more so by Blanchot's ambivalent relation to the philosopher's life and thought. This was revealed quite explicitly in a letter Blanchot wrote in 1987 at the height of the furor surrounding the revelations about Heidegger's political life, in which he returned to these pages from 1959 to put them in perspective. Although brief, Blanchot's remarks are intriguing for they indicate that he responded to the offer of the Festschrift because of the necessity of giving due recognition to Heidegger's achievement in *Being and Time*, despite the unavoidable presence within that work of the same language that would later give its voice so clearly to the cause of National Socialism. Blanchot acknowledges that his own work would not have been possible without the "veritable intellectual shock" that Heidegger's book forced him to undergo, and thus his distance from Heidegger must be measured carefully.[5] This subtle negotiation takes place in "Waiting" as an examination of the impossible burden of relation, which makes it a decidedly oblique contribution to a volume honoring Heidegger. In doing so Blanchot offers us an extremely rigorous example of how to respond to Heidegger, for "Waiting" seems to operate by rewriting Heidegger's language to the point of dissolving its meaning. This does not render it simply nonsensical but rather exposes the disturbing figurality of language itself, as that which lies within the terms of Heidegger's thought while remaining excessively exterior to them.

Blanchot reads Heidegger by rewriting him, repeating his thoughts such that they become exposed to their own exteriority. In this way he can remain loyal to the promise of Heidegger's thought while refusing its delivery, and in doing so his relation to Heidegger is also drawn out as that of an extreme intimacy that is nevertheless utterly exterior. Such a relation does not seek to relate Blanchot to Heidegger in the sense that it holds them together, but instead honors it by exposing the immense absence that lies between them. They are drawn into relation only insofar as they remain outside each other, so that their proximity to each other can only be measured by absence. A writing that can hold itself within this reserve comes from the distance sketched out *within* its proximity, in the deferral that arises out of its repetition. The waiting in this deferral "is always a waiting for waiting, resuming the beginning, suspending the end and, inside this interval, opening the interval of another waiting." In this sense waiting is close to Heidegger's understanding in "Toward a Situation of

Releasement: From a Conversation on a Country Path about Thinking," but Blanchot repeats it to the point of exposing something very different, for if waiting "is waiting for nothing" then the "impossibility of waiting belongs essentially to waiting."[6]

This is not to negate Heidegger's thought but to find within it an opacity that masks an entirely other relation, since, as Heidegger himself laboriously explored in *The Fundamental Concepts of Metaphysics*, in waiting for nothing we enter an emptiness without end. But in doing so waiting evades itself and becomes impossible, as it "opens up time to the absence of time where there is no place for waiting"; as a result it can find no fulfillment but instead exposes an other relation. Waiting thus opens onto an estrangement that can never be reconciled with itself, as it releases a dispersion that can only be brought together in the imminence of its return, for at "each step we are here and yet beyond." This other relation lies within language as that which is alongside but forever estranged from it, as "if the same word could have expressed and yet acted as a barrier to expression." Within our ordinary use of language we make use of the relation that language affords us, but for Blanchot this leaves aside the relation of language itself, which does not afford itself to us but rather desists from any affordance. This leaves us wishing "to and unable to speak; not wishing to and unable to avoid speaking; in that case, speaking-and-not-speaking, in an identical movement." Only in waiting can this impossible relation be traced, for through waiting "that which turns aside from thought returns to thought become a turning aside from itself."

Blanchot is very carefully but also very discreetly drawing out a paradoxical (im)possibility from within Heidegger's own terms, for while the repetition of his language exposes its emptiness, this is also the space of an other relation, a "space of turning aside without digression, of errancy without error."[7] The piece itself is an example of this space, as the writing of "Waiting" turns back on itself by repeating its terms such that they become fragmented and indeterminate, and in doing so Blanchot has found a means of responding to the excessive demand of the Festschrift; for this fragmentation has not arisen as the source of his response but out of the impossibility of the task. Because Blanchot's relation to Heidegger lies within his language, as that which both enables and disables it, it is only by registering this difficulty and drawing it out that an other relation arises. In this way the fragmentary emerges, but in doing so it releases an ethical and political concern, for the suspension of relation found in the fragmentary is the only relation to the other that is able to relate to it as other. I will return to this point shortly, since Blanchot is not developing an "ethics" here, but is exploring the nature of writing and the demands it places upon us, for in responding to Heidegger he has found that this is a challenge that is as unavoidable as it is unreachable, for the dispossession it issues, which results in the fragmentary, can never be acceded to. Instead, the fragmentary offers the ghost of a chance, not the void of pure absence but the ambiguous image of a word effacing itself, an approach that replaces confrontation with deferral, revealing with dissembling, resolution with patience.

This desistance indicates that the action of writing undermines its own possibility by persistently deferring relation, such that it fails to achieve any proximity to what is taking place. This failure comes from the nontransparency of language, which is unable to proceed without becoming interrupted by its own action; the fragmentation of writing is a mark of this loss. For Blanchot the fact of writing is something immeasurably dense: its presence is not of something that appears, but that which interrupts or inhibits appearance, it dis-appears, diverting us from its occurrence and removing us into absence. Obscured from appearance, writing also displaces us from its event: if "Waiting" repeatedly indicates the possibility of relation, in its writing this possibility perpetually recedes, giving way to writing as the nonencounter of an imminent return. Although there is no way to avoid the obscurity of language, it is also difficult to follow it into its passivity. The fragmentary provides a way into this nonoccurrence by its desistance, but in doing so it removes us into the imminence and dissembling of its event, and so any attempt to recover the relation to the outside must first negotiate the writing by which it retreats.

But the effacement of writing leads it into an exteriority in which the terms of its encounter with the other become indeterminate as they become exposed to endless absence; there being no presence in waiting, no encounter, only the perpetual imminence of return. Thus the encounter loses itself, such that it will have occurred and will recur but will never be present; it will desist from its own event, its lack of terms leaving it unworkable. This worklessness prevents the writing from developing and forces it to return again and again to itself, weakening its rhythm and syntax by this repetition, and resulting in words that do not reveal or conceal meaning but fragment into the neutrality and passivity of their own turning, a turning aside that renders it opaque: in speaking itself the language of literature is left speaking nothing.

The fragmenting of Blanchot's writing in "Waiting" does not expose the other toward which it attempts to draw itself, but rather provokes an emptiness and resistance that refuses to be drawn. This other relation lies alongside Blanchot's writing as a writing that is neither meaningful nor meaningless but neutral, a writing that simply returns and fragments. In doing so it does not give itself or withdraw, as the abyssal essence of language is read in Heidegger's later works, but finds in its repetition a suspension of any such relation. By neither supporting nor denying Heidegger's work, Blanchot removes himself from its encounter and thereby finds what remains without. This evasion of the terms of Heidegger's relation to poetry and language brings out in its own (interminable) terms that which remained configured within it: the writing of these terms. Such a writing does not carry an opening to the other but the impossible burden of trying to face up to that which effaces itself. It is this desistance of the other that evades Heidegger's work as he persists in marking and thereby limiting its absence. But the absence of the poetic mark is limitless, for in trying to mark itself it finds that these attempts only remove it into an endless return by which it ceaselessly effaces itself.

To approach the other without negating or assimilating it means finding a relation and a writing that does not treat it as part of a whole. To allow it to persist in itself means not incorporating it into a system, and not treating it as a present or absent element of any unity. For it to be other is for it be outside any such definitions; thus the relation and writing by which we are to approach it must leave its exteriority undiminished. The fragmentary follows this other relation not by presenting itself as part of a whole but by following its exteriority into an excessive eccentricity. The fragmentary does not refer beyond itself to a hidden unity of which it is the exposed part, but rather exists as an incompleteness that is bound to its own rupturing as that which it endlessly pursues. The fragmentary possesses a constitutive rather than an accidental incompleteness: its interruption is what brings it about, not what ruins it.

However, this needs to be distinguished from the fragment as it was understood by Novalis and Schlegel; as the Romantic writing par excellence: the form in which the transcendence of the subject could be experienced in the way that the fragment projected beyond itself into the totality that it marked. Thus this is not the fragmentary as Blanchot understood it but a strategy for the affirmation of unity (EI: 525–27/358–59). A fragmentary writing that existed outside any unity would instead require a turning aside from the autonomy of any individual meaning, or the identity of a collective meaning, into a divergence that was endless. This fragmentary would not engender meaning by linking together what is ruptured, but would insistently separate and diverge from meaning. Blanchot found this in Nietzsche, where the fragmentary seemed to arise out of its own repetition, rather than the desire for completion, and thereby exposed an other relation in which repetition operated as the spacing of difference.

To understand how the fragmentary offers a possibility of relation to the other we have to understand how the separation that exists between self and other, or "philosophy" and "poetry," is a separation without reciprocity. While there is a co-respondence between the two it is neither regular nor symmetrical: the other remains at an infinite and irreducible distance, such that its encounter cannot occur through an approach that would undermine its essential distance, but only through an interruption, leading to a disjunction of relation that leaves its distance intact. The relation to the other is thus never direct or apparent, nor does it lead to a unity in which it is assimilated to what is known. Equally, the encounter does not take place in a moment of convergence and simultaneity: "philosophy" and "poetry" do not occur together but through a movement of exclusion and displacement. But if the interruption of the other does not lead to harmony but only to further rupture, not wholeness but loss, then how can we respond to it? How "can one write in such a way that the continuity of the movement of writing might let interruption as meaning and rupture as form intervene fundamentally?" (EI: 9/8) If, moreover, we recognize the necessity of this encounter as arising from a problematic that concerns our own existence, then we are faced with a question that diverts any direct attempt to respond to it by virtue of the impossibility of coming face-to-face with that which displaces our existence. But this turning aside, which the interruption of the other brings about, sends us on an indirect path that *by* its turning responds to the turning aside of the other. For Blanchot, this is the "essential speech of detour, the 'poetry' in the turn of writing" (EI: 31/23).

But to turn aside in response to that which also turns aside is to uproot or unground the turning by making it ex-centric. For if the writing of this word comes after a point that is itself adrift, it can only turn again, deferring itself, and in doing so it brings about a turning that is in response to itself as well as to the other; thus any chance of this turning returning to itself is lost, as the "return effaces the point of departure," leaving it without origin or source (EI: 36/26). "Poetry," for Blanchot, is the name of this writing that becomes displaced by its own words, such that it becomes suspended by and in its lack of ground. Hence, the word of poetry is a (dis)semblance of this turning, that is, it is not only a turning of writing away from the other, and thus a dissembling of it, but also "a turn of the turning, the 'version' that is always in the process of inverting itself," that is, an echo or semblance of this echo (EI: 42/30). It is by way of this doubled turning that writing brings itself into relation with the other, not by revealing it, but by *miming* its turning aside, such that the word's (dis)sembling re-marks its interruption.

However, this writing never attains a proximity with the other instead, by way of its interruptions, the other removes itself from any relation such that the turning of writing can only respond to it by way of its loss, which means that "impossibility is the relation with the Outside" (EI: 66/46). But, as Blanchot points out in a remark that echoes the thought of Levinas, this relation "where the other and the same, while holding themselves in relation, *absolve themselves* of this relation . . . is language" (EI: 79/55).[8] Thus, while the demand of language persists as the impossible necessity to speak from within this infinite detour by which there is relation, the retreat of its terms means that there is no unity or horizon within this detour in which the word can be gathered. So, even if the turning of the word is always a return, this does not mean that it returns to any present or whole; rather its return is the mark of an endless displacement, its rupture leaving it outside any presence, infinitely other. Hence, although the relation of language is, as it was for Heidegger, "an interval that would be neither of being nor of non-being and that bears the Difference of speech," the terms of its relation are effaced by its turning such that it becomes an endless repetition of difference (EI: 99/69). Blanchot summarizes this by saying that poetry is, like the other itself, both "the *relation* of inaccessibility to the other, the other that this inaccessible relation sets up, and nonetheless the inaccessible *presence* of the other." Poetry, that is, the writing *of* this turning, thereby becomes a relation in the very inaccessibility of its approach, so that we have to think of it "as the infinite of a relation without terms and as the infinite termination of a term without relation" (EI: 105/74).

Thus it is in the eccentricity of poetry, its endless, elliptical turning, that we find a response to the rupturing of language that provoked Heidegger's thought. For it is precisely as a *demand* of writing that poetry persists, as an exteriority that can only be reached by a relation reserving in itself the same absence. Such an absence only occurs in "an arrangement that does not compose, but juxtaposes, that is to say, leaves each of the terms that come into relation *outside* one another," and this Blanchot finds in the fragmentary (EI: 453/308). In such a relation the fragmentary cannot relate to itself, as it only diverges; thus it loses any sense of propriety and removes writing into a plurality outside any unity, and within this dissembling its persistent turning only defers its exteriority further: for its exteriority "is always exterior to itself." As a result of this endless detour, exteriority exists *as* "the exposition of difference," for by its ex-position it is difference itself that *writes*, that is, it marks the repetition and deferral of a differentiation without term (EI: 241/161). Thus the fragmentary can only refer to itself as outside, by deferring itself, leaving it not revealed but removed and as a result, it cannot subtend any presence for it only appears by way of an effacing of presence, including its own. Thus, its effect is to "articulate the void by a void, to structure it as a void by drawing from it the strange irregularity that always from the outset specifies it as empty" (EI: 254/169). This irregularity is the self-effacing mark of repetition and exteriority that dissembles the origin, so that by its differentiation it writes and by its writing it defers, leading to an endlessly repeated rupture and suspension: the (re)turning that is (the) poetry (of writing).

This opening up of Blanchot's writing to repetition and exteriority occurs most profoundly in *The Step Not Beyond* (*Le pas au-delà*). Here the demand of responding to writing's othering leads to a radically dispossessed language that exposes his writing from any authorial center or propriety into an other spacing, a repetition of difference. That is, in opening his writing to its own exteriority, by the repetition of its limits, it is this exteriority that begins to write by way of its spacing and fission. This change comes about insofar as the fragmentation of writing approaches "the limit from which the irregularity of another speaking, non-speaking, space comes back, which effaces it or interrupts it and which one approaches only through its alterity, marked by the effect of effacement" (PAD: 72/50). This limit is the point at which writing turns back on itself and responds to its own othering, and the effect of this return, by which it becomes effaced by its own (re)writing, leaves it without origin or unity while leaving traces of its own dissembling: "To write, is perhaps to not write in rewriting—to efface (in writing over) that which is not yet written and that rewriting not only covers over, but restores obliquely in covering it over, in making us think that there was something before, a first version (a detour) or, worse, an original text engaging us thus in the process of the illusion of infinite deciphering" (PAD: 67/46). While the fragmentary effaces the writer by way of an interruption of the other, this exposes the rupture as a relation that is then effaced by its return, such that its excessive loss leads to an (in)articulation of writing by the void (PAD: 32/20). However, as noted, this fragmentation also risks becoming the mask of a subject in dissolution and thereby reconstituting itself as such, re-covering its abyssal effacement with a ground of subjecthood. This possibility is inherent in the attempt to write from out of the displacement that writing brings, from out of what Blanchot calls the *neutre*, and can only be avoided if the *neutre* is not approached as the other itself, but as "the very *relation* of the self to the other." But the result of this is that the *neutre* itself becomes a "relation always in displacement, and in displacement in regard to itself, without anything that has to displace itself, displacement also of that which would be without place. A word perhaps, nothing but a word, but a word in excess, a word too many which for that reason is always lacking. Nothing but a word" (PAD: 12–13/5). The repetition of a word, dissembling nothing.

The effect of this repetition was indicated to Blanchot by Pierre Klossowski's reading of Nietzsche's writings on the Eternal Return.[9] For Heidegger, Nietzsche's position on the Eternal Return is twofold, being both a countermovement to nihilism, insofar as its moment (*Augenblick*) is a time of decision and possibility in which the endless repetition of time can be creatively reappropriated (*Ereignis*), but equally, it is also a confrontation with the endlessness of the past and the future as impossibilities that cannot be appropriated. Thus the thought of the Eternal Return is one of the "loneliest loneliness" and "the greatest burden" whose necessity lies in thinking the affirmation of endless repetition, that is, both as an affirmation and as an endlessness. This is a "riddle" from which thinking cannot extricate itself as it holds a duplicity that cannot be decided, making it an intrinsically tragic thought since its thinking is both a transition (*Übergang*) and a decline (*Untergang*). Perhaps trying to extricate himself from the abyssal nature of this duplicity, Heidegger sees Nietzsche's thought as both the end of metaphysics and its culmination, although he does concede that as the "last thought of Western metaphysics" the Eternal Return "conceals something unthought, something which at the same time remains a sealed door to metaphysical thinking." It is thus a thought that is "wrapped in a darkness" for Heidegger, but one that we should not shrink back from, as its position at the end of metaphysics provides us with an understanding of what such an end persistently reveals and conceals (WHD: 46–47/108–9; VA1: 117–18/232–33).

As Blanchot, following Klossowski, reads it, to experience the Eternal Return is to experience the return of time in time, but there is no moment in time that could receive the return of time and so the experience of return could only occur outside of time, by way of presentiment and memory. But as a result, this would not be an experience in time but outside it, for "the demand of the return, excluding any present mode from time, would never release a now in which the same would come back to the same, to myself" (PAD: 21/11). Thus to experience the present as a return would be to not experience it at all except as a re-(experience) of it, by way of return, for in returning it displaces the present *so that* it can be experienced as a return. Thus the experience is one of derangement, removing presence into an exteriority of repetition, such that the experience of return as return is not an experience of anything, but return. However, for it also to be a recurrence of the "same" is for it to be an endless repetition of difference, which as repetition can be the "same":

> But if it is the "same" through its return, is it not the return alone that would give rise to the same, and thus it would necessarily happen that the "same" has deferred through an infinity of rounds, of times, only returning to the same by the law of return. Is it therefore not the case that nothing, in this same, comes back to the same, except *the return itself* (turn, detour, overturning) and is it not the case that the affirmation of return leads to affirming together—but without constituting a whole—the difference and the repetition, thus the non-identity of the same? (EI: 410/275)

Thus to affirm this experience is to affirm nothing, for as the Eternal Return of the Same it is also the "perpetual detour of difference," which is to say that this experience both affirms singularity as the condition of return while effacing it by its return, just as the moment of the experience is deferred by the endlessness of its return while it is thereby being affirmed (EI: 413/277). Thus what returns in the Eternal Return is nothing but the return, and so to write from within this experience is to only write by rewriting; since a writing that affirms the return can never affirm itself, for while it will recur and has already occurred it will never be present to itself; its own presence will be forgotten or erased by way of its return: "Where would this affirmation that is without return be situated? There is no moment—no instance—for the affirmation of all affirmation any more than for he who would affirm it, since its presence would mean: a lack whose lack no mark could indicate without thereby annulling itself" (EI: 418/280–281).

Thus writing at this limit is always undermining itself, for while its repetition persists by way of its turning it is thereby also lost, as its writing perpetually retreats the limit from which it returns, rendering its circle ex-centric and endless, "the circle out of circulation of all circles" (PAD: 22/12). This means that if writing occurs then it is not by taking place as a mark that in withdrawing marks itself, which is the movement of being in Heidegger's thought, but as the trace of an effacing whose singularity is marked by *un*-marking itself, the effacement of effacement, *l'iter-rature*, which leaves it without. Writing does not set itself up or bring itself forth, but ex-poses itself; it is a rupture that withdraws from tracing itself by persistently repeating its rupture, separating from itself such that its only self is this ellipsis or interval, which is endlessly displaced by its own return. But if there is a displacement here it is a displacement of the self to the other, that is, the proper dissembles itself into alterity, rupturing its event into an endless prosaic othering, exposing the receding edge of the limit of language. Is this then the basis upon which to think the ethical fragmentation of *Ereignis*?[10] For this endless detour becomes an affirmation of the return in that it holds to its turning by turning away from it, such that the fragmentary in being deferred returns: "we can only affirm the return as detour, making of affirmation that which turns away from affirming and of the detour that which hollows out the affirmation and in this hollowing out makes it return from the extreme of itself to the extreme of itself, not to coincide with it, rather to render it again more affirmative at a mobile point of extreme non-coincidence" (EI: 414/278).

Thus as its experience erases itself, the idea of recurrence itself becomes impossible, for as a "doctrine" of repetition it cannot be repeated. This reveals it as an aporia for thought, for what is revealed in the Eternal Return is that the experience of repetition cannot itself be repeated, which is also the case for the self-effacing mark of poetry. While this experience was deeply destabilizing for Hölderlin and undermined any possibility of his being an exemplar, or "poet of poets," with Heidegger the inability to re-experience the experience of repetition was evidence of its finitude, of the singularity of the *logos* whose concealment calls us to respond, but to which we can have no relation other than our own finitude. What

Blanchot has exposed is that a relation to this rupture persists *within* the movement of repetition as its detour, which does not secure it but that finds in its disruption its own language, which is the worklessness and unworking (*désoeuvrement*) *of* disruption.

Thus the fragmentary, as the writing of this rupturing, exposes the present to the impossibility of being present without repetition, which only affirms it by way of its effacement. The present is then only possible on the basis of being endlessly displaced and ruptured, which inscribes it into the past as that which has never been present but that is always already lost. In doing so, the fragmentary answers to the demand of repetition, in which what is repeated "is" not, for it is forever being displaced by its own return; hence its rupturing is the means by which there is this recurrence: it is its *relation.* The fragmentary writes the return but through its repetition both marks and retreats from it; thus what remains of this writing that un-(marks) or secretes itself is the *neutre*, which is writing as a passivity beyond all passivity, a patience or passion that is always past, each of these words marking for Blanchot the step (*pas*) that is not (*pas*) a movement by virtue of its recurrence: the (step) (not) beyond (ED: 33/16).

This is what has been exposed in the works of Hölderlin and Heidegger: the strangeness of writing (and thus literature, which is to say, "poetry" and "philosophy") as that which is without author or subject or presence, a disturbing, eccentric repetition. As repetition, writing occurs, as Blanchot writes in the epigraph of this chapter, outside being and non-being, as an endlessly deferred encounter with the other, and within this deferral the other is always on its way but never arrives; it is never present but nor is it ever fully absent; its arrival, just as its word, is to come (EI: 104/73). As well as its temporal and literary implications, the fragment also enables us to understand the nature of encounter itself as an endless approach, and thus not to see its rupture as an aporia but as the perpetual detour of difference, which thereby gives it the greatest ethical exigency. This dissembling is mobilized in the way that *The Step Not Beyond* oscillates undecidably between philosophy and literature, suspending its own encounter, its own limits, in such a way that the terms of the encounter, "philosophy" and "literature," are placed in palimpsest. This does not mean that the writing becomes meaningless, but through its repeated effacement it removes its figuring as "philosophy" or "literature" and thereby becomes rigorously indeterminate and irreducible. This double erasure or "l'iter-rature" is called *neutre* as a marker of its namelessness and evasion of terms. Literature has opened onto a strange and infinite exteriority; lacking presence or unity it appears by absenting itself and does so endlessly.

If I might be permitted the artifice, there is a particular mobilization in "l'iter-rature" that I would like to take advantage of here. As it implies, there is a reference in this phrase to a repeated erasure, moreover, to literature itself *as* a repeated erasure, that is, to an erasure that is itself erased by the iteration of literature, by its rewriting and overwriting by which it is always in palimpsest. That literature is in palimpsest is hardly a new observation, but to suggest that this is constituted by repeated erasure is significant, for it indicates that if writing is always rewriting and overwriting then it cannot be separated from erasure, and more importantly, from the repetition of erasure, by which it both forgets and inscribes itself into the palimpsest in which it occurs. This is also to suggest that Heidegger's oblivion of being, the forgetting of forgetting, fails to understand the nature of repetition as that which dissembles itself, unless it is inscribed in textual terms, which has the result of not setting up an epochal destining of being as the progressive loss of awareness, but of endlessly displacing presence in palimpsest. This deferral undermines any possibility of historical founding and sending, because it replaces the relation of being and forgetting, of the gift of being, with the neutrality of rewriting and l'iter-rature, in which the possibility of relation only arises by way of the endless detour of repeated erasure and rupture. The necessity of responding to this demand is the necessity that faces poetry after Heidegger.

... ...

The event of being, the presencing of presencing, is ambiguous as its situation is undecidable. As the presencing of presencing it is a recurrence in which the same returns to the same, but insofar as it is the event of being it is always in withdrawal. The relation between the same and the return is obviously the key to this ambiguity and the differing inflections given to it give rise to the different approaches of Heidegger and Blanchot. For Heidegger, even though the event is in withdrawal it is still part of the unity that is the recurrence of the *same*, it is thus a withdrawal *of* being. Blanchot takes the other path, emphasizing the fact that in the recurrence of the same the only aspect that returns is the *recurrence*, giving it not a unity but an endless differentiation and eccentricity. While Heidegger would agree with this reading of recurrence as differentiation, its turning cannot be recouped for Blanchot in any way, not even as withdrawal, for repetition leads to the *perpetual detour* of difference. This differentiation is itself apparent in the transition from Heidegger to Blanchot and this allows us to affirm both versions despite their divergence, which is precisely what is at stake in Blanchot's rewriting of Heidegger. For we must continue to attempt to broach the relation of language and being even as it prevents us from doing so, since in this rewriting the relation of language to being is reinscribed such that it "de-scribes" (*dé-crit*) itself by its secretive (dis)appearance, leaving it strange and other and endlessly dissimulated (ED: 17/7).

Writing has no event; it simply persists in the repetition of itself and thus arises the demand issued in poetry: the demand to write, until the difference between writing and not writing is no difference (ED: 25/12). For it is only by succumbing to this demand that we can enter into a passivity (*pathos*) and sobriety in which the un-marking of difference, of the other, persists. Although it is only in virtue of the fact that we are that we can respond to this demand, it is only in being removed that "we" can be affirmed, and in doing so it is the removal that is affirmed such that we "are" only as this dissembling. Hence, in our attempts to respond to this demand, to "come again would be to come to ex-centre oneself anew, to wander. Only the *nomadic* affirmation *remains*" (PAD: 49/33). In other words, poetry exposes thinking to language as an endless estrangement without ground or return, and as a result it is both that by virtue of which thinking *is* and that which also resists or evades thought, thereby forever undermining it. It is as such that poetry is a limit of thinking and conversely, thinking is always *of* this limit. Thus, while thinking can turn away from this limit, a thinking of poetry would have to attempt to persist within this limit as an echo of its desistance, not to shelter or preserve this mark, but to follow its ex-centric path. It is from this demand that Hölderlin's rewriting and Blanchot's fragmentary have arisen, as an endless tracing of loss. If a poem is the singular mark of this occurrence, a solitary convolution of the limits of language, a meniscus perhaps, formed as language's edge reaches beyond itself only to turn back onto itself, then thinking is what takes place out of it, such that poetry would be the diaphanous event of thinking and thinking an elliptical experience of poetry.

Consequently, what is interesting for us here are not so much Heidegger's suggestions about poetry, as the implications that arise from these suggestions. Poetry works for Heidegger insofar as it exposes thinking to the relation of being and man by language. However, the undercurrents of this exposure have proved stronger than Heidegger seems to have realized, for poetry does not expose us to the presencing of being by language as much as it ex-poses us *from* this presencing. It would perhaps be this that would serve to distinguish the endlessness of Blanchot's nomadic fragmentary from the regioning of Heidegger's topological *Gelassenheit.* For poetry exposes thought to an absence outside of any presencing, such that it is not conceivable as the absence *of* being but only as an indeterminate loss.[11] To think out of such a rupture is the concern of Heidegger's experience with language, but poetry undermines this thinking insofar as it removes any possibility of drawing out an origin, work, or figure from this experience. The writings of Blanchot and Hölderlin have pursued this interruption to the extent that it has inverted the ends to which Heidegger put it; possibility only ever arises from impossibility, relation from nonrelation, origin from repetition, use from uselessness, and figuring from disfiguring. Poetry after Heidegger must contend with these implications which, shorn of their being-historical configuration, arise as still unanswerable issues, whose impossibility directly pertains to their necessity. For what Heidegger's thought brought out most profoundly was a singularity that cannot be appropriated as it evades and disrupts any appropriation. Poetry emerges from Heidegger as an ellipsis that interrupts all creative or productive impulses, but in doing so holds out the greatest ethical possibilities if we can come to understand how ethics arises not from relation but from its other: nonrelation.

As an instance of this possibility the space between these views is itself significant, for it is evidence of the unknown that emerges between them. In the interval between Blanchot and Heidegger we do not find a compromise or reconciliation, but the presence of an unknown that does not relinquish its obscurity. Instead, there is an infinite gaping or hollowing out that language does not so much carve out as indicate by the distance it covers in skirting it. This space is not the arena of possibility, but the expanse of an impossibility that appears not as present but as the lining of juxtaposition; that which invisibly separates by the opacity of its transparency. Writing after Blanchot and Heidegger arises from this shadowy expanse, neither drawing it out nor plunging in, but maintaining the pressure of its inaccessibility as a constant echo; the fact of language's separation as the welcoming without subordinating of the unknown. In this way

Hölderlin's writings do not speak to us of the absent gods as the mark of historical determination, but as the mark of language's groundlessness that haunts being with writing. This is our ellipsis, to write that which cannot be read, other than by writing, a writing without voice or silence, fiction or reflection, a writing of endless empty echoes: *mimēsis.*

. . . "NEVER REPEAT" . . .

I cannot speak without being misheard; I cannot write without being misread, even by myself. Already I have lost my intention and your attention. I cannot speak and yet, that is all there is to say. Never can I say what I mean although I mean everything that I say. I cannot speak, and that is why I do. I can neither speak nor write, and yet that is what is going on. There is speaking and writing here but my relation to them is no relation at all. What is happening here is impossible, and yet it persists. It is the limit of all that I can do, the end, the edge, the period. It is finitude, and yet it is itself infinite, an endless repetition of ending, an infinite finitude, a repeating period: an ellipsis. What is this ellipsis? A pause, which appears between other pauses, although it doesn't appear for there is nothing there to appear. Language is nothing but this endlessly repeated encounter with its own limits, an ellipsis in which and as which it persists.

How do we speak in this? What are *we* in this ellipsis, if we are not that by which this ellipsis is? We are that against which its gaping extends *and* that which is extended. Speaking is only possible here where I speak *that* I cannot speak, where I am the extension, the repetition of that limit. What does it mean to be unable to speak and yet to be able to say that? This is a question *of* language; indeed it is *the* question of language, as it is the question that language itself raises: How can I speak of that which gives speech but cannot itself be spoken? What kind of language can I use to speak the impossibility of language? Not in such a way that I am simply speaking of impossibility, for that would be only to describe it rather than to say it, but in such a way that I would say something altogether different, which is to speak *impossibly.*

But who would hear this, and how could it be heard? And if it could not, what then would I be saying? Is not hearing necessary for language, even if it is only my own? And what if by speaking impossibly I could not hear what is said, even as I say it? What has happened to me in speaking of language is nothing less than a dispossession of my self. I can neither speak nor hear, and yet that is what is going on, or rather, language is speaking and hearing and "I" have no place in this. "I" am its limit, just as it is mine. What kind of language is this and what is it saying? Despite its closeness it is foreign to any language we know, except poetry. The question, "how can I speak?" lies at the heart of poetry, but in trying to answer it poetry is brought up against its own limits. These limits enable poetry to speak, but also prevent it from ever fully speaking; hence the question at the heart of poetry is always inflected by its own constraints. But what kind of relation could obtain between speaking and its impossibility, its other, its limit?

Even if there is misreading and mishearing at work here, that still means that there is reading and hearing going on; it is just no longer mine, or anybody's, for the word resists all possession, even its own. While it gives itself freely, what gives it is inaccessible, and so it remains outside our grasp and incomprehensible. We cannot name it or know it, as it is that which names and thereby brings to knowing, and so while it names its own name is lost. What is heard or read is paradoxical: both utterly singular but also mundane, both original and repeated. But this is no harmonious balance, as the word places us on a tightrope of extreme delicacy, of the delicacy, in fact, of a breath. A breath expired and inspired in what we call "poetry," which is the turning into the word of the word.

What is language here? This is at the heart of Derrida's inquiry in his short paper "Che cos'è la poesia?," and its commentary, "Istrice 2: Ick bünn all hier." The first is an ode to the poem and the second an interview with Maurizio Ferraris; in both Derrida attempts to sketch out the nature of this singular experience that is passed over by literary or philosophical discourse even while it is being discussed.[12] He calls this a "poematic" experience insofar as it is the experience of singularity that gives rise to a poem, which leads to a poetics grounded in singularity rather than in the generality of *poiēsis.* While Derrida has always shown an interest in the language of poets like Artaud, Mallarmé, Ponge, or Celan, and has also examined Heidegger's readings of Trakl and Hölderlin, he has avoided thinking about poetry itself and what can be thought or said about it after Heidegger, except in these two pieces. Their existence would itself appear to be strategic, in that their isolation and obscurity seems to have been used by Derrida to conceal his own thoughts on this topic, so as to prevent their being lost in the larger ambit of Heideggerian or poetic scholarship.

It is as if they have been made to remain small and hard ("brief, elliptical by vocation," he says) so as to avoid being noticed and thereby captured in philosophical discourse (PI: 291).

This tactic is inherent to the poematic experience and is illustrated for Derrida by the humility of the hedgehog, which rolls itself up into a spiky ball when threatened. This bristling maneuver is called *hérisser* in French, which gives the hedgehog (*hérisson*) its name, and in Italian—it was for an Italian journal that the first piece was written—it is *istrice.* As names these are decidedly catachrestic, hardly names at all, more like movements, subtle almost inconspicuous movements given form in word and flesh, not a hedgehog but a bristler, a thing of bristles. The name "*hérisson* is barely a name, it does not bear its name, it plays with syllables, but in any case it is neither a concept nor a thing"; it is finally no more than a clump of letters around which Derrida builds up his ode (PI: 303). In doing so, he is not simply mobilizing a metaphor to describe the poematic experience, but is actually exposing its behavior by way of the elusiveness and resistance that is the bristling of language as it turns in on itself. Here the presence of terms like *hérisson* and *istrice* is critical, because their idiomatic strangeness is irreducible and thus surfaces through the translation as that which resists or evades the movement from one language to another.

But this irreducibility is not evidence of some concretion of truth that persists across the movement of languages, but of something far more humble and vulnerable: the *idiom,* which does not subtend language as an essence but that recurs across its surface as what is inessential and cannot be translated and, as a result, is always at risk of being lost or destroyed, forgotten or neglected. As such the idiom is a mark of the poematic experience, of a singularity that does not transcend or unify language but that disappears from it as the irreplaceable marker of its instancy. The idiom is the site of the siting of language, the trace of its placing; it is that which records only to be forgotten, the intangible grit that sticks to language as it occurs.[13] Elsewhere Derrida has found other instances of this textual singularity in the proper name, the date, and the signature, all of which indicate the peculiar presence of a mark that while universal is always singular and thus most difficult to recall, for these marks distinguish a text *as* a particular text and are thus irreplaceable but also anonymous. There are no marks to distinguish the mark itself; it is already lost: as a mark of presence it is inherently absent as it cannot remark its own presence as such.

The distinctiveness of the poematic experience arises from its relation to translation, as it bears that elusive trace that marks the impossible task of translation, that is, it echoes the thematics of poetic dictation in which the poetic "would be that which you desire to learn, but from and of the other, thanks to the other and under dictation, by heart, *imparare a memoria*" (PI: 291). The text of "Che cos'è la poesia?" is littered with idiomatic phrases and their simultaneous resistance and loss is made apparent by the bilingual presentation of the text, which gives us the translation at the moment of its transition, presenting us not only with the translation itself but also with that which resists it, that which is lost or sacrificed in translation. Within this loss lies the endless desire that seeks not only to learn from the other but *of* the other, in its own tongue, its own language, which is precisely the source of its destruction as the idiom is precisely that which translation betrays. Since in crying out "do not repeat me, learn me by heart," the other calls for its own destruction, as the demand to remain true to the other, to its mark, requires following an injunction that its very translation makes impossible.

This is the "*literality of the vocable*," its letter to which we wish to remain true, but that we always betray: "literally," as we say, is itself, in its desire for an "absolute inseparation" of the meaning and the letter, "the origin of the poetic" (PI: 293–95). The poematic experience is of this impossibly "single trait," the cipher that in joining together meaning and letter nevertheless spaces them out in the rhythm or ellipsis that is the poem, and by which we then learn what it is "to learn by heart" and thus what the "heart" (*phren*) is that is at the heart of *phronēsis*, our care for the word. But as such the poetic is that which turns away from words, leaving only a mark, a residue, which refuses to be taken up in thought or language, not because it conceals some impossibly hard diamond-like truth but the opposite, because it is "the absolute nonabsolute" (PI: 295). This phrase deliberately complicates any understanding of the fragment that seeks to depict it, as Schlegel did, as being "complete in itself like a hedgehog," that is, as ab-solute, without relation, by suggesting instead that the poetic is *only* relation.[14]

To be nonabsolute is to be without the ability *not* to relate, and the poetic is this absolutely; it is entirely lacking in anything *but* relation, that is, any autonomy or completion that could render relation unnecessary. Thus it cannot even relate to itself; it evades even its own marking, which is to say that the poetic is alterity, and like the hedgehog is destined for a humble, insignificant, and endlessly repeated death, a death that cannot be recouped as sacrifice or remainder (PI: 308, 322). It is precisely the hedgehog's curling in on itself that seals its fate; it is because of its alterity that it is always appropriated; its resistance to meaning is the very condition of its thematization. The poetic "can only expose itself to accidents when it tries to save itself, and first of all to save itself from its name and to save its coming. It has no relation to itself—that is, no totalizing individuality—that does not expose it to even more death and to being-torn-apart" (PI: 303).

"It thus takes place, essentially, without one's having to do it or make it: it *lets itself* be done, without activity, without work, in the most sober *pathos*, a stranger to all production, especially to creation. The poem falls to me, benediction, coming of (or from) the other. Rhythm but dissymmetry. There is never anything but some poem, before any *poiēsis*" (PI: 297). The poematic experience indicates that there is something outside thought and language that is so intangible that we can only find its mark, and because its mark refuses even words, we find that the heart of the poetic lies in its unspeakability. But it is an unspeakability that desires repetition, even though doing so means that it is destroyed in the process, for the poetic cries out with the desire to be said again and again and what it says is "never repeat . . ." (PI: 295). This desire *is* the poetic, it is its heart; that which drives it to bristle with self-annihilation, the source of its aleatory alterity, its wandering doom: "Without a subject: poem, perhaps there is some, and perhaps it *leaves itself*, but I never write any. A poem, I never sign(s) it. The other sign(s)" (PI: 299).

. . . (REFRAIN) . . .

Heidegger was concerned with trying to find a language with which to articulate the meaning of being, and he proceeded, by way of poetry, to uncover such a language in tautology, as a saying of the same. But the repetition involved in this saying is grounded in the singular experience of our own finitude, rendering the very possibility of ontology doubtful, as it is a question of bringing the singular rupture of existence to the repetition of language. To some extent tautology enables us to respond to this singular rupture by way of its repetition, but the question remains of how it is possible for a relation to occur between finitude and repetition, as the former is both the condition of possibility and impossibility for the latter. This is the question that remains after Heidegger.

Intrinsic to Heidegger's approach to language, in common with much modernist thinking and writing, is that it manifests itself by way of an encounter with its own finitude: it is only where language reaches its own limits and begins to fall apart that it comes to appear in itself. But language does not do this in isolation; it is our language and if it encounters its limits it is only insofar as there is a concomitant encounter between ourselves and our own limits as humans. Language as such is thus a *praxis* of finitude, but this is only half of its essence, for in its encounter with its limits language repeats itself, and by way of its rupturing it dissembles and thereby differentiates itself; thus its *praxis* of finitude becomes a *pathos* of alterity as we attempt to bear out this repetition of the same of language *as* its differing. This other half is attended to in greater detail by Hölderlin and Blanchot who perceive how this *pathos* of alterity is at root the basis of history and ethics but, combined with Heidegger's emphasis on the repetition of language, these two aspects comprise the essence of *mimēsis* as the elliptical writing of being: that by which the repetition and difference of language and the human persist in their own finitude and alterity.

The significance of seeing this *mimēsis* as the writing of being is that it draws us away from an account of being in its presence and into its essence as eccentric and elliptical: *mimēsis* as the writing of the essence of language is that which resists or evades presence insofar as it is l'iter-rature, the repeated erasure by which it, and thus we, are always in palimpsest. As was found with the earth and the caesura, there are aspects of presencing that secrete themselves, that is, they not only withdraw but also reproduce themselves, and withdraw *by* reproducing themselves, thereby leaving a palimpsest of repeated and thus unmarked erasure. This necessarily rewrites Heidegger's history of the forgetting of being, by which being withdraws and this withdrawal also disappears, by indicating that there is a *traumatic* side to this history, a side that cannot be recalled but that also is not forgotten as it persists in and by its own repeated erasure.[15] This is what is at issue in Hölderlin's understanding of modernity and in Blanchot's work on relation: an unresolved *pathos* of alterity, a bearing of the other in its otherness, which is in some way to be approached as and in a new kind of writing.

By drawing out the peculiar nature of trauma we can see some of the demands to which this new kind of writing must respond, for psychiatric studies have shown that trauma is very hard to isolate in terms of what we ordinarily understand by "experience."[16] The event that leads to the trauma is precisely that which is *not* experienced in any mode of comprehension or representation. What occurs leaves an unconscious mark that only comes to awareness at some later point, and even then it may not be experienced as such for it is likely that its recurrence is by way of some displacement. The structure of the trauma is thus highly complex as it only occurs by way of its recurrence, which is to say that it exists as a temporal and symbolic doubling that persistently resists assimilation and narrativization. The "experience" of trauma then, is of recurrence, of that which was not experienced recurring by way of something else, leaving it strictly uncanny and inaccessible. It is this evanescence that constitutes its singularity, for it renders it irreducible and unrecountable.

This temporal anomaly indicates something particular about memory, for it lets us see how a memory can persist without being available for recall, while still recurring by itself. Attached to this recurrence is the forgetting attendant on its displacement, since within each recurrence what recurs remains hidden in oblivion, meaning that its recurrence is uncannily marked as being always for the first time. Therapeutic treatment of trauma works from this point of first recognizing the trauma *as* recurrent and thereby opening paths to begin a comprehension of what lies behind this recurrence, thus slowly assimilating its concealed origin. However, this can of course only work in those instances where there is a *particular* wound to address, for it may be the case that there is in this mode of recurrence and oblivion some more profound indication of our temporal existence as such. Between the point of the traumatic event and its recurrence there is only an absence without end, the absence of an open-ended waiting in which there is no awareness of waiting or absence but only a peculiar suspension in which one might be said to persist in the oblivion of the past, that is, to be withdrawn from presencing. This is what Blanchot has described as the sheer passivity of the disaster, which indicates a more extreme withdrawal into what there is (*il y a*) of being—what remains—than Heidegger has countenanced, for it is an absolute limit to *Andenken.*

While in the poetic experience there is an event that has occurred whose recurrence is then awaited, exposing the poet to *l'attente de l'avenir*, in trauma there is no original experience that can be recalled or awaited, yet there is recurrence, a return of what was never present and never experienced, which had no event and did not occur, an uncanny presence that then divides the present against itself, displacing it into a waiting that is forgetting, that is a memory of the present, *déjà vu*, without future or passing. In this phantom encounter, in which there is the incomprehensible feeling of having seen or known something before that cannot be verified or dispelled, we come across the essentially undecidable truth that abyssally underpins all of Heidegger's readings of poetic language. For despite his insistence in the preface to the *Elucidations* that his readings will lead us to think that we have understood Hölderlin's poems in this way all along, the ambiguity of *déjà vu* displaces any such assurance into an awareness that there is something here that can never be brought to a decisive understanding, something that evades thought by way of its irreducible and singular absence, something of the uncanniness of the literary, which in both its reading and writing is never just a homecoming, or return to the familiar, but also and undecidably so, a radical estrangement from the familiar into an errancy without end.[17]

This ambiguous *déjà vu* exposes the traumatized to the demand of language, insofar as the absolute past is the time *of* language, to which we have always already been enjoined. This makes clear that the claim of language is inherent to trauma, a claim to speak or write where this cannot be done, as language only ever desists from or deceives our approaches, thereby extending its own inaccessibility and inescapability. Thus while the mark of pain is that which inscribes memories for us, this is only a modification of the original forgetting that is the pain of language itself, which of course has no language in which it can be recounted and thereby assimilated. This is perhaps the basic trauma that is at the heart of some of Blanchot's or Celan's later works, and indicates the intense demand to interrogate the limits of language as a means to respond to its recurrent absence.

Consequently, we can appreciate how Hölderlin and Blanchot have developed, practically and theoretically, an understanding of writing as a repetition of interruption, a fragmentary rewriting, which effectively pursues the ellipses that opened up in Heidegger's thought where it encountered the extreme displacement of the earth and the draw-ing. From this new kind of writing both Hölderlin and Blanchot uncover a new mode of relation drawn from the repetition of interruption, which responds to the difficulties of addressing the evasion and resistance of ethical and historical relations, which characterizes our modernity, by recognizing how this writing persists in palimpsest with ethics and history by virtue of its rewriting of relation as l'iter-rature, as the repeated erasure of its terms. While Heidegger's thinking does not entertain this possibility, his work is central for any attempt to understand how this rewriting has developed and also how it brings about an encounter with our own finitude, as a repeated encounter of singularity. While there is an extreme divergence between their writings, the works of Blanchot, Hölderlin, and Heidegger are linked by way of this divergence, as it is the same divergence of language, its *partage* (sharing and dividing) and *excriture* (exscription), as Jean-Luc Nancy would say, that is at issue in each, in its alterity and finitude, its *pathos* and *praxis*, and its tragedy and truth.[18]

To respond to the earth as the ground of language is thus a twofold task, for it requires a response that is yet free, as only this can answer to the earth as earth. The mutual demand between earth and response holds them together even as they turn aside from each other, since the demand of each risks undermining the possibility of the other. As a result, a path must be found in which the response answers most closely to the earth, and in its materiality and dissembling the only option would appear to be that which occurs in writing and specifically, that writing that is neither silent nor spoken but simply repeats. The importance of this lies in the fact that there is a traumatic desistance to the earth that cannot be encompassed by the answering of truth to the call of the clearing. For the earth as earth is traumatic; it is a memory that cannot be forgotten, but that also cannot be fully recalled. The free response to this lies only in writing, because it too carries this passage between presence and absence, which indicates how its *praxis* arises from a sober *pathos*, and as a result this writing perhaps needs to be approached not in terms of an ontology but rather in some as yet undeveloped form of *pathology*.

Writing is the chattering of inedible words, the free echo of the iterations of the earth. Hölderlin found a way to this echo in the translation of tragedy, Blanchot in the fragmentation of relation, for in both of these ways there is a response to the desistance of the earth that still preserves it, a way of commemorating *and* surviving, by repeating the earth into its difference, which is not so much a recovery or retrieval as a recapitulation. This brings us close to Nancy's understanding of the *partage* of language in the experience of freedom, but also brings to his reading a much stronger *pathos*, and thus an awareness of the sobriety of this bearing out of iteration. This is the essence of *mimēsis*, since it is by way of this *pathos* that *mimēsis* is borne and as such claims us; the *mimēsis* of the ethical and historical is what exercises us in language, tracing out its steno-graphy, the mark of our bearing straits.

Notes

INTRODUCTION

1. Maurice Blanchot, *The Space of Literature*, tr. Ann Smock (Lincoln: University of Nebraska Press, 1982), 43. Blanchot is responding to Mallarmé's question: "Does something like Literature (*les Lettres*) exist?" Let me emphasize this point by way of caution; I do not see an equivalence between Blanchot's use of *littérature* and Heidegger's use of *Dichtung*, but nor is it the case that there is an a priori distinction between the two in terms of what we understand as "prose" and "poetry." However, for both, but in significantly differing ways, which this work will endeavor to unravel, there is an attempt to approach a certain mode of language that is concerned with its own status and nature, whether in poetry or prose.

2. Martin Heidegger, *Nietzsche: The Will to Power as Art*, tr. David Farrell Krell (New York: Harper, 1979), 198; *Plato's 'Sophist,'* tr. Richard Rojcewicz and André Schuwer (Bloomington: Indiana University Press, 1997), 297. Claudia Baracchi, *Of Myth, Life, and War in Plato's 'Republic'* (Bloomington: Indiana University Press, 2002), 98–109, 117–26, emphasizes this ambivalence of *mimēsis* in Plato by indicating that it is both unavoidable *and* elusive.

3. Rüdiger Safranski, *Martin Heidegger: Between Good and Evil*, tr. Ewald Osers (Cambridge: Harvard University Press, 1998), 281.

4. Heidegger, *Logik als die Frage nach dem Wesen der Sprache*, ed. Günter Seubold (Frankfurt am Main: Vittorio Klostermann, 1998), 170.

5. Rudolf Carnap, "The Overcoming of Metaphysics through Logical Analysis of Language," tr. Arthur Pap, in *Heidegger and Modern Philosophy: Critical Essays*, ed. Michael Murray (New Haven: Yale University Press, 1978), 23–34.

6. Heidegger, *The Metaphysical Foundations of Logic*, tr. Michael Heim (Bloomington: Indiana University Press, 1984), 154–59; Heidegger, *Kant and the Problem of Metaphysics*, tr. Richard Taft (Bloomington: Indiana University Press, 1997), 163.

7. Heidegger returns to this point six years later, making it the guiding thread of his 1935 *Introduction to Metaphysics* lectures (EM: 24–30/24–29). See also this remark from his lectures on Nietzsche's fundamental metaphysical position, *Nietzsche: The Eternal Recurrence of the Same*, tr. David Farrell Krell (New York: Harper, 1984), 195, two years

later: "the most durable and unfailing touchstone of genuineness and forcefulness of thought in a philosopher is the question as to whether or not he or she experiences in a direct and fundamental manner the nearness of nothing in the being of beings. Whoever fails to experience it remains forever outside the realm of philosophy, without hope of entry." Richard Polt provides a useful overview in "The Question of Nothing," in *A Companion to Heidegger's 'Introduction to Metaphysics,'* eds. Polt and Gregory Fried (New Haven: Yale University Press, 2001), 57–82.

8. Ludwig Wittgenstein, "Zu Heidegger," in Friedrich Waismann, *Wittgenstein und der Wiener Kreis,* ed. Brian F. McGuinness (Oxford: Blackwell, 1967), 68; tr. Michael Murray as "On Heidegger on Being and Dread," in *Heidegger and Modern Philosophy,* ed. Murray, 80.

9. Robert Bernasconi's *The Question of Language in Heidegger's History of Being* (Atlantic Highlands, NJ: Humanities Press, 1985), is an excellent if somewhat reserved reading of Heidegger's encounters with Hölderlin and George; tending to lean more to the philosophical contextualization of poetic language rather than to its challenges to traditional thinking. The excluded conclusion on Heidegger's "The Way to Language," "The Transformation of Language at Another Beginning," in *Heidegger in Question: The Art of Existing* (Atlantic Highlands, NJ: Humanities Press, 1993), 190–210, is a necessary rejoinder to this weakness. Gerald L. Bruns's *Heidegger's Estrangements: Language, Truth, and Poetry in the Later Writings* (New Haven: Yale University Press, 1989), fully embraces Heidegger's radical rethinking of language but ultimately fails to see the impact of its ontological grounding, and thus neglects its philosophical implications. The work of Christopher Fynsk has gone farthest in balancing these two trends in *Heidegger: Thought and Historicity* (Ithaca: Cornell University Press, 1993), and *Language and Relation: . . . that there is language* (Stanford: Stanford University Press, 1996). The first provides strong readings of Heidegger's encounters with Nietzsche and Hölderlin, while the second has chapters on "The Essence of Language" and "The Way to Language."

10. David White, *Heidegger and the Language of Poetry* (Lincoln: University of Nebraska Press, 1978); and David Halliburton, *Poetic Thinking: An Approach to Heidegger* (Chicago: University of Chicago Press, 1981), are both good general introductions but neither treat the later works and thus fail (White especially) to see the impact that poetry had on Heidegger's thinking of language. Edited collections on this topic have followed similar paths; see Joseph J. Kockelmans, *On Heidegger and Language* (Evanston, IL: Northwestern University Press, 1972); William V. Spanos, *Martin Heidegger and the Question of Literature: Toward a Postmodern Literary Hermeneutics* (Bloomington: Indiana University Press, 1979); David Wood, *Heidegger and Language* (Warwick, UK: Parousia Press, 1981); and John Sallis, *Heidegger and Hölderlin,* special issue, *Research in Phenomenology* 19, (1989). Many of the most useful essays from these collections have been recollected in *Martin Heidegger: Critical Assessments.* Vol. 3, *Language,* ed. Christopher Macann (London: Routledge, 1992); see especially those by Parvis Emad, Theodore Kisiel, John Sallis, and Friedrich-Wilhelm von Herrmann. Paul de Man's work on Hölderlin and Heidegger, particularly "Heidegger's Exegeses of Hölderlin," tr. Wlad Godzich, in *Blindness and Insight: Essays in the Rhetoric of Contemporary Criticism* (London: Routledge, 1983), 246–66, has been very influential in the literary reception of Heidegger's work, despite or because of its misreading of Heidegger, and seems to exemplify an approach that refuses any "philo-

sophical" treatment of poetic language, preferring instead to see such language as beyond the sphere of philosophical reading. Despite many incisive points Véronique M. Fóti's *Heidegger and the Poets: Poiēsis/Sophia/Technē* (Atlantic Highlands, NJ: Humanities Press, 1992), all too often falls into this trap.

CHAPTER 1. REPEAT

1. For background on Lask and Heidegger's early thoughts on logic see Theodore Kisiel, *The Genesis of Heidegger's 'Being and Time'* (Berkeley: University of California Press, 1993), 25–59; and "Why students of Heidegger will have to read Emil Lask," in *Heidegger's Way of Thought: Critical and Interpretative Signposts*, eds. Alfred Denker and Marion Heinz (New York: Continuum, 2002), 101–36; and Steven Galt Crowell, *Husserl, Heidegger, and the Space of Meaning: Paths toward Transcendental Phenomenology* (Evanston, IL: Northwestern University Press, 2001).

2. Kisiel, *The Genesis of Heidegger's 'Being and Time,'* 37. Like all students of Heidegger I must indicate how indebted I am to Kisiel's monumental work, without which any analysis of Heidegger's origins, including this brief sketch, would be impossible.

3. Heidegger, "Comments on Karl Jaspers' *Psychology of Worldviews*," tr. John van Buren, in *Supplements: From the Earliest Essays to 'Being and Time' and Beyond*, ed. John van Buren (Albany: State University of New York Press, 2002), 94–95.

4. Ibid., 82.

5. The literature on Heidegger and Aristotle is extensive, but the following are particularly useful: William McNeill, *The Glance of the Eye: Heidegger, Aristotle, and the Ends of Theory* (Albany: State University of New York Press, 1999); and Walter Brogan, *Heidegger and Aristotle: The Twofoldness of Being* (Albany: State University of New York Press, 2005).

6. Heidegger, "Phenomenological Interpretations in Connection with Aristotle: An Indication of the Hermeneutical Situation," tr. John van Buren, in *Supplements*, 121.

7. For the analysis of *phronēsis* see the 1922 report, "Phenomenological Interpretations in Connection with Aristotle," in *Supplements*, 134–36; and the course of winter 1924–25, *Plato's 'Sophist,'* 34–39, 93–115.

8. The discussion of *pathos* as the horizon of *logos* is in the summer course of 1924, *Grundbegriffe der aristotelischen Philosophie*, ed. Mark Michalski (Frankfurt am Main: Vittorio Klostermann, 2002), §§ 16, 18. P. Christopher Smith, in *The Hermeneutics of Original Argument: Demonstration, Dialectic, Rhetoric* (Evanston, IL: Northwestern University Press, 1998), 13–34, shows how Heidegger's retrieval of the *pathos* of the Aristotelian *logos* leads to his later emphasis on the rhetorical dimension of hermeneutics; see also *Heidegger and Rhetoric*, eds. Daniel M. Gross and Ansgar Kemmann (Albany: State University of New York Press, 2005).

9. Heidegger, *History of the Concept of Time: Prolegomena*, tr. Kisiel (Bloomington: Indiana University Press, 1985), 272.

10. In *Being and Time*, Heidegger remarks, "In 'poetical' discourse, the communication of the existential possibilities of one's disposition can become an aim in itself, and this amounts to a disclosing of existence" (SZ: 162/205). Then in the summer course of 1927, *The Basic Problems of Phenomenology*, tr. Albert Hofstadter (Bloomington: Indiana University Press, 1982), 171–72, that is, directly after the publication of *Being and Time*, he states, "Poetry is nothing but the elementary emergence into words, the becoming-uncovered, of existence as being-in-the-world." In his courses of 1929–31 the position of poetry becomes more tacit, but no less significant, as it is repeatedly mentioned in his attempts to understand how philosophy relates to other forms of ontological inquiry. See Heidegger, *The Fundamental Concepts of Metaphysics: World, Finitude, Solitude*, tr. William McNeill and Nicholas Walker (Bloomington: Indiana University Press, 1995), 5; Heidegger, *Hegel's 'Phenomenology of Spirit,'* tr. Parvis Emad and Kenneth Maly (Bloomington: Indiana University Press, 1988), 147; Heidegger, *Aristotle's 'Metaphysics' Theta 1–3: On the Essence and Actuality of Force*, tr. Walter Brogan and Peter Warnek (Bloomington: Indiana University Press, 1995), 109; and Heidegger, *The Essence of Truth: On Plato's Cave Allegory and 'Theaetetus,'* tr. Ted Sadler (London: Athlone, 2002), 47. In the last instance Heidegger returns to the earlier formulations by saying that "poetry makes beings more being (*seiender*)."

11. Heidegger, *Logik: Die Frage nach die Wahrheit*, ed. Walter Biemel (Frankfurt am Main: Vittorio Klostermann, 1995), 197–207. David Farrell Krell provides a detailed interrogation of this failed path in his *Intimations of Mortality: Time, Truth, and Finitude in Heidegger's Thinking of Being* (University Park: Pennsylvania State University Press, 1986), 27–63.

12. The remark on the "destructuring" of logic comes from a letter Heidegger wrote to Karl Löwith in March 1925, which stated that his forthcoming book on "Time" would re-establish his thinking "in the context in which it was elaborated—as a ground for the destructuring of Greek ontology and logic," cited in Kisiel, *The Genesis of Heidegger's 'Being and Time,'* 479. Heidegger discusses the possibility of finding an alternative logic in rhetoric and poetics in *Logik: Die Frage nach die Wahrheit*, 130.

13. Jean-Luc Nancy provides a very strong analysis of these pages in "Sharing Voices," tr. Gayle L. Ormiston, in *Transforming the Hermeneutic Context: From Nietzsche to Nancy*, eds. Ormiston and Alan D. Schrift (Albany: State University of New York Press, 1990), 216–24.

14. Heidegger, *Plato's 'Sophist,'* 39.

15. Heidegger, *Logik als die Frage nach dem Wesen der Sprache*, 170.

16. See Erasmus Schöfer, "Heidegger's Language: Metalogical Forms of Thought and Grammatical Specialties," in *On Heidegger and Language*, tr. and ed. Joseph J. Kockelmans (Evanston, Ill: Northwestern University Press, 1972), 297–301; and Herman Rapaport, *Heidegger and Derrida: Reflections on Time and Language* (Lincoln: University of Nebraska Press, 1989), 108–9.

17. As Blanchot remarks, Plato's reading of *alētheia* in the *Cratylus* is as *alē-theia*, meaning "divine wandering" or "the straying of the gods," which in etymological terms has as much weight as *a-lētheia* (ED: 148/94).

18. As Heidegger remarked in his letter to William Richardson in April 1962: "Naturally only someone who is thinking too briefly, or not at all, could content themselves with the construction: Heidegger grasps truth as unconcealment," see his preface to Richardson's *Heidegger: Through Phenomenology to Thought* (The Hague: Martinus Nijhoff, 1963), xii.

19. It is worth pointing out that, as with all his readings of the Presocratics, Heidegger is following the versions collected and edited by Hermann Diels. However, despite the invaluable philological work done by Diels, recent work has meant that most commentators would now doubt the accuracy of some of his readings. This line of Parmenides is a case in point, as modern readings claim that *eukukleos* should be replaced by *eupeitheos*, "well-persuasive," which considerably alters Heidegger's rereading by suggesting a rhetorical essence to truth. See Alexander P. D. Mourelatos, *The Route of Parmenides: A Study of Word, Image, and Argument in the Fragments* (New Haven: Yale University Press, 1970), 154–58. While these discoveries do not invalidate Heidegger's readings, they direct us to the instability of the philological "text," which is bound by the ambiguity and historicity of the translator's practice. This reflects Heidegger's concern with the indeterminacy of the word, which is particularly appropriate for any translation of Presocratic thought in which each word offers variable and contentious possibilities and "accuracy" has an uncertain meaning. Of course, it is in response to this demand that Heidegger develops his own readings.

20. Bernasconi provides a helpful commentary on this transformation, including its reasons and implications, in *The Question of Language in Heidegger's History of Being*, 15–27.

21. On the implications of this point see Jean-François Courtine, "Phenomenology and/or Tautology," tr. Jeffrey S. Librett, in *Reading Heidegger: Commemorations*, ed. John Sallis (Bloomington: Indiana University Press, 1993), 241–57; and O. Bradley Bassler, "The Birthplace of Thinking: Heidegger's Late Thoughts on Tautology," *Heidegger Studies* 17 (2001): 117–33.

22. Blanchot's citation of this line contains a curious mistake in that he replaces *seyn* with *sei*, changing the meaning from "will be open" to "may open." This may be evidence of the speed with which he wrote this article or, as Leslie Hill has remarked in relation to the couplet that closes Blanchot's essay, it could suggest a deliberate but subtle rewriting; see Hill, *Blanchot: Extreme Contemporary* (London: Routledge, 1997), 90–91.

23. David Constantine, *Hölderlin* (Oxford: Clarendon Press, 1988), 119, 240; Charlie Louth, *Hölderlin and the Dynamics of Translation* (Oxford: Legenda, 1998), 179.

24. Friedrich Hölderlin, *Poems and Fragments*, tr. Michael Hamburger (London: Anvil Press, 2004), 462–67.

25. See Hölderlin, *Sämtliche Werke: Frankfurter Ausgabe*, eds. Dieter Eberhard Sattler et al., *Bande 7 und 8: Gesänge* (Frankfurt am Main: Stroemfeld, 2000), 94–107, 541–59.

26. Timothy Torno's full-length study of "As when on a holiday . . ." *Finding Time: Reading for Temporality in Hölderlin and Heidegger* (New York: Peter Lang, 1995), reads the holiday as a *kairos*, or time of decision. While this is an important aspect of Hölderlin's poem, my concern here is with the textual basis of this possibility.

CHAPTER 2. HIDING

1. The notes from 1931 to 1932 have been published as "Vom Ursprung des Kunstwerks: Erste Ausarbeitung," ed. Hermann Heidegger, *Heidegger Studies* 5 (1989): 5–22; and those from 1934 as "Zur Überwindung des Aesthetik: Zu 'Ursprung des Kunstwerks,'" ed. Friedrich-Wilhelm von Herrmann, *Heidegger Studies* 6 (1990): 5–7. Bernasconi reviews the whole period in "The Greatness of the Work of Art," in *Heidegger in Question*, 99–116. Françoise Dastur, in "Heidegger's Freiburg Version of the Origin of the Work of Art," in *Heidegger toward the Turn: Essays on the Work of the 1930s*, ed. James Risser (Albany: State University of New York Press, 1999), 119–42; and Jacques Taminiaux in "The Origin of 'The Origin of the Work of Art,'" in *Reading Heidegger*, ed. Sallis, 392–404, compare the final lectures of 1936 with the 1935 version, which is to be published in volume 80 of the *Gesamtausgabe: Vorträge.*

2. Heinrich Wiegand Petzet, *Encounters and Dialogues with Martin Heidegger 1929–1976*, tr. Parvis Emad and Kenneth Maly (Chicago: University of Chicago Press, 1993), 149. Günter Seubold has attempted to draw out the implications of Heidegger's brief notes on Klee in his *Kunst als Enteignis: Heideggers Weg zu einer nicht mehr metaphysischen Kunst* (Bonn: Bouvier Verlag, 1996), 119–34.

3. Heidegger, *The Essence of Truth: On Plato's Cave Allegory and 'Theaetetus,'* 89–106. At the same time as he was delivering this last course Heidegger was composing his first notes on the origin of the work of art, during which he remarked that "truth is essentially earthy," see Heidegger, "Vom Ursprung des Kunstwerks," *Heidegger Studies* 5 (1989): 21.

4. In a footnote added to the 1960 edition of *Holzwege* Heidegger places next to this use of *Sagen* the following remark: "*Verlauten, Sprechen*" (sounding, speaking), seemingly to indicate the dimensions of saying in what might still be termed their earthly and worldly modes. This suggests a late emendation of his thoughts on language along such lines as to bring out an added physical or material dimension that he must have felt had not been adequately indicated earlier. The difficulty of bringing out this dimension of language will become an increasingly important point as we proceed.

5. This point has attracted important commentaries from Sallis, *Echoes: After Heidegger* (Bloomington: Indiana University Press, 1990), 184–85; Fynsk, *Heidegger*, 148–50; and Marc Froment-Meurice, *That Is to Say: Heidegger's Poetics*, tr. Jan Plug (Stanford: Stanford University Press, 1998), 170–74. While Sallis feels that "mimesis can be rethought and reinscribed in Heidegger's poetics," Fynsk urges us to see it as being a limit for Heidegger's thinking by virtue of its resistance to figuration. For my own purposes, in exploring the nature of repetition in Heidegger's writings on language, I will move between these concerns; while *mimēsis* is a limit *for* Heidegger's thought, it is also an aspect *of* his understanding of the finitude of language. See also Arne Melberg, *Theories of Mimesis* (Cambridge: Cambridge University Press, 1995), 153–67; and Samuel IJsseling, *Mimesis: On Appearing and Being*, tr. Hester IJsseling and Jeffrey Bloechl (Kampen, Netherlands: Kok Pharos, 1997), 59–77. Philippe Lacoue-Labarthe's critique of Heidegger's thinking of *mimēsis* will be examined in chapter 3.

6. The possibility that the shoes in van Gogh's painting are not actually a pair is not addressed by Heidegger, but is taken up by Jacques Derrida in "Restitutions of the Truth

in Pointing," in *The Truth in Painting*, tr. Geoffrey Bennington and Ian McLeod (Chicago: University of Chicago Press, 1987), 264–65, 332–33, 373–77, where he makes much of their useless and disfiguring asymmetry. Such shoes are emphatically not "footgear" but are, as a result of their material repetition, closer to the dissembling of being.

7. In his *Force of Imagination: The Sense of the Elemental* (Bloomington: Indiana University Press, 2000), 124–27, Sallis uses "drawing" to designate the verbal and nominal horizons of a work. This graphological point is pursued in Rodolphe Gasché's essay "Joining the Text," in *Of Minimal Things: Studies on the Notion of Relation* (Stanford: Stanford University Press, 1999), 221–41, which asks whether Derrida's reading of *Riß*, in "The *Retrait* of Metaphor," tr. Frieda Gasdner et al., *Enclitic* 2 (1978): 27–33, allows us to answer Gérard Granel's key question of whether Derrida's "text" is a "translation" of Heidegger's "being."

8. It is by this move that we can, according to Lacoue-Labarthe, recognize the action of the *Ungeheure* as that of the sublime; see Lacoue-Labarthe, "Sublime Truth," tr. Jeffrey S. Librett, in *Of the Sublime: Presence in Question* (Albany: State University of New York Press, 1993), 94–95.

9. Despite the perceived distance between Heidegger's thinking in this essay and the radical approaches of "modern art," Heidegger is nothing but "modernist" in his understanding of art, as we can see by his later appreciation of not only Klee and Cézanne, but also Japanese calligraphy (see Fóti, "Heidegger and 'The Way of Art': The Empty Origin and Contemporary Abstraction," *Continental Philosophy Review* 31 (1998): 337–51), and the work of the Basque sculptor Eduardo Chillida, to whom the essay "Art and Space" was dedicated (see Miguel de Beistegui, *The New Heidegger* [London: Continuum, 2005], 146–49). The question that remains however is precisely that of the relation between "modernism" and "modern art," for it could be argued that the basis of the former lies in an opening of the truth of appearance, which the latter only ever puts into question. But the crudity of these terms, "modernism" and "modern art," places this distinction in doubt such that we would perhaps be better served by addressing the issue of what such an "opening of the truth of appearance" entails, when each of these terms involves an abyssal repetition.

10. Fynsk, *Heidegger*, 137–39, provides a very focused analysis of this point.

11. A note of caution is necessary here for the etymological link between *dicht* and *Dichtung* is unsustainable, as will be shown in chapter 3 (although the relation between *Lichtung* and *Dickung*, "density," which itself directly pertains to the essence of *Dichtung*, is made explicit in "The End of Philosophy and the Task of Thinking" [ZSD: 72/65]). But this does not prevent Heidegger from overlaying the meaning of *Dichtung* with that of terms that appear related, like *Verdichtung* and *gedichtet*. This deliberate complication suggests that we should not question Heidegger's thinking on the grounds that it is based in "arbitrary" etymological games, but see these as part of a broader strategy of estranging our overfamiliar use of words, not to reveal their "original" meaning, but rather their dissembling.

12. A very similar note was also added to "The Way to Language," where a remark on "the sounding of the word" was expanded by the note: "*Lauten und Leiben—Leib und Schrift*" (sounding and bodying—body and writing) (US: 249/129).

13. This is the point at which Lacoue-Labarthe's critique of Heidegger, in "Typography," tr. Eduardo Cadava, in *Typography: Mimesis, Philosophy, Politics*, ed. Christopher Fynsk (Stanford: Stanford University Press, 1989), 63–95, loses some of its strength: Although his analysis of Heidegger's elaboration of the setting-up of the work of art reveals the pervasive if tacit presence of *technē* as production, it fails to address the linguistic ground from which this elaboration arises, which is that the *logos* of *technē* is itself already engaged in an ungrounding of this sense of production by virtue of its repetition. As I will show, the repetition of the *logos* is always both the placing and displacing of any sense of work.

14. Blanchot, *The Space of Literature*, 243. As Blanchot points out, a work of art that seeks to resemble the essence of what is will find itself resembling nothing, but the dissembling of being as the sheer power of semblance. Thus, this will not be a language *of* images or figures, "but one that is its own image, an image of language . . . a language that no one speaks, that is to say, that speaks from out of its own absence," *The Space of Literature*, 34, cf. 263–64.

CHAPTER 3. BEYOND

1. This is in itself a significant occasion, being Heidegger's first publication, apart from "Hölderlin and the Essence of Poetry" in 1936, in twelve years, since "What Is Metaphysics?," "On the Essence of Ground," and *Kant and the Problem of Metaphysics* in 1929, and marking the beginning of his later publishing career.

2. Heidegger, *Hölderlin's Hymn 'The Ister,'* tr. William McNeill and Julia Davis (Bloomington: Indiana University Press, 1992), 8.

3. Heidegger, *Hölderlins Hymnen 'Germanien' und 'Der Rhein,'* ed. Susanne Ziegler (Frankfurt am Main: Vittorio Klostermann, 1989), 29.

4. Heidegger uses *poiēsis* sparingly in his later works and then only in the way that I have just sketched out; see, for example, "The Question Concerning Technology," where it is a term that bridges the revealing and bringing-forth of *phusis* and *technē* (VA1: 11–12/10–13). It is as such that we should treat poetry as *poiēsis*, as opposed to any sense of "creation" or "production," for as the relation with *phusis* and *technē* makes clear, revealing and bringing-forth only take place by way of a prior concealing and withdrawing. It is partly as a result of this potential confusion that I have opted to emphasize the mimetic rather than the poietic nature of poetry, although the main reason is to draw out the role of repetition. However, as is apparent, the necessity for rethinking *poiēsis* along these lines itself arises out of the question of *mimēsis*.

5. Fóti's work in *Heidegger and the Poets*, esp. 44–59; and "Heidegger, Hölderlin, and Sophoclean Tragedy," in *Heidegger toward the Turn*, ed. Risser, 163–86, exemplifies this particular critique of Heidegger's apparent appropriation of poetry, which she claims follows a "totalizing" trend that has its roots in an implicit political agenda that Heidegger brings to poetry, which leads him to "a disregard for poetic finitude." While this is undoubtedly a valid and necessary critique, it falls into the trap of "totalizing" Heidegger

by imposing one reading on him at the expense of his own very careful ambiguity. See the review by John T. Lysaker, "Heidegger after the Fall," *Research in Phenomenology* 23 (1993): 201–11.

6. Hans-Jost Frey, *Studies in Poetic Discourse: Mallarmé, Baudelaire, Rimbaud, Hölderlin*, tr. William Whobrey (Stanford: Stanford University Press, 1996), 178–91. See also Timothy Bahti, *Ends of the Lyric: Direction and Consequence in Western Poetry* (Baltimore: Johns Hopkins University Press, 1996), 102–14.

7. Heidegger, "Brief an Max Kommerell" (4. August 1942), in Max Kommerell, *Briefe und Aufzeichnungen, 1919–1944*, ed. Inge Jens (Olten: Walter Verlag, 1967), 405:

> Sie haben recht, die Schrift *ist* ein "Unglück". Auch *Sein und Zeit* war eine Verunglückung. Und jede unmittelbare Darstellung meines Denkens wäre heute das größte Unglück. Vielleicht liegt darin ein erstes Zeugnis dafür, daß meine Versuche zuweilen in die Nähe eines echten *Denkens* kommen. Alles aufrichtige Denken ist zum Unterschied der Dichter in seinem unmittelbaren Wirken eine Verunglückung. Daraus ersehen Sie schon, daß ich mich nicht und nirgends mit Hölderlin identifizieren *kann*. Hier ist die Auseinandersetzung eines Denkens mit einem Dichter im Gang, wobei die Aus-einander-setzung sogar den Entgegnenden erst setzt. Ist das Willkür oder höchste Freiheit?

8. Paul Davies has some especially good pages on this in his "A Linear Narrative? Blanchot with Heidegger in the Work of Levinas," in *Philosophers' Poets*, ed. David Wood (London: Routledge, 1990), 59–66.

9. I owe this point to Froment-Meurice, *That Is to Say*, 63, but its development is my own. Although he calls it a "monstrology," Sallis regards this change in the mode of phenomenology to be a necessary mutation if it is to move away from a grounding in presence and reorient itself to the self-showing of things themselves; see Sallis, *Force of Imagination*, 41–42, 104–5.

10. The tendency to see Blanchot's reading of Heidegger in these opposing terms is demonstrated by Rapaport, *Heidegger and Derrida*, 115–23; and by Hill, *Blanchot*, 82–91, who view the relationship of Blanchot's essay to Heidegger's reading as *either* compatible *or* incompatible. It should be recalled, however, that Heidegger himself on reading Blanchot's essay was led to remark that he felt a "great affinity" with the author, such that he could pronounce him "the best mind in France" (*la meilleure tête pensante française*), but considering that he made the strikingly uncharacteristic mistake of attributing the essay to Georges Bataille, rather than to Blanchot, then perhaps we should not overestimate the accuracy of Heidegger's reading. See Hill, "A Fragmentary Demand," in *The Power of Contestation: Perspectives on Maurice Blanchot*, eds. Kevin Hart and Geoffrey H. Hartman (Baltimore: Johns Hopkins University Press, 2004), 108 and footnote 16.

11. Paul de Man makes the rather literal claim that Hölderlin's "depiction" of his failure is omitted by Heidegger because he does not want to accept it; see de Man, "Patterns of Temporality in Hölderlin's 'Wie wenn am Feiertage . . .'" in *Romanticism and Contemporary Criticism: The Gauss Seminar and Other Papers*, eds. Ellen S. Burt, Kevin Newmark, and Andrzej Warminski (Baltimore: Johns Hopkins University Press, 1993), 65.

12. Peter Szondi suggested this in "The Other Arrow: On the Genesis of the Late Hymnic Style," tr. Harvey Mendelsohn, in *On Textual Understanding and Other Essays*, ed. Michael Hays (Minneapolis: University of Minnesota Press, 1986), 23–42.

13. Fynsk, *Heidegger*, 190–94, develops the point that Heidegger may be seeking to limit the destabilizing effect of the poet's position precisely by figuring him in this way, which would have the direct result of leading Heidegger into a figuring of his own position by recapitulating the traditional philosophical treatment of the poet as a *pharmakos.*

14. See also Heidegger, *Nietzsche: The Will to Power as Art*, 168–87; although the wider context of these remarks needs to be placed next to his earlier reading in *Plato's 'Sophist,'* §§ 58, 62, which demonstrates the tantalizing ambiguity of Plato's position.

15. Lacoue-Labarthe, *Heidegger, Art and Politics: The Fiction of the Political*, tr. Chris Turner (Oxford: Blackwell, 1990), 83–84. This analysis is drawn from his longer discussion in "Typography," in *Typography*, 77–86, of Heidegger's reading of *mimēsis* in the Nietzsche lectures on the will to power as art. As noted in chapter 2, I cannot entirely agree with this reading, that Heidegger's understanding of the work of art is pervasively guided by a thinking of *technē* as production, nor with its corollary that Heidegger refuses "to take seriously the concept of *mimesis.*" Although *mimēsis* is never addressed by Heidegger in any original manner, his thinking of the repetition of presencing is such that we should ask whether it supports or undermines the "mimetological" thinking of *mimēsis* as production, as Lacoue-Labarthe calls it in "Transcendence Ends in Politics," tr. Peter Caws, in *Typography*, 297–300. That is, we must try and find what a Heideggerian thinking of *mimēsis* might be, given his thinking of repetition, the ur-reference for this rethinking is of course Derrida's "The Double Session," tr. Barbara Johnson, in *Dissemination* (Chicago: University of Chicago Press, 1981), esp. 190–93; but see also Sallis, *Crossings: Nietzsche and the Space of Tragedy* (Chicago: University of Chicago Press, 1991), 82–101, for whom Nietzsche's understanding of the Dionysian suggests a reading of *mimēsis* as the (un)grounding of existence, thus marking it as an essentially tragic space.

16. These details are from Roger Munier, as cited by Lacoue-Labarthe in his *Poetry as Experience*, tr. Andrea Tarnowski (Stanford: Stanford University Press, 1999), 128 n. 15.

CHAPTER 4. SUSPENDING

1. "Let us note: *Nachtrag* has a precise meaning in the realm of letters: appendix, codicil, postscript. The text we call present may be deciphered only at the bottom of the page, in a footnote or postscript. Before the recurrence, the present is only the call for a footnote." Derrida, "Freud and the Scene of Writing," tr. Alan Bass, in *Writing and Difference* (London: Routledge, 1978), 212.

2. Lacoue-Labarthe, "The Caesura of the Speculative," tr. Robert Eisenhauer, in *Typography*, 209–10.

3. The idea that Heidegger was disinterested in Hölderlin's theoretical works needs to be balanced by an awareness of his persistent negotiation with issues of history and translation in his three courses on Hölderlin's hymns, particularly in his examination of Hölder-

lin's phrase "the free use of the proper," as well as his readings of the chiasmic historicity of time-space in *Contributions to Philosophy (From Ereignis)*, §§ 238–42; and of the relation of *genesis* and *phthora* in *Basic Concepts*, tr. Gary E. Aylesworth (Bloomington: Indiana University Press, 1993), §§ 22–24.

4. The philosophical basis of Hölderlin's thoughts on tragedy constitute a key turning point not only for his own work but also for his contemporaries, as has been promoted by Dieter Henrich in contradistinction to Heidegger's extraction of the poet from his time; see Henrich, *The Course of Remembrance and Other Essays on Hölderlin*, tr. Abraham Anderson and Taylor Carman, ed. Eckart Förster (Stanford: Stanford University Press, 1997). But see Dastur, "Tragédie et modernité," in *Hölderlin: Le retournement natal* (La Versanne, France: Encre marine, 1997), 25–96, who emphasizes the radical distortion of speculative thought that Hölderlin's work entails. More generally, the history of the concept of tragedy has been studied by Dennis J. Schmidt, *On Germans and Other Greeks: Tragedy and Ethical Life* (Bloomington: Indiana University Press, 2001).

5. Heidegger's work on Empedocles suffered a similar fate, as this remark relating to a 92-page manuscript from 1938 indicates: "This manuscript—because insufficient (*unzureichend*)—destroyed," see *Zu Hölderlin: Griechenlandreisen*, ed. Curd Ochwadt (Frankfurt am Main: Vittorio Klostermann, 2000), 404.

6. As Michel Haar points out in his *The Song of the Earth: Heidegger and the Grounds of the History of Being*, tr. Reginald Lilly (Bloomington: Indiana University Press, 1993), 108, this dynamic opposition, which Hölderlin adopted from Schelling and Rousseau, found its way into Nietzsche's reading of tragedy as comprising Dionysian and Apollonian tendencies, and also, he suggests, into Heidegger's use of earth and world in his understanding of the work of art.

7. Lacoue-Labarthe, "The Caesura of the Speculative," in *Typography*, 226–27.

8. For Hölderlin's refiguring of this Kantian aporia see Courtine's essay, "Of Tragic Metaphor," tr. Jonathan Derbyshire, in *Philosophy and Tragedy*, eds. Miguel de Beistegui and Simon Sparks (London: Routledge, 2000), 59–77. See also Nancy, "Hyperion's Joy," tr. Christine Laennec and Michael Syrotinski, in *The Birth to Presence* (Stanford: Stanford University Press, 1993), 58–81, for a broader account of Hölderlin's relation to Kant.

9. Robin B. Harrison, *Hölderlin and Greek Literature* (Oxford: Oxford University Press, 1975), 169–92; and George Steiner, *Antigones: How the Antigone Legend has Endured in Western Literature, Art, and Thought* (Oxford: Oxford University Press, 1984), 66–103, both provide useful introductions to these translations.

10. See also Froment-Meurice, *That Is to Say*, 135–37. However, the reading of the "Nationelle" that Heidegger offers here needs to be supplemented by the extensive meditations on the destiny of the Occident that he provides in "Das abendländische Gespräch" in *Zu Hölderlin*, 59–196, recently studied by Peter Trawny, in *Heidegger und Hölderlin, oder Der Europäische Morgen* (Würzburg: Königshausen and Neumann, 2004).

11. This process has attracted an extensive literature ranging from Szondi's reading in "Hölderlin's Overcoming of Classicism," tr. Timothy Bahti, *Comparative Criticism* 5 (1983): 251–70; to the more nuanced approach of Dastur, in "Hölderlin and the Orientalisation of Greece," tr. Hector Kollias, *Pli* 10 (2000): 156–73.

12. Walter Benjamin, "Goethe's *Elective Affinities*," tr. Stanley Corngold, in *Selected Writings: Vol. 1, 1913–1926*, eds. Marcus Bullock and Michael W. Jennings (Cambridge: Belknap Press, 1996), 340–41. The differences between Benjamin's and Heidegger's readings of Hölderlin are profound and complex and I will not attempt to address them here; however, my own reading of Hölderlin follows the relation of language to history in which is found the crux of their differences. Lacoue-Labarthe has explored this further in "Poetry's Courage," tr. Simon Sparks, in *The Solid Letter: Readings of Friedrich Hölderlin*, ed. Aris Fioretos (Stanford: Stanford University Press, 1999), 74–93.

13. Andrzej Warminski, *Readings in Interpretation: Hölderlin, Hegel, Heidegger* (Minneapolis: University of Minnesota Press, 1987), 17; Fóti, *Heidegger and the Poets*, 73–74; and Krell, "A Small Number of Houses in the Tragic Universe," in *The Tragic Absolute: German Idealism and the Languishing of God* (Bloomington: Indiana University Press, 2005), 307–8, all mention this point but do not pursue it.

14. Lacoue-Labarthe, "The Caesura of the Speculative," in *Typography*, 221. On this point see also in the same volume "Hölderlin and the Greeks," tr. Judi Olson, 246–47.

15. Hölderlin, "Hyperion, or the Hermit in Greece," tr. Willard R. Trask and Daniel Schwarz, in '*Hyperion*' *and Selected Poems*, ed. Eric L. Santner (New York: Continuum, 1990), 67. By replacing *diapheromenon* in Heraclitus' fragment 51, which reads, "a thing agrees at variance (*diapheromenon*) with itself," with *diapheron*, Hölderlin makes it into an active rather than a passive construction, which might indicate an added emphasis on the enduring dynamism at work in nature (Kahn: 65). For this see Melberg, "Turns and Echoes: Two Examples of Hölderlin's Poetics," in *The Solid Letter*, ed. Fioretos, 341.

16. Sophocles, *The Three Theban Plays: Antigone, Oedipus the King, Oedipus at Colonus*, tr. Robert Fagles (Harmondsworth, UK: Penguin, 1984), 60. For an English version of Hölderlin's translations see *Hölderlin's Sophocles: Oedipus and Antigone*, tr. David Constantine (Tarset, UK: Bloodaxe, 2001), this line is on page 71. The background and implications of Hölderlin's translation of this line have been analyzed by Aris Fioretos in "Color Read: Hölderlin and Translation," in *The Solid Letter*, ed. Fioretos, 268–87.

17. Antoine Berman, *The Experience of the Foreign: Culture and Translation in Romantic Germany*, tr. Stefaan Heyvaert (Albany: State University of New York Press, 1992); and Louth, *Hölderlin and the Dynamics of Translation*, 5–53, are both helpful guides to the different approaches to translation prevalent during the period of Hölderlin's work. Louth's work is especially good at demonstrating how translation and rewriting gradually became the central focus for Hölderlin's poetic practice. See also Rainer Nägele, *Echoes of Translation: Reading between Texts* (Baltimore: Johns Hopkins University Press, 1997); and Sallis, *On Translation* (Bloomington: Indiana University Press, 2002), for inquiries into what this changed sense of translation brings to our understanding of literature.

18. It is precisely this movement that Benjamin proposes in "The Task of the Translator," tr. Harry Zohn, in *Selected Writings*, 253–63, and for which he sees Hölderlin's Sophocles translations as exemplary.

19. For Krell, *Lunar Voices: Of Tragedy, Poetry, Fiction, and Thought* (Chicago: University of Chicago Press, 1995), 33–36, this endless suffering is *the* distinguishing mark of modern, as opposed to Greek tragedy. This is also Dastur's conclusion in "Tragédie et

modernité," in *Hölderlin*, 64–65, although she goes on to ask whether it is still possible to associate modernity with "tragedy" insofar as Hölderlin's failure with *Empedocles* may indicate that tragedy is no longer possible. Instead, she suggests, we should look to the relation of modernity with lyric poetry as the means for exposing its *dysmoron*. Although this seems to pick up on Lacoue-Labarthe's suggestion that it is the relation of modernity to "a new kind of writing" that must now be explored I would counter that it is the prosaic rather than the lyrical that is the mark of modernity. For as Benjamin pointed out in the epigraph of this chapter, the development of Hölderlin's poetry is marked by the principle of sobriety, in which the lyrical is subjected to a prosaic fragmentation as it seeks to respond to the endlessness that is the temporal mode of modernity. However, it should be recalled that Benjamin's understanding of prose as "the *idea* of poetry" arises from Schlegel's valorization of the fragment and is thus utterly distinct from Hölderlin's "sobriety," I will return to these issues in chapter 6.

20. My translation here deliberately parallels that of Heidegger's distinction between dying (*Sterben*) and perishing (*Verenden*) in order to suggest a difference in their approaches to death (SZ: 241/284). For while Hölderlin's distinction would seem to follow Heidegger's in suggesting that it is only the "deadly factive" word that is authentic, it does so in terms of a history that suggests that such authentic dying no longer exists and that instead there now holds a far less decisive and "proper" relation with death as a limit (*peras, Ende*). This also leads into the relation between language and dying, which for Heidegger does not pertain for those that do not die, but only perish (US: 203/107). But for Hölderlin there is now no possibility of dying other than to perish and this relation to the limit, which means that "packed up in any container we very quietly move away from the realm of the living," would suggest that if there is a relation between language and dying then it is also by way of this endless sober ending, rather than by any appropriative decision.

21. Benjamin, "The Concept of Criticism in German Romanticism," tr. David Lachterman, Howard Eiland, and Ian Balfour, in *Selected Writings*, 175–76.

22. On this point see Werner Hamacher, "Hermeneutic Ellipses: Writing the Hermeneutical Circle in Schleiermacher," tr. Timothy Bahti, in *Transforming the Hermeneutic Context*, eds. Ormiston and Schrift, 200:

> Ellipsis is the rhetorical equivalent of writing: it de-completes, in order to make ideational totalities possible—but each whole gained with its assistance remains imprinted with the trace of the original elimination. At the same time it also withdraws, like writing, from every alternative of presence and absence, whole and part, proper and foreign, because it is only on its—perpetually self-hollowing—ground that such conceptual oppositions can develop: it withdraws from its own proper concept. Ellipsis eclipses (itself). It is the "figure" of figuration: the area no figure can contain.

Chapter 5. A Void

1. Heidegger, *Heraklit*, ed. Manfred S. Frings (Frankfurt am Main: Vittorio Klostermann, 1994), 27. Apologies to Gilbert Adair for the title of this chapter.

2. See, for example, Beistegui, *Heidegger and the Political: Dystopias* (London: Routledge, 1998), 122–31; Warminski, "Monstrous History: Heidegger Reading Hölderlin," in *The Solid Letter*, ed. Fioretos, 201–14; McNeill, "A 'scarcely pondered word.' The Place of Tragedy: Heidegger, Aristotle, Sophocles," in *Philosophy and Tragedy*, eds. Beistegui and Sparks, 169–89; and Dastur, "Heidegger on Anaximander: Being and Justice," in *Interrogating the Tradition: Hermeneutics and the History of Philosophy*, eds. Charles E. Scott and John Sallis (Albany: State University of New York Press, 2000), 179–90.

3. Plato, "Ion," in *Early Socratic Dialogues*, tr. and ed. Trevor J. Saunders (Harmondsworth, UK: Penguin, 1987), 49–65. Timothy Clark has some very useful pages on the mimetic instability of Ion's position in *The Theory of Inspiration: Composition as a Crisis of Subjectivity in Romantic and Post-Romantic Writing* (Manchester, UK: Manchester University Press, 1997), 50–56.

4. Peter Fenves analyzes the ramifications of this distinction through a number of readings in *Arresting Language: From Leibniz to Benjamin* (Stanford: Stanford University Press, 2001).

5. In 1955 Heidegger referred to *pathos*, which he translates as "at-tunement (*Gestimmtheit*) and de-termination (*Be-stimmtheit*)," as the *archē*, or constant source and guidance of philosophy, that which "carries (*trägt*) and pervades (*durchherrscht*)" it; see *What Is Philosophy?* tr. William Kluback and Janet T. Wilde (London: Vision Press, 1958), 81–83.

6. Heidegger, "The Theological Discussion of 'The Problem of Nonobjectifying Thinking and Speaking in Today's Theology'—Some Pointers to its Major Aspects," tr. James G. Hart and John C. Maraldo, in *Pathmarks*, ed. William McNeill (Cambridge: Cambridge University Press, 1998), 55.

7. Heidegger, "Conversation on a Country Path about Thinking," in *Discourse on Thinking*, tr. John M. Anderson and E. Hans Freund (New York: Harper, 1966), 76.

8. For Nancy this repetition and division constitutes the "voice" of language, which links together poet, rhapsode, and thinker through the *singularity* of their interpretations; see Nancy, "Sharing Voices," in *Transforming the Hermeneutic Context*, 243–47.

9. For Blanchot, as we will see in chapter 6, this rewriting of Heidegger's fourfold opens it onto "areas of dislocation, the four winds of spirit's absence, breath from nowhere—the names of thought, when it lets itself come undone and, by writing, fragment. Outside. Neutral. Disaster. Return. Surely these names form no system" (ED: 95/57–58).

10. The interaction of these terms, *Gelassenheit* and *Abgeschiedenheit*, are central to the thought of Meister Eckhart where they are understood as "letting-be" and "detachment," see John D. Caputo, *The Mystical Element in Heidegger's Thought* (Athens: Ohio University Press, 1978), 173–83.

11. Derrida's remarks on these pages in "Différance" are still highly illuminating; see *Margins: Of Philosophy*, tr. Alan Bass (Hemel Hempstead, UK: Harvester Wheatsheaf, 1982), 23–27.

12. Heidegger, "The Turning," tr. William Lovitt, in *The Question Concerning Technology and Other Essays* (New York: Harper, 1977), 39.

13. Bruns, *Heidegger's Estrangements*, 99–149; Herrmann, "'The Flower of the Mouth': Hölderlin's Hint for Heidegger's Thinking of the Essence of Language," tr. Parvis Emad and Kenneth Maly, in *Martin Heidegger*, ed. Macann, 277–92; and Fynsk, *Language and Relation*, 39–85, are still the only worthwhile readings of this key essay.

14. It is on this point that Heidegger's later works open onto the writings of Blanchot. As I will show in chapter 6, what needs to be developed to understand this relation is not so much the terms of their delineation, as the divergence brought about by their differing approaches to the *use* (*Brauch* or *désoeuvrement*) of this (im)possibility as finitude or alterity.

15. Fynsk, *Language and Relation*, 52. We might also recall an aside from Heidegger's 1935 lecture: "Language is, i.e. it stands in the written image of the word, in the written signs, in the letters, *grammata*" (EM: 68/68).

16. Otto Pöggeler, *Martin Heidegger's Path of Thinking*, tr. Daniel Magurshak and Sigmund Barber (Atlantic Highlands, NJ: Humanities Press, 1987), 230–40.

17. See especially on this point, Gasché, "Perhaps: A Modality?" in *Of Minimal Things*, 173–91.

18. The transformation of the guideword recalls a formulation added in 1949 to Heidegger, "On the Essence of Truth": "The question of the essence of truth finds its answer in the proposition: *the essence of truth is the truth of essence*" (W: 96/153). Much could be made of the translation from "truth" to "language" between the two phrases, but perhaps the most important point is the *manner* of its rewriting; the displacement from a proposition into parataxis through the withdrawal of the copula "is," which suggests a move away from an ontological understanding of essence as that which *is* and thereby guarantees presence, into the rupture of this relation in and by language. See Derrida's note to Dastur in *Of Spirit: Heidegger and the Question*, tr. Geoffrey Bennington and Rachel Bowlby (Chicago: University of Chicago Press, 1989), esp. 135.

19. Heidegger, "Conversation on a Country Path about Thinking," in *Discourse on Thinking*, 71.

20. Interestingly, this directly counters the movement of "de-distancing" (*Ent-fernung*) that Heidegger used to describe the way in which distance is revealed (as absent) as things, rather than words, are brought close (SZ: 105/139–40).

CHAPTER 6. FRAGMENTING

1. I must mention here Nancy's article, "Elliptical Sense," tr. Peter Connor, *Research in Phenomenology* 20 (1990): 175–90, which discusses Derrida's reading of Edmond Jabès, and that explicates exactly this movement of repetition without return that makes up the relation of writing.

2. Beistegui delivers a substantial corrective to this tendency by stressing how it was by way of his readings of poetry that Heidegger was able to rethink the language of politics; see Beistegui, *Heidegger and the Political*, 87–113.

3. On this point I can only concur with the criticisms raised by Dominique Janicaud in *The Shadow of That Thought: Heidegger and the Question of Politics*, tr. Michael Gendre (Evanston, Ill.: Northwestern University Press, 1996), 85–93, about Lacoue-Labarthe's response to Heidegger's silence in *Heidegger, Art and Politics* and *Poetry as Experience*: that we cannot condemn Heidegger on this point while still accepting his history of being, as the former is implied in the latter. The unraveling of this history and its relations to truth and language is thus the measure of any work that would now attempt to come after Heidegger.

4. This understanding of the relation of *philia* as that which loses itself distinguishes Blanchot's writing from Heidegger's, as Derrida has explored in "Heidegger's Ear: Philopolemology (*Geschlecht* IV)," tr. John P. Leavey Jr., in *Reading Heidegger*, ed. Sallis, 179–96; and Derrida, *Politics of Friendship*, tr. George Collins (London: Verso, 1997), 293–302. It is notable that while *philia* is understood by Heidegger out of its relation to *phusis* and *sophia*, as that which articulates its relation to the other in terms of favoring, reciprocity, unity, correspondence, accord, and belonging, for Blanchot, *philia* as such needs to be replaced by an understanding of the demands of friendship as that which can only persist in a relation without sharing, need, reciprocity, symmetry, or bond. See especially his extraordinary testimony to Bataille, "Friendship," tr. Elizabeth Rottenberg, in *Friendship* (Stanford: Stanford University Press, 1997), 289–92; as well as the writing of his extended relations with Levinas, Derrida, and Nancy.

5. Blanchot, "Thinking the Apocalypse: A Letter from Maurice Blanchot to Catherine David," tr. Paula Wissing, *Critical Inquiry* 15 (1989): 479.

6. For the overlap between these textual experiments see Clark, *Derrida, Heidegger, Blanchot: Sources of Derrida's Notion and Practice of Literature* (Cambridge: Cambridge University Press, 1991), 89–107.

7. All citations in the previous two paragraphs come from Blanchot, "Waiting," tr. Michael Holland, in *The Blanchot Reader* (Oxford: Blackwell, 1995), 272–78. Hill provides details on the background of this piece in "A Fragmentary Demand," in *The Power of Contestation*, 101–20; more generally, Ann Smock provides a particularly fine reading of the convolutions of Blanchot's writing in *What Is There to Say?* (Lincoln: University of Nebraska Press, 2003), 1–20.

8. See Emmanuel Levinas's argument in *Totality and Infinity: An Essay on Exteriority*, tr. Alphonso Lingis (Pittsburgh: Duquesne University Press, 1969), esp. 72–77. Although Blanchot's reading of Heidegger often goes by way of Levinas's criticisms, it just as often works against this tendency; emphasizing the strangeness and subtlety of Heidegger's language that Levinas all too often overlooks. Careful examinations of the relations between the three are not widespread but Davies, "A Fine Risk: Reading Blanchot Reading Levinas," in *Re-Reading Levinas*, eds. Robert Bernasconi and Simon Critchley (Bloomington: Indiana University Press, 1991), 201–26; Hill, *Blanchot*, 158–84; and Hent de Vries, "'Lapsus Absolu': Notes on Maurice Blanchot's *The Instant of My Death*," *Yale French Studies* 93 (1998): 30–59, provide good starting places.

9. Pierre Klossowski, *Nietzsche and the Vicious Circle*, tr. Daniel W. Smith (London: Athlone, 1997), esp. 55–73.

10. I can only point to Wittgenstein's comments on Heidegger's "What Is Metaphysics?" here, as they were recorded by Waismann and appended to Wittgenstein's "Lecture on Ethics" without the first sentence or title:

> I can easily think what Heidegger means by being and anxiety. Man has that drive to run up against the limits of language. Think, for example, of the astonishment that something exists. This astonishment cannot become expressed into the form of a question, and there is also no answer to it. Everything that we would like to say can, a priori, only be nonsense. Nevertheless we run up against the limits of language. This running-up against Kierkegaard also saw and even designated it in a wholly similar way (as running-up against paradox). This running-up against the limits of language is *ethics.*

See Wittgenstein, "Zu Heidegger," in *Wittgenstein und der Wiener Kreis,* 68; "On Heidegger on Being and Dread," in *Heidegger and Modern Philosophy,* 80.

11. Lacoue-Labarthe has stated somewhat polemically that talk of an alterity "beyond" being is misguided or incoherent, for the idea of an "otherwise than being," as Levinas proposed, is still the "same" as Heidegger's "Being": Since the alterity of the other *is* its being, "which always 'is' and can only 'be' Being," there can be no "otherwise" or "beyond" that does not already involve being, see Lacoue-Labarthe, *Poetry as Experience,* 66. This would seem to underestimate what is at issue in poetic writing, which is precisely concerned with an alterity that persists as a self-effacing trace of absence, and as such "is" only as the limits of language. As Derrida has remarked in his introduction to Lacoue-Labarthe's *Typography,* the "sameness" that Lacoue-Labarthe sees here does not do justice to the "desistance" that he himself has responded to in Heidegger's language, which evades its own terms and that leads to an opening that is always other and thus is neither Heideggerian nor Levinasian. See Derrida, "Desistance," tr. Christopher Fynsk, in *Typography,* 23. It is the double-sidedness of this liminality that I have endeavored to pursue here: the language that recedes within that which grants.

12. Clark draws out the ode-like structure of Derrida's essay in *The Theory of Inspiration,* 266–71.

13. The relation between a poem and the poetics it gives rise to is addressed by Derrida by way of a reading of Celan's poem "Aschenglorie" in "Poetics and Politics of Witnessing," tr. Outi Pasanen, in *Sovereignties in Question: The Poetics of Paul Celan,* eds. Thomas Dutoit and Outi Pasanen (New York: Fordham University Press, 2005), 65–96. Here the poetics of a poem is that which occupies the impossible position of the witness, who has to answer for the impossibility of answering, to speak of the impossibility of speaking, thereby bearing the poem to us but in doing so finding its own position undermined, for while the pain of a poem needs a witness, "no-one / bears witness for the witness."

14. See Lacoue-Labarthe and Nancy, *The Literary Absolute: The Theory of Literature in German Romanticism,* tr. Philip Barnard and Cheryl Lester (Albany: State University of New York Press, 1988), 43–44.

15. Krell has begun to explore this possibility in "God's Trauma," in *The Tragic Absolute,* 104–48.

16. Cathy Caruth, *Unclaimed Experience: Trauma, Narrative, and History* (Baltimore: Johns Hopkins University Press, 1996), provides an excellent overview.

17.

> Whatever an elucidation can or cannot do, this is always true of it: in order that what has been composed (*Gedichtete*) purely into a poem may stand forth (*dastehe*) a little clearer, the elucidating speech must each time shatter itself and what it had attempted to do. For the sake of preserving what has been put into the poem (*Gedichteten*), the elucidation of the poem must strive to make itself superfluous. The last, but also the most difficult step of every interpretation, consists in its disappearing, along with its elucidations, before the pure standing (*Dastehen*) of the poem. The poem, which then stands in its own right (*eigenen Gesetz stehende*), itself throws light directly on the other poems. This explains why in rereading the poems we think we had understood them in this way all along. It is well for us to believe this (EHD: 8/22).

Further analysis of the hermeneutic traps of *déjà vu* can be found in Nicholas Royle's *The Uncanny* (Manchester, UK: Manchester University Press, 2003), 172–86.

18. *Partage* is discussed in Nancy's article, "Sharing Voices," in *Transforming the Hermeneutic Context*, while *excriture* is scattered across many of the pages of *The Birth to Presence*, and not just in the article of the same name.

Index